# The Patchwork City

# The Patchwork City

*Class, Space, and Politics in
Metro Manila*

MARCO Z. GARRIDO

*The University of Chicago Press   Chicago and London*

PUBLICATION OF THIS BOOK HAS BEEN AIDED BY A GRANT FROM
THE BEVINGTON FUND.

The University of Chicago Press, Chicago 60637
The University of Chicago Press, Ltd., London

28  27  26  25  24  23  22  21  20  19      1  2  3  4  5

ISBN-13: 978-0-226-64300-7 (cloth)
ISBN-13: 978-0-226-64314-4 (paper)
ISBN-13: 978-0-226-64328-1 (e-book)
DOI: https://doi.org/10.7208/chicago/9780226643281.001.0001

Library of Congress Cataloging-in-Publication Data

Names: Garrido, Marco Z., author.
Title: The patchwork city : class, space, and politics in Metro Manila /
    Marco Z. Garrido.
Description: Chicago ; London : The University of Chicago Press,
2019. | Includes bibliographical references and index.
Identifiers: LCCN 2018054724 | ISBN 9780226643007 (cloth) | ISBN
9780226643144 (pbk.) | ISBN 9780226643281 (e-book)
Subjects: LCSH: Manila Metropolitan Area (Philippines)—Social
    conditions | Metropolitan areas—Social aspects—Philippines. |
    Social classes—Philippines—Manila Metropolitan Area. |
    Urban poor—Philippines—Manila Metropolitan Area—Social
    conditions. | Middle class—Philippines—Manila Metropolitan
    Area. | Equality—Philippines—Manila Metropolitan Area. |
    Social conflict—Philippines—Manila Metropolitan Area. | Urban
    poor—Political activity—Philippines—Manila Metropolitan
    Area. | Middle class—Political activity—Philippines—Manila
    Metropolitan Area. | Manila Metropolitan Area (Philippines)—
    Politics and government
Classification: LCC HT334.M3 G37 2019 |
    DDC 307.76/40959916—dc23
LC record available at https://lccn.loc.gov/2018054724

# Contents

# Acknowledgments

I have incurred a number of debts in the research and writing of this book, and I'm afraid that the most I can do at this point is to acknowledge them. My fieldwork was greatly enabled by the Cayton family. Both "Mommy" and "Daddy" provided me with contacts in various government agencies. They fed and housed me. They indulged my questions about Philippine politics. Mommy transcribed most of my interviews and helped me acquire local copyright permissions. Daddy continued to serve as my "consultant" long after I had left the field. My debt to them is too great to square. Nene also took care of me. She was, moreover, my companion during my "years in the desert." It's not enough to simply thank her. Uncle Jun Santillana put me in contact with some of my informants. Rafael Calinisan helped me get aboard Erap's bus on his sortie through Laguna. The officials of various housing agencies and municipal governments passed along data. I thank my informants, of course. My fieldwork was funded by the Fulbright-Hays Program, the Ford Foundation, Rackham School of Graduate Studies at the University of Michigan, and the Asia Research Institute at the National University of Singapore.

My advisers at the University of Michigan supported my project in seed form: Jeffrey Paige, Gavin Shatkin, Fred Wherry, Jun Aguilar, Allen Hicken, and Howard Kimeldorf. I would single out Howard. His faith in my work has been unflagging. There have been days when it has surpassed my own and been the thing I have held onto in the effort to keep afloat. I keep his example in my head as the picture of the kind of adviser I hope to become.

At the University of Chicago, my work has matured under the guidance of colleagues, particularly Lis Clemens, Andy Abbott, Jenny Trinatopoli, and Andreas Glaeser. The Politics, History, and Society workshop and the write-ins at the Center for International Social Science Research (CISSR) have given me a sense of being at home intellectually. A book workshop sponsored by the CISSR made a crucial intervention. It helped me reimagine the project in ways that spoke to a broader audience. The readers were Patrick Heller, Michael Pinches, Erhard Berner, and Claudio Benzecry. I would also add Brodie Fischer. I'm grateful for their having engaged my work so vigorously.

A number of very smart people commented on parts of the manuscript in early forms, including Rob Jansen, Aries Arguay, Avi Astor, Dingxin Zhao, Robert Vargas, and Steve Raudenbush. I'm surely forgetting many others. Emily Osborn helped me come up with the title of the book. Several students provided invaluable research assistance: Austin Kozlowski, Ben Ross, John Hadaway, and especially Pranathi Diwakar.

Early versions of chapters 3 and 7 appeared in *International Journal of Urban and Regional Research* (29, no. 3 [2018]: 442–60) and *American Journal of Sociology* (123, no. 3 [2017]: 1–39), respectively. I'm grateful to the *Philippine Daily Inquirer* and Pol Medina for allowing me to use images they owned. My editors at the University of Chicago Press deserve thanks: Doug Mitchell, for always taking my side, and Kyle Wagner, for seeing the project through.

Pa[2] and Ma[2], for always being there, despite me. Mica, for being my rock. She was there for nearly every interview as my notetaker. She's the other part of the "we" I slip into occasionally in the text. She's also been there for nearly every other thing. She's the other part of the "we" I invoke regularly, to myself, beyond the text.

# Glossary

| | |
|---|---|
| *Ate* | Older sister. |
| barangay | The smallest administrative division in cities, akin to the barrio or neighborhood; the barangay also refers to the administrative body at that level, the neighborhood government. |
| CMP | Community Mortgage Program. |
| CO | Community organization, usually of the urban poor. |
| Cory | Corazon Aquino. |
| Crame | Military camp in Manila. |
| DAHHA | Don Antonio Heights Homeowners Association. |
| EDSA | Epifanio de los Santos Avenue: the massive demonstrations held around the shrine along EDSA were called Edsa 1 (against Marcos), Edsa 2 (against Estrada), and Edsa 3 (in support of Estrada). |
| Erap | Estrada's nickname; *erap* is *pare* ("buddy") in reverse. |
| FPJ | Fernando Poe Jr., a movie star and Arroyo's chief rival in the 2004 presidential election. |
| GMA | Gloria Macapagal Arroyo. |
| *hakot* | Pulled; to say that the Edsa 3 demonstrators were *hakot* means that they were pulled to participate by politicians who promised them payment or food and transported them to the demonstration. |
| Hello Garci | A scandal indicating that Arroyo committed electoral fraud in 2004. |
| HLURB | Housing and Land Use Regulatory Board. |
| *jueteng* | An illegal lottery game. |
| *kagawad* | Barangay councilor. |
| *kusang loob* | Voluntary. |

| | |
|---|---|
| Lina Law | Urban Development and Housing Act of 1992; the bill came to be known for its sponsor, Joey Lina. |
| *masa* | The Philippine masses; the word connotes vulgarity and backwardness. |
| Malacañang | The presidential palace. |
| MMDA | Metropolitan Manila Development Authority. |
| N3T | A federation of community organizations in San Roque opposed to Estrada. |
| NBN-ZTE | National Broadband Network–Zhongxing Telecommunications Equipment (Corporation). A scandal involving senior officials in the Arroyo administration. The officials were accused of receiving bribes from ZTE in exchange for ensuring that the company was awarded the contract for building the country's broadband network. |
| NHA | National Housing Authority. |
| Noli | Noli de Castro, a popular news broadcaster and Arroyo's vice president. |
| Noynoy | Benigno Aquino III. |
| *pang-masa* | Suited for the *masa*, or masses. |
| *pamanhikan* | A Filipino custom in which the family of the prospective groom formally asks the family of the prospective bride for her hand in marriage; *pamanhikan* usually take place over a meal. |
| *pare* | Buddy. |
| PCUP | Presidential Commission on the Urban Poor. |
| people power | May refer in general to the method of using popular demonstrations to remove unpopular leaders, or may refer specifically to Edsa 1 or Edsa 2. |
| PHAI | Phil-Am Homeowners Association Incorporated. |
| PHHC | People's Homesite and Housing Corporation. |
| PMAP | People's Movement against Poverty. |
| PO | People's organization, including the community organizations of the urban poor. |
| SOP | Standard Operating Procedure; in context, bribes. |
| SRCC | San Roque Community Council, a federation of community organizations in San Roque supporting Estrada. |
| *tanod* | Barangay security officer. |
| UDHA | Urban Development and Housing Act, also known as the Lina Law. |
| village | Residential subdivision. |

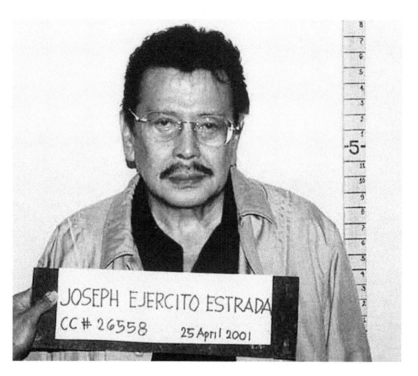

*The face that launched a thousand jeeps*

# Introduction

It was the spectacle of Joseph Estrada being taken into police custody on April 25, 2001, that instigated the largest single protest in Philippine history. An estimated 1.5 million people gathered around a landmark shrine along the Epifanio de los Santos Avenue (Edsa) in Manila. The Edsa shrine was where the demonstrations that toppled the dictator Ferdinand Marcos in 1986 (Edsa 1), and Estrada three months earlier (Edsa 2), had taken place. Now Edsa 3, as the demonstration came to be known—albeit grudgingly, with some quarters unwilling to confer Edsa status upon it—was an attempt by Estrada's supporters to reinstall him as president. It lasted a full week and culminated with upward of fifty thousand protestors marching up to the gates of the presidential palace before they were violently routed. Most remarkably, the protestors largely consisted of the urban poor, a population generally considered risk-averse and fragmented and thus unlikely to mobilize as a group. Why, then, did they turn out in unprecedented numbers for Joseph Estrada?

Joseph Estrada was elected president in 1998 by 40 percent of the vote, a plurality of more than twice the votes obtained by his nearest rival. Not long after being elected, his popularity declined precipitously among the middle- and upper-class segments of his constituency amid reports of his cronyism, serial indiscretions involving women, and extravagance. Discontent with Estrada came to a head when a disgruntled crony publicly accused him of receiving kickbacks from *jueteng*, an illegal gambling game. Organizing for Estrada's ouster was galvanized by the revelation, and the following month Estrada was impeached. The impeachment trial was aborted on January 16, 2001, when Estrada's allies in the Senate blocked a key piece of evidence: an envelope allegedly containing information on bank accounts for which Estrada had signed under an alias. In response, the prosecution staged a walkout. Text messages circulated furiously—two hundred million between January 16 and January 20 (Bautista 2001, 189)—expressing outrage and calling people to gather at the Edsa shrine. Soon a crowd of several hundred thousand mainly young, mainly middle-class demonstrators had assembled around the shrine. Merely three days later, on January 19, the military defected, and the mood of the crowd, never particularly solemn to begin with, turned positively festive. On the fifth day of what was already being touted as Edsa 2, the presidential oath was administered to vice president Gloria Macapagal Arroyo at the Edsa shrine. Estrada, meanwhile, had absconded by boat through the Pasig River at the rear of the palace and taken refuge in his home in San Juan. Estrada's supporters seemed to accept the development—that is, until the Arroyo government moved to arrest Estrada three months later.

On word of Estrada's impending arrest, several hundred supporters, mostly urban poor, began to gather outside the wealthy enclave where he lived. Their core had been organized by a political organization with an extensive network in several urban poor communities. At the time, politicians allied with Estrada had been hyping the idea of an "Edsa 3." The mobilization of such a large number of people would not have been possible, however, had the government's move to arrest Estrada not aroused a deep feeling of injustice among the urban poor. On the day of Estrada's arrest, the supporters who were camped outside poured inside the enclave, their numbers swelled by streams of people coming mainly from slum areas. The *Philippine Daily Inquirer* estimated that ten thousand supporters had come to Estrada's defense. The irony of the scene is rich: the urban poor storming a gated subdivision to protect its wealthiest resident from the police. On any other day, the urban poor would have been kept out of the place by security guards. This day, however, they blockaded the gates of Estrada's mansion with their bodies. Estrada reportedly called his neighbors to apologize for the inconvenience caused by the crowd.[1]

1. Rina Jimenez-David, "Little Drama, Much Significance," *Philippine Daily Inquirer*, April 26, 2001.

The demonstrators hijacked two water delivery trucks to use as barricades against the police. A few proceeded to wash themselves with water from the tankers. While doing so, they cried out in response to a newspaper article deriding them as "bathless and toothless": "Who says we're 'bathless and toothless'? Now we've got two water tankers here and are taking a bath!" The journalist reporting the incident quipped that little, however, could be done for the toothless among them.[2] Some three hundred police set upon the crowd with truncheons, tear gas, and water cannons. It took them four hours to fight their way through. Upon reaching Estrada's mansion, they rappelled over the walls and opened the gates from the inside. They drove in and collected Estrada. He went with them "meek as a lamb" while his supporters all but ran riot: [3] "Women wailed, men screamed curses, choppers thundered overhead, and battle-ready police formed a wall of flesh outside the high brown gate of No. 1 Polk Street in North Greenhills, San Juan."[4]

The major dailies hailed Estrada's arrest as "a turning point in Philippine politics," "a watershed in our historical struggle to create a working democracy," and "a powerful reminder that no one is above the law."[5] Leftist groups held a victory party. The urban poor, however, responded with lamentation. "I've never ever cried for my husband, but now I'm crying because of what you're doing to our president," one woman told a reporter, "her face drenched in tears."[6] In particular, the urban poor reacted fiercely to the publication of Estrada's mug shot in the front pages of all the dailies. An astute columnist noted: "Later, I would learn from talking to people that one detail in particular stuck out with [the Edsa 3 demonstrators]. It was not the phalanx of shielded police that came to escort Erap, it was not the women that shed tears of grief for their idol, it was not even the bloodied faces of the men that fought off the truncheon-wielding anti-riot squads. It was the sight of Erap [Estrada] being photographed left, right, and front like a common thief."[7] The image proved incendiary. It served to redouble the num-

---

2. Max V. Soliven, "The Greeks Had a Word for It," *Philippine Star*, April 26, 2001.

3. Non Alquitran, Jose Rodel Clapano, and Jaime Laude, "Erap Jailed for Plunder," *Philippine Star*, April 26, 2001.

4. Volt Contreras, Blanche S. Rivera, and Agnes E. Donato, "Erap's Biggest Box-Office Hit," *Philippine Daily Inquirer*, April 26, 2001.

5. Amando Doronila, "Estrada Arrest a Turning Point in RP Politics," *Philippine Daily Inquirer*, April 26, 2001; Jimenez-David, "Little Drama"; *Philippine Star*, "Editorial: No One Is above the Law," April 26, 2001.

6. Contreras et al., "Erap's Biggest Box-Office Hit."

7. Conrado de Quiros, "Again, the 'Dumb' Masa," *Philippine Daily Inquirer*, May 1, 2001.

bers massing at the Edsa shrine. With Estrada's arrest the stock market soared by eighteen points; with the onset of Edsa 3 it plummeted by twenty-five.[8]

The case of Estrada is a case of what the political philosopher Jacques Rancière (1999) calls dissensus (*mésentente*). Dissensus is not a matter of different parties misconstruing each other's meaning. It has to do with them not being able to comprehend what the other is talking about. The object of dissensus is constructed in different and incommensurable ways. The middle class, in general, saw Estrada as incompetent and vulgar and thus framed Edsa 3 as illegitimate, the result of the poor being manipulated by Estrada's political allies and cronies. The urban poor, in general, saw Estrada as someone who sincerely cared about the poor—indeed, for some, he was a figure worthy of devotion—and thus framed Edsa 3 as a legitimate response to the injustice of Estrada's ouster.

A state of political dissensus, one that cut largely along class lines, represented something new in Philippine history. The urban poor usually follow the lead of the middle class politically. Here, they broke sharply with that class. The urban poor usually mobilize around parochial issues and for instrumental reasons. Here they mobilized around a grievance, the arrest of *their* president, a grievance, moreover, that struck them collectively. The last time the urban poor marched to Malacañang, the presidential palace, was in 1974. Five thousand residents of informal settlements along the Tondo foreshore went to protest Marcos's plan to raze their homes. They met with the president and extracted a promise to preserve the area (van Naerssen 1993). In contrast, the march in 2001 drew well over fifty thousand participants, many from slum areas across the metro area. Finally, contention cut along the housing divide between the urban poor and middle class. One could say that both Estrada's strongest support and his strongest opposition were based in Manila, but in slums and enclaves, respectively. To be sure, the Edsa 3 forces did not consist entirely of the urban poor. They also included the members of two religious organizations that supported Estrada: the Filipinized Christian church Iglesia ni Cristo and the Catholic charismatic sect El Shaddai. The membership of these organizations was largely lower middle class (Rivera 2001). Nevertheless, the evidence—my data included—suggests that slum res-

---

8. Max V. Soliven, "Is It 'Poor People' Power, EDSA TRES, or Just Plain Hakot-Power?" *Philippine Star*, April 27, 2001.

idents heavily supported Estrada and enclave residents heavily opposed him. With respect to Estrada, the housing divide approximated a political cleavage. *This* was new.

How do we explain the state of political dissensus and the class division it traced? Why was Estrada such a polarizing figure? How was someone who was *bad* for the poor, at least in terms of their material interests, able to command their support as a group? Why had the housing divide become politically salient? Let me suggest that the answers to these questions are connected.

## The Project

This is not a book about Estrada or Edsa 3. It is not a community study of the urban poor or middle class in Manila. This is a book about the relationship between the urban poor and middle class as located in slums and enclaves (and in Manila they have become increasingly so). The project is to connect this relationship with urban structure on the one hand and political dissensus on the other, and, in the process, highlight the role of class in shaping urban space, social life, and politics. Indeed, I argue that class has become more important than ever in the wake of urban restructuring.

The title of the book, *The Patchwork City*, refers to the fragmentation of Manila into a patchwork of classed spaces, particularly slums and upper- and middle-class enclaves. This is a book not just about urban fragmentation, however, but also about its effects on class relations and politics. I make the argument that the proliferation of slums and enclaves and their subsequent proximity to each other have intensified class relations. For enclave residents, the proximity of slums constitutes a source of insecurity. They feel besieged and thus compelled to impose spatial boundaries on slum residents. For slum residents, the regular imposition of boundaries has made a sense of discrimination a common sense. Thus we see class boundaries clarify along the housing divide and the urban poor and middle class emerge as class actors—not as labor and capital but as squatters and "villagers" (in Manila, residential subdivisions are called villages).

The first part of my argument, covered in part 1 of the book, traces the emergence of class identities shaped by experiences of siege and discrimination. The second part of the argument, covered in part 2, focuses on the politicization of these identities. I trace their influence on the political thinking of the urban poor and middle class with respect to the populist president Joseph Estrada. A sense of being discriminated against made many slum residents susceptible to Estrada's appeals, which were predicated, fundamentally, on the negation of their stigma as poor people and squatters. Meanwhile, a sense of electoral, not simply territorial, siege led many in the middle class to reject Estrada as another lumpen politician, not just corrupt but also vulgar, and to push for his ouster extraconstitutionally. In Edsa 3, the class divide crystallized politically in the form of dissensus over Estrada.

The book, then, traces the processes connecting segregation, class relations, and contentious politics. These topics are usually taken separately by scholars, but if we keep our eyes on the class boundary as it manifests spatially, morally, and politically, they become hard to separate. It becomes apparent that class as a social structure is as indispensable to the study of Manila—and of many other cities of the Global South—as race is to the study of American cities.

# ONE

# The Stakes and Approach

## The Stakes

### Urban Restructuring

This story fits into a larger one about the restructuring of cities in an era of globalization. It begins with the global process of economic restructuring in the 1970s and 1980s. Restructuring involved a shift in production from manufacturing to services, a transition to more open markets, and developments in transportation and information technology. It led to increased capital mobility and greater global economic integration. Consequently, we see the dispersal of economic activities globally but also their concentration in "global cities." Friedmann and Wolff (1982), Sassen (1991), and Knox and Taylor (1995), among others, depict global cities as the command centers of the world economy. They function as hubs for corporate services as well as major sites of production.

This literature tells a story of social polarization in global and globalizing cities. It highlights the bifurcation of the labor market between high- and low-skilled service work. Although the opportunities for those at the top have expanded, the situation of those at the bottom has worsened as work is rendered "flexible" or contingent, welfare provisions rolled back, and the power of organized labor diminished. We see a contraction of the middle class, greater inequality, and the growth of informal work. Although restructuring is not making cities socially dual—they remain stratified along various, crosscutting lines—it has led to a process of dualization. Soja (1989), Mollenkopf and Castells (1991), Sassen (1994), and others have pointed to the formation of an organized core of professionals and managers and a disorganized periphery of low-wage service workers. Workers on the periphery are disorganized because they are socially heterogeneous and occupationally fragmented.

Corporate building and social polarization manifest spatially in gentrification, gating, racial and cultural segregation, eviction, homelessness, and the consolidation of "ghetto" areas. We see a restructuring of urban space distinguished, Marcuse and van Kempen (2000) contend, by two broad developments: one, the proliferation of distinct, self-contained, and relatively exclusive social spaces (e.g., residential and commercial enclaves, business and industrial districts, cultural quarters, ghettos) and, two, the emergence of new and stronger spatial divisions, both physical and symbolic. "Social contact across class lines has always been limited," they write; "what is different today is the sharpness of the spatial boundaries inhibiting such contact, the extent of the concentration by class within those boundaries" (252). They describe urban space being "quartered" along lines of race, ethnicity, class, and occupation—quartered in the sense of being fragmented but also in the sense of being pulled apart.

Soja (1989) describes the post-Fordist geography of Los Angeles as "kaleidoscopic." He depicts a city fragmented into a mosaic of spaces coexisting uneasily with one another. Davis (1990) portrays the city as increasingly forbidding. He cites building characterized by "an architecture of fear," well-heeled residents resorting to private security services, and public spaces designed to deter the wrong public (i.e., the poor and homeless). Wilson (1987) links economic restructuring to the consolidation of ghettos in Chicago. The deindustrialization of the city and the emergence of new service industries in the suburbs and other parts of the country precipitated the exodus of middle- and working-class blacks from the inner city. The "truly disadvantaged" were left behind in areas that had come to be characterized by the concentration of poverty. The literature on neighborhood effects describes these areas as "poverty traps," places where social disadvantages compound (Sampson and Morenoff 2006). Wacquant (2008), meanwhile, emphasizes a process of stigmatization that is not just racial but also territorial. While the residents of Chicago's ghettos are stigmatized, foremost, by race, the stigma attached to *banlieue* residents in France is primarily territorial. Stigma can be avoided so long as person and place are dissociated.

Urban restructuring has given rise to contestation over urban space in the form of, for example, struggles for affordable housing or against gentrification. The globalizing city has becomes a stage for marginal groups to assert their "right to the city." The notion of a right to the city has been advanced by various scholars as a way of highlighting issues of spatial justice. It means more than just the right to urban space and resources. It means the right to urban life (Lefebvre 1996) or urban presence (Sassen 1999)—essentially, the right to remake the city in one's image over and against the interests of capital (Harvey 2003).

Abu-Lughod (1999) cautions against seeing the effects of restructuring as uniform across cities. She observes significant variation in the effects of restructuring on New York, Chicago, and Los Angeles. Social polarization is a function not purely of globalization, she contends, but of different, city-specific causes. Brenner (2001) agrees that restructuring is path-dependent and welcomes thicker, more contextually embedded scholarship. He argues, nonetheless, that it marks a break with earlier phases of urbanization, one distinguished by the globalization of urban processes. The variation in outcomes represents different expressions of the same process.

Cities in the Global South also underwent an urban restructuring, but to understand the impact of that, we cannot simply extrapolate from the experience of cities in the Global North. The effects of restructuring on the Global South have differed in significant ways. We see growth in high-value corporate services but also in manufacturing, particularly across Asia and in parts of Latin America. We cannot really speak of deindustrialization when, in most countries, there was little industrialization to begin with. Instead, economists talk about countries "leapfrogging" industrialization by wholeheartedly embracing services. The implementation of market reforms accelerated the inflow of foreign direct investment (FDI) into metro regions, spectacularly remaking urban landscapes in many primate cities. A market orientation generally promoted economic growth and led to significant reductions in poverty (eventually, if not initially), but it also worsened conditions of work. Employers increasingly turned to nonregular, unprotected forms of employment. The informal sector, already large, expanded in some countries. Overall, work became even more precarious (Kalleberg and Hewison 2013; Portes and Roberts 2005).

Although there is growing income inequality and a bifurcation between professional and precarious work, social polarization in the developing world is not quite the same thing as social polarization in the developed one. For one, we see a thickening, not a thinning, of the middle class in the developing world. Economic restructuring led to the growth of the middle class as an economic group as well as to its greater sense of identity as a social one. In Latin America and the Caribbean, for instance, the middle class expanded by 50 percent, from 103 million to 152 million, between 2003 and 2009 (Ferreira et al. 2013). It now accounts for about 30 percent of the region's population, with most of the rest consisting of the poor and near poor, at 38 percent and 30 percent, respectively. Second, if restructuring in the Global North led to the emergence of problems related to a new precarity among workers (e.g., the growth of an informal economy, spreading homelessness, consolidation of the ghetto), social polarization in the Global South has meant the worsening of old problems associated with "overurbanization," notably, precarious work and informal housing.

Scholars in the 1950s and 1960s diagnosed "Third World" cities as being overurbanized. By this they meant that urban growth had "run ahead" of the city's capacity to absorb the population (Davis and Golden 1954; Hoselitz 1957; Gugler and Flanagan 1976).[1] There wasn't enough industrialization or economic development relative to urban growth; specifically, there weren't enough jobs, housing, and services. The problem, though, was not simply a lack of jobs; it was that most of the urban population had no other option but casual work—work characterized by the insecurity of employment and income (Bromley and Gerry 1979). These jobs were not so much occupations as means of getting by. Overurbanization also manifested in the growth of slums. Slums were not only a general problem affecting Third World cities— market economies, specifically—across the board. They proved a persistent problem. A third of the urban population in developing countries continues to live in slums. This figure represents a slight decline proportionally (from about 35 percent to 40 percent in the 1970s) but a breathtaking increase in absolute numbers. The slum population in cities of the Global South grew from one hundred million in 1960 to nearly nine hundred million in 2014 (UN Habitat 2016).

Urban restructuring in the 1990s was distinguished most evidently by widespread enclavization. This includes the enclosure of the rich and middle class behind the walls of gated subdivisions and closed condominiums (heavily guarded high-rises), the building of corporate and commercial enclaves, and the bundling of various functions

---

1. In counterpoint, Sovani (1964) argued that claims of overurbanization were overstated and the concept Eurocentric.

within the same exclusive spaces. Enclavization has been driven by the unprecedented inflow of FDI and remittances, as well as by middle-class demand. The real estate industries in cities of the Global South have focused not only on meeting this demand but also on helping create it by marketing enclaves as the very definition of modern housing (e.g., Connell 1999).

In some cities, the proliferation of slums and enclaves has produced a pattern of segregation characterized by the proximity of spaces sharply distinguished by their class character. This pattern—mixed at the macro level and intensely segregated at the micro level—has been described as "cellular segregation" (Thibert and Osorio 2013), "perverse integration" (Portes, Itzigsohn, and Cabral 1994), and "proximity and walls" (Caldeira 2000) in certain Latin American cities.[2] There is evidence of a similar kind of fragmentation in other cities across the Global South, including Manila (Shatkin 2008), Mumbai (Patel 2007), Jakarta (Firman 2004), Istanbul (Genis 2007), and Cairo (Abaza 2001). For this set of cities, we can say, in general, that the urban middle class and poor have moved closer together in space and that their spaces have become more sharply distinguished. In Manila, as we will see, the interspersion of slums and enclaves is especially pronounced.

As a result of these spatial sorting processes, many Global Southern cities have become more clearly dual. We see spatial boundaries proliferating and becoming sharper. As a number of scholars have observed (Gonzáles de la Rocha et al. 2004; Koonings and Krujit 2009; Sandhu and Sandhu 2007), the experience of stigma and exclusion has become salient. The stigma is primarily territorial; the exclusion primarily spatial. In a survey of favela residents in Rio de Janeiro, Perlman (2010) found that living in a favela constituted a greater source of discrimination than being dark-skinned, looking a certain way, or originating outside the city. In Manila, class boundaries are clarifying and calcifying along the boundary between slums and enclaves. We are seeing class formation along the housing divide. We need to understand this process relationally, that is, as driven by class interaction. It is through such interaction that boundaries take shape and class groups acquire definition. What restructuring is changing, I argue, is the extent and quality of class interaction. It is this thread I pick up and develop throughout this book.

What has restructuring meant for urban experience? What has it

2. See also Bosdorf, Hidalgo, and Sánchez (2007); Coy and Pöhler (2002); Ribiero and Lago (1995); and Sabatini (2003).

meant, specifically, for the experience of class relations in cities of the Global South? A number of studies already focus on the plight of the urban poor or middle class under restructuring.[3] It is not just the one or the other group being transformed, however, but their relationship. It is their dynamic, not their individual situations, that is producing a new spatiality, sociality, and politics. I focus, therefore, on the changing experience of class relations. It is this aspect that I seek to integrate more fully into the larger story. After all, urban restructuring involves more than just the transformation of social and spatial structures. It involves the formation of distinct subjectivities and a particular economy of practices. The two elements, structure and experience, are bound together, and so by integrating them, we can get a better account of social processes at stake. We also will be better able to see how restructuring has shaped subjectivity and practice and how these, in turn, reproduce emergent social and spatial structures. In the case of Manila, I show a pattern of segregation to affect the extent and quality of class interaction and give rise to logics of practice that, enacted, further entrench segregation and underscore class boundaries.

Further, by incorporating experience into the story, we are able to see beyond the usual plotlines. We are able to extend the story beyond space and class and into the realm of politics. I show how the experience of the urban poor and middle class as class actors shapes their subjectivity as political actors. I show how it leads to contention not just over the right to the city but also over the right to speak and be heard. It leads to contention over democracy.

### Democracy and Inequality

Democracy Distorted

For Tocqueville ([1835] 2003), democracy is more than just a form of government; it is a type of society based on equality. He was struck by the general equality of conditions prevailing in early nineteenth-century America among freemen of European origin. Social equality was coupled with a remarkable social mobility such that, Tocqueville recounts, most of the wealthy men he encountered had come from poverty. As he saw it, the situation fostered democratic relations. Com-

---

3. In addition to work previously cited, see Anjaria (2016); Baviskar and Ray (2011); Fernandes (2006); Ghertner (2015); Harms (2013); Robison and Goodman (1996); Takashi and Phongpaichit (2008); Weinstein (2014); and Zhang (2010).

pared to the situation in Europe, interaction was simple, easy, uncomplicated by status concerns, and unencumbered by ceremony. The influence of social equality on the imagination was profound. It became easy to imagine oneself in the place of others, and thus people were better able to conceive "a general compassion" for one another. It became easy to imagine oneself along with everyone else as part of the same nation. This led, naturally, to a feeling of solidarity. Because it was easy to place oneself within the nation as a whole, the notion that the majority possessed moral authority appeared self-evident, and the legitimacy of representative government could be taken for granted. In contrast, in an aristocratic nation, where social inequality has been formalized into a hierarchy of status groups, members of the different groups "scarcely believe that they belong to the same human race" (650).

Tocqueville illustrates this difference with reference to the master-servant relationship. In aristocratic nations, masters and servants form "two social groups, one lying above the other, always clearly defined by parallel principles" (663). But in America the difference between masters and servants is situational more than it is social. Their common status as citizens takes precedence over their occupational or class identities. Servants are not seen as inferior to masters by nature; "they become so only temporarily by contract." "Within the terms of this contract," Tocqueville continues, "one is servant, one is master; beyond that they are two citizens, two men" (667). To put the matter another way, general equality creates a democratic ethos that negates specific situations of hierarchy, "a sort of imaginary equality in spite of the actual inequality of their social condition" (668).

We might add a contemporary contrast. In India, domestic servants form an essential part of middle-class households, and yet they are considered socially distinct from their employers. According to Qayum and Ray (2011), this distinction has blurred with the spread of mass culture. Employers complain that servants are no longer as easily identifiable by their dress or deportment. This becomes a cause for anxiety, for "if female servants 'pass' as middle-class women, then employers could mistakenly socialize with them, talk to them as peers and, most worryingly of all, conceivably fall in love with them" (267). The threat of pollution, the fact that servants can only pass and never *be*, reveals the nature of the divide between the groups. They are seen as unequal not only in condition and capability but also in kind and worth. To use Charles Tilly's phrase (1998), they are categorically unequal.

Categorical inequality blocks the democratic imagination. In India and other countries in the Global South, members of the upper strata are unable to imagine the political body as continuous and whole. They conceive of it, rather, as segmented, consisting of us few and the many thems. They view the masses as lacking an equal capacity for discernment and thus discount their political participation. When the majority is believed to lack moral authority, elections become a form of tyranny. The nature and desirability of democracy is thrown into question. Extreme inequality, Lipset (1960, 66) wrote, creates a situation in which the upper class treats the lower class as "vulgar" and "innately inferior." The lower class's notion of having a share in power strikes the upper class as "essentially absurd and immoral."

This situation remains relevant to a number of third-wave democracies in the Global South—Brazil, for instance. Weffort (1992, 24) describes Brazil as "Belindia," "meaning that the rich Brazil is small like Belgium, and the poor Brazil is big like India." "What is the meaning of political democracy," he asks, "if governments are elected by people from 'India' and the real power is controlled by people from 'Belgium'?" He goes on to argue that extreme social inequality stunts the consolidation of democracy. Consolidation means that "the rules of the game" (the game being democracy) are widely shared, and even taken for granted, by the population. It refers to the institutionalization not just of democratic procedure but of a democratic ethos. In contrast are polities characterized by a gap between formal rules and actual behavior, polities where formal rules are regularly overwhelmed by informal and particularistic practices (see O'Donnell 1999). Of course, in countries like "Belindia," such practices are necessary. They represent a means of incorporating the substantial population falling outside formal structures of governance. Extreme inequality, in short, encourages political dualism.

Chatterjee (2004) identifies two distinct modes of politics in India: civil society and political society. Civil society in his sense does not encompass the entire domain of nonstate organization (as it does in the classical sense). It is limited to the associational activities of people possessing a certain amount of property and education—"a small set of culturally equipped citizens" (41)—and thus represents something of a bourgeois public sphere. In these hands, the project of civil society is the project of modernization, or, in other words, "to make subjects citizens" (31). Political society, in contrast, refers to the substantial domain of political negotiation occurring, for the most part, outside the law and formal channels. It is mediated by relationships with politicians and government agencies and largely comprises the accommodation of claims to shelter, livelihood, and development. Politicians and bureaucrats negotiate out of electoral or pastoral considerations, that is, in response to political mobilization or as a way of carrying out a welfare mandate. Chatterjee astutely observes that such accommodations allow for an incremental modification of property relations—which, given the extent of deprivation, is inescapable—without fundamentally threatening their constitutional basis.

The distinction between civil and political society has been criticized for its simplicity. The distinction does not always align so neatly with the distinctions between legal and illegal or paralegal, or between formal and informal (Baviskar and Sundar 2008). Fernandes (2006) points out that, one, civil society is not equivalent to middle-class society. It also includes organized labor. Two, civil society is not monolithic. The issues taken up within civil society are highly diverse and sometimes at cross-purposes. Three, the middle class does not operate only through civil society; it also engages with the state in significant ways (in Fernandes's example, by campaigning for beautification projects designed to clear the streets of squatters and hawkers). Moreover, the middle class continues to rely on informal modes of political influence, including patronage, bribery, and social networks. These are all good points. They complicate the distinction between civil and political society in ways that sharpen our picture of the situation. But they do not invalidate it. I find the distinction useful not only because it draws our attention to different spheres of political activity but because it highlights the tension between them—the tension between the project of modernization on the one hand and practices of democratic accommodation on the other. Given the prevalence of such practices, Chatterjee (2004, 41) notes, "one is liable to hear complaints from the protagonists of civil society and the constitutional state that modernity is facing an unexpected rival in the form of democracy."

Lipset (1960), following Aristotle, identifies a large middle class as being crucial to democracy. He cites its role in tempering social division and promoting democratic norms. The middle class in the Global South is not large, but it is growing and becoming more assertive. Its greater presence and activity, however, seem to be worsening categorical inequality. The middle class in India, Fernandes (2006) writes, feel a sense of alienation from normal politics. They come to view it as dirty, and democracy as vulgar (see also Anjaria 2016; Hansen 1999; Harriss 2006). At the same time, they feel it incumbent upon themselves to engage in a different sort of politics. Thus, we see increasing involvement in civil society, as defined by Chatterjee. Activism in civil society, Harriss (2006, 461) claims, has become "a part of what it means to be 'middle class.'" The problem is that civil society is an exclusive sphere of activity. It is constructed on a number of distinctions: against the backward masses, a venal state, a dissolute elite, and a demoralized middle class. It partakes in a moral discourse premised on civility, or, more exactly, opposed to vulgarity, corruption, disorder, and filth. It promotes a vision of the city as slum-free (Ghertner 2015). It does not reject democracy so much as seek to discipline it by proscribing certain forms of political mediation (e.g., clientelism) as "corruption." In general, civil society adopts a paternalistic attitude toward the poor. Although a lot of activism is dedicated to helping the poor, it is frequently with the aim of transforming them. This becomes a precondition of real democracy: the education or "conscientization" of the masses. Only then will they be able to participate in politics properly. This attitude ends up reproducing the distinction between citizens and "people 'to be done unto'" (Harriss 2006, 462). It has the effect, in other words, of reinforcing categorical inequality and thus undermining the development of a democratic ethos.

This is where my story comes in. I describe the situation of a middle class that sees itself as a moral minority, possessing the right values and yet outnumbered and outvoted by people possessing the wrong ones. Their sense of electoral siege informs their political calculations: whether to support "winnable" candidates over those who reflect their values, whether to abide crooked leaders to avoid populist ones. It informs their efforts to teach their workers, household help, and neighboring slum residents how to make good political choices. The sense of electoral siege among Manila's middle class has grown stronger with the proliferation of populist candidates in the 2000s. It has bred a palpable frustration with democracy. This is significant because these are the same people who championed democracy in the 1980s. We are witnessing their disenchantment.

Disjunctive Democracy

If the middle class begins with the fact of categorical inequality and from there questions the viability of democracy, then the urban poor begin with the promise of equality heralded by democracy and ask why they continue to be treated as second-class citizens.

DaMatta (1991), writing about Brazil in the 1970s, observed that the upper class, when confronted by lowly state authorities—when pulled over by traffic police, for instance—commonly rebuff them by saying,

"Do you know who you're talking to?" The question is an assertion of hierarchy, a way of putting social inferiors in their place. Its widespread use, he argued, belies the conceit that everybody is equal before the law. It undermines the status of citizenship. Holston (2008) reports the difference democracy has made. He recalls standing in line at a bank in São Paulo in the mid-1990s. By that time, Brazil had been democratic for nearly a decade. A teenager nonchalantly cut the line. When people grumbled, a well-dressed man spoke up for the teen. He claimed to "authorize" the cut. The manicurist standing behind the man protested immediately. "'This is a public space,' she asserted, 'and I have my rights. Here, you don't authorize anything'" (17). The teenager skulked to the back of the line. Holston tells the story to make the point that class relations have changed with democratization. Citizenship has become meaningful even for the poor.

Latin American scholars have noted that democratization has made the urban poor more rights conscious (Gonzáles de la Rocha et al. 2004). A rights discourse has become widespread as a result of social movements pushing for democracy and nongovernmental organizations (NGOs) framing their advocacy in terms of rights. At the same time, the urban poor have become more conscious of the disjunction between their political rights and their social inequality. Despite having an equal vote, they continue to be treated unequally in society. They face discrimination in the courts and by the police, in hospitals, at schools and government agencies, and in their everyday interactions with the "rich." Their settlements are demolished without due process. Furthermore, they are criminalized and targeted by the police. They lack recourse in the courts. Weak civil rights undermine their status as citizens (Holston and Caldeira 1998; Oxhorn 2003). This situation has generated a powerful demand for their equal recognition as citizens.

As Hobsbawm (1962) discovered, the French Revolution had a similar effect on the English working class in the early nineteenth century. It inspired what he called a "Jacobin consciousness." This consciousness combined with and reinforced their proletarian consciousness. The two kinds of consciousness were distinct, however—the one shaped by democratic ideals and the other by the experience of exploitation. We might keep this distinction in mind moving forward. The urban poor may have accepted a democratic ethos and become less willing to tolerate class discrimination, but I argue something else: they are experiencing *more* discrimination in the wake of urban restructuring. I see this as driving their support for populism.

Populism in the Global South should be understood against the backdrop of stigmatization and exclusion. It takes shape in contexts distinguished by extreme social inequality and historically weak forms of institutional representation. Populism thus functions as a mode of political incorporation through the person of the leader (in contrast to incorporation through government bureaucracy, political parties, or social movements). Within these contexts, effective populist leaders speak to people's need to be seen as possessing social worth. Perlman (2010) writes of the importance, for *favelados* in Rio, of being *gente* (somebody). My urban poor informants often complained of being treated as if they were not people—of being disregarded, dismissed, and disrespected. They spoke of the humiliation that came with such mistreatment. My data speak to the importance of a politics of recognition among the urban poor. This kind of politics has been discussed mainly in the context of multicultural regimes in the Global North. It is seen as involving the assertion of ethnic or cultural difference over and against liberal policies of dedifferentiation (Fraser 1997; Taylor 1994). In the Global South, however, a politics of recognition involves stigmatized groups asserting their equal dignity. This politics is central to populism. Allow me to illustrate.

The social historian Daniel James (1988) situates workers' support for Juan Perón against the backdrop of Argentina's *década infame*, a period stretching from 1930 to 1943 marked by economic depression and widespread public cynicism in the wake of relentless corruption scandals. Workers experienced this period as profoundly disempowering. What Peronism did was "give public utterance to what had until then been internalised, lived as private experience" (30). Its "heretical" power derived from symbolic inversion; it made those on the margins the protagonists of national renewal. Nothing exemplified this better than the positive resignification of the word *descamisado* (shirtless one), once used to disparage workers. The term came to connote one's status as a Perón supporter. Peronism was found more credible than the discourse of traditional working-class parties because it dealt with the concrete economic situation of workers. Other parties, in contrast, favored "woolly generalities concerning national renovation and civic virtue" (21). Peronism took workers as they were and not as they needed to become in order to fulfill some historical role. Unlike his political rivals, Perón affirmed workers' lifestyle and values. He addressed them in a popular idiom without moralizing or judgment. This recognition, James argues, was the key to Peronism's appeal.

This argument reflects Weber's insight into charisma; namely, it is the product of recognition (rather than the cause of it). That is, leaders appear extraordinary because their supporters recognize them as such. Supporters feel compelled to recognize leaders in light of their having proved themselves through some extraordinary quality or act,[4] which resonates in a particular context of meaning. Perón's recognition of workers was beheld as extraordinary given the context of the *década infame*. Consequently, workers responded, in Weber's language, with "devotion to the corresponding revelation," that is, by recognizing Perón's claim to leadership.

Taking Weber seriously means shifting our focus from leaders to the relationship between leaders and supporters. It means looking not only at the leader's qualities but also at the context in which those qualities are received. It means asking why those qualities speak to supporters. Consider Venezuela's Hugo Chávez, for example. Most explanations of his appeal focus on his attributes, rhetoric, and tactics. The problem with this approach is that scholars end up emphasizing different things. For Weyland (2003, 844), Chávez's charisma had to do with "the attraction of his crude diction and belligerent rhetoric." Roberts (2003, 70) cites "his modest upbringing, mixed racial features, blunt discourse, and penchant for playing baseball." Sylvia and Danopolous (2003, 67) include "his dark complexion and coarse hair [which] identify him racially with the vast majority of Venezuelans," his invocation of the nationalist icon Simón Bolívar, and his use of media to communicate directly and regularly with the poor. López and Lander (2000) explain Chávez's appeal with reference to several qualities, including his rhetoric (as antielitist, nationalist, and culturally resonant), his outsider status, his working-class roots, his deft use of symbols and rituals, his military background, and his physical features. Clearly, charisma functions as a kind of catchall for any number of appealing qualities; consequently, it explains very little. The analytical challenge is not to enumerate the leader's populist credentials but to explain why they work. We cannot do this without taking into account the perspective of supporters.[5]

4. According to Weber ([1922] 1978, 242): "It is recognition on the part of those subject to authority which is decisive for the validity of charisma. This recognition is freely given and guaranteed by what is held to be a proof, originally always a miracle, and consists in devotion to the corresponding revelation, hero worship, or absolute trust in the leader."

5. See, for example, Javier Auyero's (2001) work on clientelism. Auyero is adept at illuminating urban poor politics "from the inside."

I argue that Estrada's tremendous support among the urban poor derives from a political performance that actively negates their sense of stigma. Slum residents explain his appeal by recounting stories of his visiting them, sharing meals with them, hugging them without hesitation, and generally attending to them as decent human beings. This simple performance resonates because they expect to be treated otherwise, to be discriminated against because of where they live. Hence, Estrada's consideration strikes them as revelatory. They see him as sincere, as someone who truly cares about them in a field of politicians who merely use them for electoral gain, and thus they support him unreservedly. Recognition succeeds in annulling the stigma, if not the reality, of poverty— hence its power to drive political support.

## Dissensus

I make sense of Edsa 3 using Rancière's notion of dissensus. In the original French, Rancière uses the word *mésentente*, which has been translated in English as both "dissensus" and "disagreement." The word means "both 'the fact of not hearing, of not understanding' and 'quarrel, disagreement'" (Rancière 2004, 5). On one level, dissensus refers to a situation of cognitive disjunction in which different parties view the same object or event differently, even antithetically: "While clearly understanding what Y is saying, X cannot *see* the object Y is talking about; or else, X understands and is bound to understand, sees, and attempts to make visible another object using the same name, another reason within the same argument" (Rancière 1999, xi). Dissensus is not the result of ignorance about the true nature of the object or misunderstanding the other side's representation of it. It cannot be resolved by supplying the facts or by clarifying positions all around. It cannot be "corrected," so to speak. The views at stake are fundamentally at odds because they are informed by different beliefs and expectations.

Dissensus is not just a matter of cognitive disjunction, however. There is more at stake than disagreement over the true nature of an object or event. It is an essentially political phenomenon. The dissenting parties are not just any two social actors but two parts of society, the one dominant and the other excluded. In Rancière's terms, dissensus involves a conflict between the part that counts (and does the counting—that is, whose view of things normally prevails) and "the part that has no part." Dissensus thus represents politics in action—indeed, Rancière defines politics *as* dissensus—insofar as it disrupts the "natural" social order (domination presented as consensus) and makes exclusion visible.

Rancière begins with the Aristotelian definition of the political animal as a speaking animal. Not everyone, however, possesses the capacity to speak. Aristotle distinguished those who possess language from those, like slaves, women, and workers, who merely understand it. To illustrate the distinction, Rancière cites Ballanche's account of the plebeian secession on the Aventine Hill in ancient Rome. He reads the conflict between patricians and plebeians as being "above all, one over what it was to speak" (2004, 5):

Plebeians, gathered on the Aventine Hill, demanded a treaty with the patricians. The patricians responded that this was impossible, because to make a treaty meant giving one's word: since the plebeians did not have human speech, they could not give what they did not have. They possessed only a "sort of bellowing which was a sign of need and not a manifestation of intelligence." In order to understand what the plebeians said, then, it had first to be admitted that they spoke. And this required a novel perceptual universe, one where—contrary to all perceptible evidence—those who worked for a living had affairs in common with free men and a voice to designate and argue these common affairs.

This is what "disagreement [*mésentente*]" means.

Dissensus, he writes elsewhere, "is not a discussion between speaking people who would confront their interests and values. It is a conflict about who speaks and who does not speak" (2011, 2).

For Rancière, the question defining politics is not the standard one given in political science textbooks. It is not who governs or who gets what, when, and how. The question he would have us ask is, Who counts? This question cuts to the very heart of Edsa 3. Senator Miriam Santiago, an Estrada partisan, watching the people mass along Edsa, proclaimed that "this is just a numbers game"—meaning that once Edsa 3 had surpassed Edsa 2 in size, the government would have no choice but to capitulate. Well, it did surpass Edsa 2—according to one estimate, by as many as half a million people—and yet it failed anyway. Clearly, the issue was not how many, which presumes an equal weighting of the people involved in the two demonstrations, but who counts. Despite their greater number, the people participating in Edsa 3 counted for less. We know why. My qualitative chapters make the fact of categorical inequality painfully clear.

Because categorical inequality is ordinarily taken as given, it represents a stopping of politics—what Rancière calls "consensus." Dissensus represents a break with this order and the reinstitution of politics. It counterposes a different logic of counting, the logic of democracy, against the prevailing logic. This assertion alone does not overrule the order of things, but it does serve to expose its contingency by disclosing "the presence of two worlds in one." "The essential work of politics," Rancière writes (2010, 37), "is to make the world of its subjects seen." Politics brings "a universe previously thought of as domestic [i.e., as consisting of private grievances] into public visibility. It [makes] the inhabitants of that world visible as beings belonging to the same (public) world to which others [belong], that is, as beings capable of common speech and thought" (2004, 7). In this respect, Edsa 3 succeeded.

A regard for dissensus informs not only my analysis of Edsa 3 but also my approach to studying class contention generally. I try to do justice to both sides. I try to present the predicaments of the urban poor and middle class sympathetically and to represent their perspectives faithfully. This is reflected in the structure of the book. I make it a point to air both sides. In chapter 8, I focus on the urban poor's experience of Edsa 3, but this is necessary to counterbalance the dominant account. I have not adopted this approach to be more "objective." My aim is to keep dissensus in view because it is always in danger of being occluded and because visibility—of the groups and situations that belie the stories we tell ourselves—is good for democracy. It may not always lead to understanding, but at least we can't help but receive an invitation to understand.

In the previous two sections, a key word was *experience*. The book sheds light on the experience of class relations in the wake of urban restructuring, and on the experience of democracy in an unequal society. Here the key word is *understanding, Verstehen*, an analytical and empathic apprehension not just of the one side or the other's plight but also of a collective situation of which dissensus is an ineradicable part. Not every situation of dissensus can be amended by deliberation. People cannot always be persuaded by the other side. Indeed, efforts to persuade may end up driving them farther away. What is needed is not necessarily more or better "communicative action" but rather a capacity for understanding. Understanding the other side does not mean that we cannot judge that side to be right or wrong in our own view. It just means suspending judgment for a moment (the moment, here, representing an analytical rather than a temporal interval). Understanding is the step that precedes and hopefully conditions judgment. It is good for democracy because simply to make the effort requires an evaluation of worth. It means viewing the other group as worth understanding and as people who can be understood. It may even mean imagining ourselves believing and behaving similarly were we in their place. This is the opposite of disregarding and dismissing, the opposite of treating people as categorically unequal. Such, in capsule form, is the politics of my political ethnography.[6]

## The Analytical Approach

### *Class*

I employ Bourdieu's (1984, 1987, 1991) conceptualization of social class. For Bourdieu, class maps onto location in what he calls social space. Social space represents a structure of relative positions determined by the distribution of capital. Capital is Bourdieu's way of talking about power. He constructs social space mainly with respect to three types of capital: economic, cultural, and social. The first refers to property and money, the second to competencies acquired through education and other modes of socialization, and the third to resources derived from membership in social networks. One's position in social space depends not just on the volume of capital but also on its composition and trajectory, that is, how much there is of one type vis-à-vis another and whether one's stock is projected to grow over time (e.g., as with students). Thus conceived, social space is multidimensional, implicating both market situation and social honor (Weberian class and status), and it is dynamic. Importantly, it is also continuous.

Social space represents an uneven terrain but one without clear divisions. This means that we can posit social classes on the basis of objective inequalities, but that does not make them "real." It does not mean that people actually think of themselves in terms of class. There is a difference, in other words, between class as an analytical group and class as a social group, between "classes on paper" and "real classes." People need to believe in class for it to exist. They need to use class to make sense of their lives. Getting this to happen takes work, specifically, symbolic labor. The inequality between two populations must be represented as a categorical inequality, that is, as a difference between groups. This work is done by expressing preferences and engaging in practices that distinguish the people occupying one part of social space

---

6. Benzecry and Baiocchi (2017) encourage us to make these positions explicit.

from the people occupying another. These practices serve to define the boundary between groups, which is to say, they define class relations. For Bourdieu, class struggle is primarily a "classification struggle" to delineate the groups in contention. In this struggle, the parties are unequally armed. Those possessing more capital or the right type of capital will appear to have greater authority (symbolic capital) in making pronouncements about what is proper and who belongs where.

In *Distinction*, Bourdieu (1984) highlights the role of aesthetic preferences or taste in demarcating class groups. The literature on the new middle class in Asia emphasizes the role of consumption practices in making the "new rich" visible as a group (Leichty 2003; Robison and Goodman 1996; Zhang 2010). In this book, I focus on the imposition of spatial boundaries.[7] Boundary imposition creates not just class groups but class spaces. Indeed, the latter become symbolic of the former. This means that spatial boundaries do not just align with but come to define class boundaries. Moreover, the spatialization of class boundaries has the effect of hardening them, of making them both more determinate and durable.

Class also becomes "real" through the intermediation of a spokesperson—a person or group able to claim, credibly, to speak for the group as a whole. By speaking in the name of the group, the spokesperson helps constitute it. Bourdieu (1987, 1991) called this existence by delegation. He warned that it comes at the cost of usurpation. People surrender the power to speak for themselves to the delegate, who speaks for them. I show that Estrada became symbolic of the urban poor, that he came to represent them. On the one hand, this meant that they could be mobilized as a group, as manifest in Edsa 3. On the other hand, it meant that their solidarity was tethered to the figure of Estrada. This limited their political imagination and agenda. They were not a class for itself but a class *through* Estrada.

### Categorical Inequality

As demographic categories, "urban poor" and "middle class" are not well defined. The terms themselves are woefully imprecise. For the most part, the urban poor are not poor by official measures, just poor relative to the middle class. They are not just poor but workers. Latin American scholars prefer the term *popular sector* for these reasons. The

---

7. The sociological literature on boundaries is vast, spanning from Abbot (1995) to Zerubavel (1991), and I have no intention of retreading it. See Lamont and Molnar (2002) for a useful review.

term *middle class* is also ambiguous. It is not clear where to draw the upper and lower boundaries that distinguish the group. As social groups, however, the difference between the urban poor and middle class is unmistakable. They are distinguished by their different positions in the labor market, their differential ability to access property in the formal housing market, and their drastically divergent life chances. They are distinguished most markedly by the differential attribution of social honor. Indeed, the social difference between groups is of the extreme kind Weber described as "ethnic," with one side stigmatized and considered physically polluting. Social interaction, therefore, takes on a categorical form, as interaction between different and unequal groups.

A categorically unequal relationship, following Tilly (1998), is both unequal and hierarchical, as illustrated here:

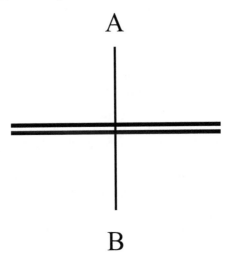

This means that A has more power than B, or even that A has power over B (the vertical line connecting A and B). This power may be cultural as well as economic, with A possessing the knowledge and knowhow to appear authoritative in general. Second, the relationship is marked by a categorical difference (the double line between A and B). It is organized around a social boundary. The difference between A and B, in other words, is not continuous: B cannot equal A simply by acquiring more money and knowledge. She must be transformed socially, that is, collectively recognized as belonging in the A group. In the context of the Philippines, the word *masa* captures the qualitative difference at stake. *Masa*, literally "the masses," connotes a vulgarity and backwardness associated with a lack of means, refinement, and "proper" knowledge. As a noun, *masa* describes "the great unwashed" or hoi polloi. As an adjective, the word is commonly used to denounce something as lowbrow or in bad taste. (One middle-class informant, for instance, described her maid's wedding dress as *pang-masa*, or fit only for the *masa*.) What is important to realize is that the poor are not just poor but *masa*. The sense that they are different is so strong that they are stigmatized or marked by social dishonor. This mark is thought to manifest in every aspect of their person. As the ethnographer Michael Pinches (1991, 178) eloquently describes, countless attributes expose the urban poor's categorical inequality and bring them shame:

The labels of poverty, propertylessness, and uncertain employment are inescapable—they are embedded in one's speech and language skills, in one's command of etiquette and bureaucratic procedure; they are evident in the texture and usually the color of one's skin, or in the condition of one's teeth, dentures, and hair; they can often be seen in one's posture and gait, or in the quality of one's attire, jewelry, and makeup, in the type of food one buys, in the location of one's home, workplace, and school, and in the company one keeps. In Manila, both rich and poor have an acute sensitivity to these signs and symbols of human value.

"Squatters" are a subcategory of the *masa*. The stigma they bear is primarily territorial and communicates, specifically, crime and the threat of encroachment.

Categorical inequality describes a form of social interaction. Following Simmel (1909), we can distinguish form from content. The form of interaction refers to its structure, and the content to its practical meaning, that is, the specific purposes or interests animating it. The distinction matters because the same form can have different contents—for example, one marriage may be characterized by amity and another by enmity, but both possess the same form. Conversely, the same content may take different forms; for example, economic interest may take the form of cooperation or competition. On the one hand, Simmel recognizes that the distinction between form and content is purely analytical. We cannot just "wring out" the meaning from sociological phenomena and derive its form. Form and content, practically speaking, are inextricable. On the other hand, the distinction provides insight into the nature of a relationship beyond its variable contents. As we will see, categorically unequal interaction may encompass different contents: feelings of charity as well as hostility, efforts to uplift as well as to exclude. It is important, however, to keep sight of the social boundary that organizes class relations. Whether boundaries are maintained or negated matters more than the specific character of interaction. Charity conducted in terms of categorical inequality, though intended to uplift, keeps class actors in their place. Meanwhile, boundaries that have been negated release enormous energy. The person doing the negating gains the appreciation and support of the people whose stigma is negated, however temporarily. Boundary negation, in short, confers symbolic power. This fact has political implications, as we will discover.

## Class Identity

I am interested in the class identities of the urban poor and middle class. I use the term *class identity* partly to avoid the connotations stuck to the term *class consciousness*, which might otherwise have been acceptable. *Class consciousness* has come to mean class actors, workers in particular, becoming conscious of, one, their real interests as a class and, two, the conflict between their interests and those of capitalists. Class consciousness is usually understood to be a collective state of mind that workers "awaken to" or achieve in the course of class struggle. As Thompson (1978, 149) wrote, it represents "the last, not the first, stage in the real historical process." By the term *class identity*, I have in mind something much more general.

I understand identity in terms of the identity theory developed by Stryker and associates (Stryker 1980; Stryker and Burke 2000; Stets and Burke 2000). They present a view of identity as shaped by social interaction, and interaction as shaped by social—and, I would add, spatial—structures. In identity theory, society is conceived as made up of relatively durable patterns of social interaction. In interaction, we occupy positions and play roles invested with specific meanings and expectations. By making these meanings our own and defining ourselves through them, we take on identities. We have as many identities as distinct positions we occupy or roles we play. Class is only one among several social identities, and it is not always the most salient one.

Class identity, then, refers to shared understandings, interpretations, and propensities formed in the course of a specific type of social interaction: class interaction. It also includes dispositions activated reflexively in the form of bodily schemas. Thus, I often speak of informants possessing a sense of class. The focus of this definition is not on the "truth" of their beliefs, ideas, and feelings but on the extent to which they form a class subjectivity. A class identity, thus defined, does not imply a capacity for autonomous collective action. It does not entail class organization or a political agenda. The politicization and mobilization of class groups constitute a separate process contingent on a particular set of factors (well elaborated by social movement scholars). Class subjectivity is important in its own right, however. As I will show, it colors the everyday experience of class interaction, it affects how class actors navigate urban space, and it shapes political opinions and the character of political contention.

### Slums and Enclaves

I study the urban poor and middle class by focusing on residents of slums and enclaves. To a significant extent, the urban poor and middle class are located along the divide between slums and enclaves. The overlap is imperfect, however. Not all urban poor live in slums, and not all middle class live in enclaves. By focusing on polar forms, we overlook intermediate spaces: mixed neighborhoods in older parts of the metro, socialized housing, rental units in apartment buildings, rooming houses. We also overlook the urban poor incorporated into middle-class households as domestics. These omissions must be acknowledged as deficits of vision—blind spots (which I collect at the end of the chapter). At the same time, slums and enclaves are not just where we happen to find the urban poor and middle class; these spaces are implicated in their formation as groups. The social difference between them is in large part constituted spatially, that is, on the basis of their residence in classed spaces. By being sorted into slums and enclaves, they become more sharply divided not only spatially but also socially. In this respect, it makes sense to focus on slum and enclave residents as a way of getting at class relations. The housing divide doesn't just organize class differences; it's an important site of class differentiation in itself.

The terms *slum* and *enclave* require heavy unpacking. The United Nations (2003) uses the word *slum* as a general term for a low-income settlement distinguished by some combination of the following: inadequate infrastructure and services, substandard housing, overcrowding, and tenure insecurity. As a number of scholars have pointed out, the term masks considerable heterogeneity. Low-income settlement takes many forms. Informal or squatter settlements represent the modal form and generally what the United Nation means by slums, but the term may also include classic slums (run-down housing in poor districts), "popular" subdivisions on the urban fringe, public housing high-rises, rooming houses, row houses, emergency housing, and the urban spaces—pavements, riverbanks, bridges, railways—overtaken by the poor (for one typology, see Leeds 1974). Further, tenure arrangements vary. Settlements may be illegally occupied, legally occupied but self-built or "irregular" from a planning perspective, or occupied with the permission of the owner (Gilbert and Gugler 1992). Residents may own the house and land they occupy, own the house but not the land, or rent in illegal settlements. Finally, slums are socioeconomically heterogeneous. They are not just places for the poor but also are home to a significant portion of the lower middle class: schoolteachers, security guards, clerks, and other service workers.

Despite such heterogeneity, the term *slum* has analytical coherence, particularly in relation to upper- and middle-class spaces. The people who live in slums share a similar market situation. First, although they may not be uniformly poor, they are priced out of the formal housing market in the areas where they make their living, it is not feasible for them to commute long distances because of cost and time, and thus they have little choice but to settle in informal areas. Second, slums tend to be physically distinctive. They stand out for their irregularity, density, and the improvised or dilapidated aspect of dwellings. Slums may include formal neighborhoods—usually in older parts of the city that have fallen into disrepair—as well as settlements that have been formalized but remain irregular and lacking in services. Third, and perhaps most important, slums are stigmatized places. They tend to be associated with crime, disorder, disease, populism, and general backwardness. The word *slum* has been criticized as derogatory (Gilbert 2007), and indeed it is, but the stigma it connotes tells us something important about how these settlements are perceived. The middle class does not differentiate these settlements by housing type or tenure status. They simply react to their physical irregularity and apparent poverty as indicating disvalued places in general. This perception affects how slum residents are treated. In Manila, the word *squatter* has come to refer to slum dwellers whether actually squatters or not. Technically, the term *squatter* refers to illegal settlers and the term *slum* to the physical condition of settlements. This distinction matters to slum residents, for whom formalization means improved status, and they often take pains to underscore it (see Berner 1997, 175). It matters less for class relations. To the upper and middle classes, slums, even ones that have been upgraded or formalized, are where the poor—"squatters"—live (Murphy 1993, v). Taking into account this stigma keys us in to understanding slums relationally, that is, as a category distinguished from "normal" housing.[8]

8. Weinstein (2014, 8–11) also thinks that the term *slum* remains useful despite its lack of precision and negative connotation. It highlights real inequalities in housing quality and service

By the term *enclaves* I mean enclosed upper- and middle-class spaces. These spaces include residential subdivisions ("villages" in Manila) and condominiums as well as exclusive malls and commercial centers. Mainly, I focus on villages. Typically, enclaves are private, physically bounded, and socially exclusive. Not all villages were originally built as gated communities; many are only recently enclosed. What distinguishes these spaces is their class character and their physical and symbolic boundedness. What is important to the argument is their social exclusivity. As does the term *slum*, the term *enclave* describes a heterogeneous domain. Enclaves fall along the class spectrum between middle and upper class, encompassing the famous compounds of the rich (Forbes Park, Ayala Alabang—names synonymous with the Philippine elite) and the numerous, unremarkable subdivisions of anonymous middle-class workers. Enclaves are distinguished by their relative prestige. High-class Ayala Alabang is a world away from middle-class BF Homes, even though the two subdivisions are a stone's throw from each other. Within BF Homes, residents are sensitive to class differences between the various subdivisions of the subdivision, between Executive Village and Sector 10, for instance. These distinctions matter for the upper and middle classes because they reveal relative class standing. They pale, however, in comparison to the division between slums and enclaves, which traces a social boundary. Thus, the terms *slum* and *enclave*, though broad, acquire definition relationally.

### Spatial Mechanisms

My research highlights the role of spatial mechanisms in shaping class identities. In sociology at least, space continues to be treated more as location than mechanism: where things happen as opposed to that which makes things happen. In particular, sociologists differ over the proper role of space in determining social phenomena. The essence of this difference is captured by a debate between Herbert Gans and Thomas Gieryn in the pages of the journal *City and Community*. Gans (2002) ascribes space a largely passive role. He argues that space mostly mediates social action, and hence the focus should be on how social actors use it. Public spaces do not automatically foster democratic behavior, he points out. They may just as easily be used for antidemocratic ends. What matters is how they are used, how much, and by whom.

provision, it points to the local politics behind labeling certain kinds of settlements as slums, and, most important, it enjoys currency on the ground (in her case, Mumbai).

In rebuttal, Gieryn (2002) argues that space has effects that cannot be reduced to social factors. Gans errs, according to Gieryn, in assuming an ontological break between "the material stuff and the social stuff" and in yielding to the latter complete explanatory power. He fails to recognize the "agentic capacity" of physical reality, says Gieryn.

These different conceptions are reflected in how space is incorporated into sociological explanations. Gould (1991), writing on the Paris Commune, is a good example of Gans's minimal approach. He found that members of the same battalions in the National Guard were frequently neighbors. The overlay of organizational and informal ties facilitated mobilization and led to greater solidarity. Overlapping enlistment, moreover, exposed insurgents to neighborhoods around the city and resulted in the scaling up of collective action from a neighborhood to a citywide effort. Gould calls attention to the spatial organization of social networks, but, ultimately, it is the networks doing the work, not space. Space merely functions to contain social powers. For Zhao (1998), in contrast, space—specifically, the layout and design of a university campus—is ascribed autonomous power. He shows that campus ecology helped shape and strengthen activist social networks. That students were packed into dorms, that dorms were all located in one part of campus, that campuses were near each other, and that their layout was such that students regularly traversed certain routes and gathered around natural hubs contributed to the spread of dissident ideas, the formation of student networks, a dynamic of interuniversity competition for activism, and the development of "ecology-dependent" collective action strategies. These effects were distinctly spatial. Both Gould and Zhao factor space into explanations of political mobilization, but only in Zhao's account is space as such actually doing something.

It's one thing to accept the analytical value of spatial mechanisms, but how should we understand space to operate? What about *space*, that black hole of a term, is actually doing the work? Here I find Simmel's ([1908] 1997) account, written more than a century ago, particularly instructive. Simmel views spatial effects as being produced at the conjunction of spatial and social forms (and thus irreducible to either). It is not space, he argues, but spatial form that matters. Space is ineffectual except insofar as it mediates social forces. In doing so, it takes spatial form. Spatial form consists of several "fundamental qualities" that serve to distinguish a space from its environment. Of these qualities Simmel discusses five: exclusivity, boundaries, fixity, proximity, and mobility. These qualities have the effect of modifying social relations. For example, proximity has the potential to make relations more intense, partly because it enables people to interact on a sensory level (here Simmel emphasizes the ability to see and especially smell each other). Because of this potential, proximate relations tend to be characterized by restraint, by people maintaining "an inner distance," and by a dulling of the senses. Thus, proximity does not always strengthen social ties but may, more generally, weaken them "in reserve or repulsion" (156). In either case, Simmel shows that proximity makes a difference in social relationships. In discussing this and other aspects of spatial form, Simmel's focus is clear and delimited and therefore most useful: "Thus, in the interest of ascertaining the forms of sociation [social interaction], we enquire into the significance that the spatial conditions of sociation possess sociologically" (138). He is interested, that is, in how spatial relations modify, not merely mediate, social interaction.

Simmel also describes space having a symbolic effect. If, in the first case, spatial form affects social interaction, then in the second, spatialization affects social perceptions. Social relations, by being spatialized, are transformed in a way that alters our perception of them and, consequently, the character of interaction. Simmel discusses spatialization with regard to boundaries. When a social boundary is spatialized, it "hardens," acquiring "a clarity and security," "a certain rigidity" that it lacked previously (144). If it had not been "projected into a sensory formation" through spatialization or some other mode of objectification, it would have remained inchoate. Spatial distinctiveness, he suggests, affects how we perceive the space. We become conscious of it as a discrete entity. The people associated with it—being inside it or standing in relation to it—acquire social coherence ("a sociological centripetality"), and they themselves acquire a greater consciousness of social unity. This is the idea behind Amos Hawley's (1944) argument that segregation strengthens perceptions of groupness. Segregated groups do not just stand out; they also appear homogeneous. Group difference acquires "an aspect of concreteness" that conducts prejudice and stereotyping.

In the chapters that follow, I show the spatial form of Manila to be *doing something*. One, the spatialization of the urban poor and middle class—their identification with slums and enclaves, respectively—has clarified class boundaries. Two, the proximity of slums and enclaves has facilitated the categorically unequal interaction of their residents. Sharper class boundaries and greater unequal interaction make the housing divide salient as a class cleavage.

## Data and Methods

I conducted an ethnographic study of relations between slum and enclave residents in Metro Manila. My data consist of 221 interviews: 104 with slum residents, 81 with enclave residents, and 36 with the representatives of various government, civic, and urban poor organizations. I selected four cases of neighboring enclave and slum areas: two cases in Quezon City, one in Parañaque City, and one in Makati City. The cases are spread out across Metro Manila (fig. 1.1). In the appendix, I discuss the criteria guiding case selection and how I obtained access to my informants.

Direct observation provided an equally important source of data. I drew on observation to document the spatial situation and social environment of each site, how informants interacted with one another and with me on site, and how Estrada interacted with his supporters. I managed to accompany the former president on a campaign sortie through the provinces south of Manila in the months leading up to the May 2010 presidential elections. The data were collected over the course of sixteen months between 2009 and 2010 and in 2014. The fieldwork, however, builds on several years of research, since 2001, in the Philippines.

My qualitative account is corroborated by considerable archival research. First, I collected demographic and spatial data from government offices, libraries, and the internet. I use these data to situate the urban poor and middle class socially and spatially. Second, I went through the country's leading newspaper, the *Philippine Daily Inquirer,* cover to cover, for the six-month period spanning Estrada's impeachment trial, Edsa 2, and Edsa 3. I use these data in chapter 8 to construct a deep historical account of Edsa 3.

My research was designed to document the state of relations between slum and enclave residents. To this end, I focused on stories of class interaction. I asked informants about their interactions with the residents of nearby slums and enclaves and with the *masa* and "rich" in general. I inquired about the context, extent, and nature of interaction. I discounted vague sentiments of class feeling in favor of concrete descriptions of interaction. I did so bearing in mind the literature in social psychology showing attitudes to be malleable, in some cases held unconsciously, and generally unreliable as predictors of behavior (Banaji and Heiphetz 2010). To the extent I could, therefore, I inferred cognition directly from behavior, observed or recounted.

**FIGURE 1.1** Field sites in Metro Manila.

## Blind Spots

I understand that class relations do not constitute a pure or univocal object. They are complicated by other social divisions. They are mediated by various political arrangements. They encompass more than just contention but also cooperation and even friendship. They reflect mutual obligation as well as resentment. Thus, my focus on class relations, on categorical inequality particularly, involves a degree of abstraction. I abstract in order to better follow the object at the heart of phenomena—urban fragmentation, class division, and political dissensus—usually taken separately. In essence, my approach is to follow the class boundary as it manifests spatially, morally, and politically. This approach admits several blind spots, some of which I have already touched on and others I touch on in the chapters that follow. Before moving forward, I want to collect them here, but not because I think I am able to correct them. It is my sense that these deficits are, to varying degrees, congenital to my approach. Correction would thus require a different research focus. I flag them in order to acknowledge how they constrain my field of vision.

First, by focusing on class identities, I miss other social identities based on ethnicity or provincial origin, religion, and civic association. Depending on the situation, these identities may be more salient than class. They certainly complicate the picture in ways I do not pay enough attention to. Second, by focusing on slums and enclaves, I overlook intermediate spaces and the lower middle class likely residing in them. Third, by focusing on the social difference between slum and enclave residents, I gloss over the social heterogeneity within slums and enclaves. In slums particularly residents differ considerably in terms of socioeconomic capacity, culture, and belief. Simone (2014) described these areas as "hodgepodge" for this reason. Studies focused on a single community over a long period of time are better able to bring out the texture of heterogeneity. A lot of these studies already exist, however, and I cite the ones pertaining to Manila throughout the book. Fourth, and finally, by focusing on the boundary between slums and enclaves, I end up de-emphasizing variation in the social and spatial situations of my cases. I try to keep this variation in view but only insofar as it affects relations between slum and enclave residents, which, again, constitute my primary focus.[9]

Having rehearsed the deficits of my approach, I might do well to remind readers of its value. Class is an essentially relational phenomenon, and so it should be studied relationally. Class relations in the form of categorical inequality are productive not just of urban social life but of urban space and politics. Everything that follows is aimed at demonstrating the point.

9. In Tilly's (1984) terms, my comparative strategy aims to universalize rather than to find variation.

# TWO

# The Argument

This chapter narrates the historical developments leading up to the current state of class relations. It traces the formation of the urban poor and middle class as class groups. It emphasizes, particularly, the impacts of economic restructuring and democratization. This history provides the essential context for the "spatial" argument I set up in the last part of the chapter and pursue in the first half of the book. I take issue with the common depiction of the urban poor as subordinate to middle-class leadership. This view overlooks the effects of urban fragmentation on class identities and fails to take into account the extent to which the urban environment has become a source of class contention and grievance.

## The Class Formation of the Urban Poor, 1950s–1980s

The following sentiments, I would argue, are not merely an artifact of different sites and different informants; they are emblematic of the urban poor's class identity in different periods: the immediate postwar decades, the 1970s and 1980s, and the post-Marcos period since 1986:

"In four years, we'll change places with all the rich in Forbes Park. We'll stay there and they'll come here." She laughs without rancor, thinking of the rich matrons bending over the *batya* (washbasin) at the faucet, washing clothes. (Stone and Marsella 1968, 83)

When I asked a group of men what they thought about the people living in Forbes Park, one of Manila's most plush residential suburbs, they simply replied: "Those people are our enemy." Pinches (1985, 155)

It's a different story in Rockwell [an upscale mall in Makati City]. People look at you. You could have a thousand pesos burning in your pocket and they would still look at you. They know you don't belong. (Fieldwork in 2009)

In this section, I trace the urban poor's changing experience of class relations from the postwar decades through the 1980s. The slum population exploded after World War II. Observers regarded this growth with alarm. Slums were viewed as incubators of radicalism. The conditions in Manila and other Third World cities, Abrams (1964, 287) warned, "recall the scene that made the *Communist Manifesto* an alluring document in nineteenth-century Europe." This, though, proved a misreading of the situation. Two facts colored the urban poor's experience of class relations. The first was that migration took place in the context of rapid industrial growth. The Philippine state began pursuing import substitution industrialization in the 1950s. Although industrialization was shallow and small scale—it largely involved the processing of agricultural products—these limitations would not become apparent until the 1970s. In the early 1960s, the country was heralded for its level of industrialization. In Asia, it was second only to Japan. The second fact was the mentality of migrants. Migrants were defined by their aspirations, particularly for their children. A survey of three poor neighborhoods found that residents held "great expectations for the next generation" (Guerrero 1973). They accorded education an "almost magical role" in bringing about social mobility (220). These communities were marked by optimism, not despair or alienation, as would be predicted by culture of poverty and marginality arguments. Scholars at the time viewed the urban poor's situation as dynamic. Laquian (1969) portrayed the slum as "a zone of transition," a way station between provincial and urban life, and a necessary one at that. In the slum, migrants could find their feet economically and socially, become integrated politically, and develop a personality type suited to "modern" society.

Migrants to Manila encountered a complex social scene. Class divisions were less clear-cut than in provincial areas, where the difference between "big" and "little" people was all but social fact (Lynch 1959). There was greater social differentiation, including a small but amorphous middle class. The upper class was racially divided into white, mestizo, and Filipino segments (Fox and Lynch 1956). There were also Chinese and South Asian capitalists who possessed wealth but lacked social status given their racial identity. The slums themselves were divided along ethnic and regional lines, reflecting a process of chain migration from provincial localities.

Finally, the way in which migrants were incorporated into urban society bred an experience of class relations distinguished by dependency. Migrants formed multiple ties with local politicians and upper-class patrons. They had to do this, given their illegal status and precarious situation. These ties constituted their primary means of securing basic needs. Stone and Marsella (1968) describe the founding of Mahirap, an informal settlement in Makati. Not long after the first residents arrived, politicians came courting. They provided electricity, a central faucet, and a well. This assistance was instrumental to establishing the community, but it also bound residents to those political patrons. The same politicians who protected residents from ejectment could threaten them with it should their electoral support flag. In short, the urban poor came to be integrated politically but as clients.

Slums were stigmatized from the start, and their residents faced discrimination as squatters. The slum dweller, for Jocano (1975, 191–92), is "a nobody, a non-entity in the structure of social relationships in many places." He is discounted as a matter of course. He is made to wait at welfare agencies, hospitals, and various offices until the clerks "finish powdering their noses or talking to one another." He must forbear being cut in line by "'influential-looking' people" despite having been standing there for hours. In the 1950s and 1960s, this state of affairs appears to have been largely accepted. Early ethnographies of the urban poor emphasize their adaptation to city life, a process they managed by avoiding confrontation, deferring to authority, and enduring slights. Carroll (1966, 584) provides a telling account of wealthy businessmen in Manila playing blackjack at a party:

The stakes got higher and higher, and as my informant watched he noticed that a group of drivers gathered around the fence was also watching the game. There was more money on the table there than any one of them handled in a year, and he thought to himself what a mistake it was to make such a display in front of them, and how likely to create bitterness and resentment. Then he looked at the faces of the drivers, and suddenly realized there *was* no resentment in those faces, only the most intense interest in the game; and that each of those drivers was "rooting" with all he was worth for the success of his particular boss or "master."

As the anecdote suggests, the poor had a clear understanding of their "place." They saw themselves as small people in subordinate roles, a "humble class," as Whiteford (1964) characterized the poor in Colombia.

This sense of deference and dependency was reflected in the character of the urban poor's political action. They were politically active to the extent that they had to be, but they could hardly be considered radical. Their collective action was largely parochial and instrumental. They favored petitions over protests and addressed politicians as sup plicants rather than entitled citizens. They were apt to view radical political activity as costly, risky, and impractical. Almost no one in Guerrero's (1973) survey had ever joined a demonstration or strike, and most (77 percent) said that they would not participate in one if given the opportunity to do so. In general, then, Portes and Walton's (1976, 108) assessment of the Latin American urban poor in the 1960s applies in this case as well: the urban poor played the role of "audiences and followers, not one of initiators." They represented a symbolic more than an actual threat. The prospect of a radical and united *masa* may have energized activists, but it bore little relation to the reality on the ground.

The 1970s saw the development of a new kind of political action. A social movement of the urban poor emerged. The Zone One Tondo Organization (ZOTO) was founded in 1970 as a federation of twenty community organizations from the Tondo district of Manila. ZOTO was supported by the Philippine Ecumenical Council on Community Organizing (PECCO), a nongovernmental organization comprising clergy and social workers. PECCO provided resources and introduced organizing techniques that had been developed by the American community organizer Saul Alinsky. By the mid-1970s, ZOTO had expanded to encompass an even greater number of community organizations from Tondo and neighboring municipalities. Several events raised ZOTO's profile, including an audience with the pope in 1971 and a march to Malacañang in 1974 to protest President Marcos's plans to redevelop the Tondo foreshore area. The leaders of the march managed to persuade Marcos to accommodate some of their demands, including establishing a nearby relocation site.

ZOTO's evolution from community organization to social movement, Karaos (1995) argues, reflected the urban poor's changing relationship with the state at the time. Marcos declared martial law in 1972. He criminalized squatting in 1975 and made slum clearance an integral component of his urban development plans. Demolitions were frequent and often massive in scope. Concerted state action had the effect of redrawing the lines of contention. Squatters' illegality was no longer subject to negotiation between individual communities and local politicians. It had become the object of contention between the urban poor as a whole and the state.

From 1970 to 1975, ZOTO focused mainly on issues of community and land tenure. By 1976, however, it had aligned with the underground Communist Party. Community issues fell by the wayside, and the struggle against the "US-Marcos dictatorship" took center stage. ZOTO's leaders, moreover, had come to frame the urban poor's situation ideologically. Within this framework, the main problem besetting the urban poor was not their illegality or tenure insecurity, but the evil trinity of "imperialism, bureaucratic-capitalism, and feudalism." The new hard line alienated many in the grass roots. They felt it drew the focus away from traditional concerns of the urban poor and invited repression unnecessarily. It also led to ZOTO's split with PECCO. The radicalized ZOTO, in Rüland's (1984) estimation, had ceased to represent the urban poor.[1]

ZOTO is significant because it marked the emergence of the urban poor as a political actor on the national stage. It did not, however, mark the urban poor's formation as a class in the Marxist sense. The movement was limited in scope to Tondo and neighboring areas. It is not clear that the urban poor as a whole had become more likely to engage in large-scale political actions without direct bearing on their welfare. Indeed, hardly anyone in Smokey Mountain, another slum area in Tondo, participated in the Edsa protests against Marcos. Residents were too preoccupied with eking out a living, and the event seemed irrelevant to their immediate concerns (Brillantes 1991). Ultimately, the case of ZOTO tells us little about the urban poor's experience of class relations. The collective identity developed as part of ZOTO was defined in relation to the state, not in relation to other classes. It was an identity largely defined by the Left, particularly during ZOTO's latter phase. It was thus a political identity more than a class identity, and, as we will see, that identity changed when the urban poor's relationship to the state changed.

---

1. This story is reminiscent of Castells's account (1983, 201) of the *pobladores* movement in Chile, which he described as directed by political parties: "We should actually speak of the pobladores' branch of each party," he wrote, "rather than of a 'squatters' movement.'" Partisan divisions limited its scope as a social movement, and eventually, it fragmented along partisan lines. There was a disjunction, moreover, between the movement's cadres and ordinary adherents. Cadres saw themselves as engaged in a revolutionary struggle; for the grass roots, tenure security remained paramount.

There is evidence, nonetheless, that class relations had worsened by the 1980s. The urban poor no longer simply accepted their subordination but had become acutely sensitive to it. Their material want and social disvalue had become a source of humiliation and cause for resentment. What happened?

Slums had become entrenched. They were not just populated by migrants anymore but also by their children and grandchildren. Slums could no longer be considered way stations toward formal urban life. They were places where urban lives were lived out. The prospect of social mobility, once so bright in the 1950s, had dimmed considerably. Entrenchment was compounded by economic stagnation. Marcos had embarked on a program of export-oriented industrialization in 1972, partly to combat persistent unemployment. The shift led to the collapse of several import substitution industries (Ofreneo 2015). Meanwhile, the new export industries—garments in the 1970s and electronics in the 1980s—were capital-intensive and not well integrated into the domestic economy. They failed to alleviate the unemployment problem. The political events surrounding Marcos's ouster in 1986 worsened the situation. Recession marked the 1980s, and economists wrote the decade off as "lost" in terms of the country's economic growth.

Within Manila's slums, ethnic and regional identities had become less important than a class identity defined by the experience of wage labor. The anthropologist Michael Pinches conducted fieldwork in the slum community of Tatalon throughout the 1980s (1985, 1987, 1991, 1992). His work highlights the centrality of wage labor in the experience of the urban poor. Tatalon's residents installed elevators (an occupation concentrated in the locality) and worked in factories and construction. They worked as domestics, drivers, salespeople, and clerks. Wage labor kept Tatalon's informal economy afloat. Wages provided the capital behind informal ventures such as food stalls and sari-sari (variety) stores. Wage workers were primarily the ones patronizing these enterprises. Unemployment, therefore, posed a threat not just to the worker and his family but to the community at large. That threat hung over the community like a sword, making the search for work a constant preoccupation and permanent source of anxiety.

Tatalon's residents experienced wage labor as exploitative. They complained to Pinches about being overworked, underpaid, underfed, physically abused, sexually harassed, cheated, coerced, and belittled. At the same time, they recognized that wage labor offered the best means of making ends meet. Self-employment was fine as a stopgap or sideline but rarely sufficient as a household's only source of income. Pinches's informants were either desperately looking for work or chafing desperately under its subordination. The experience of wage labor was not just something workers held in common; it was something they shared with one another through discussion. Workers were occupationally heterogeneous, but they also lived together, and the slum functioned as a kind of shop floor mediating the experience of work. Tatalon's residents spent an inordinate amount of time talking about work: where to find it, how to endure it, and whether to opt for a less demeaning but more precarious mode of livelihood. They also, inevitably, shared stories of mistreatment at the hands of employers. These stories built up over time into a store of public knowledge, with the same stories "often repeated in conversation to illustrate a particular point or argument" (1987, 130). They formed a common sense about class relations, a class subjectivity, including a conception of the rich as haughty, selfish, and contemptuous of the poor. Such moral boundary work had the effect of distinguishing the slum as "an alternative moral setting," a haven from degradations suffered on the "outside" (1991, 180).

Pinches acknowledged two other arenas of class interaction besides employment: institutions such as courts, hospitals, and government agencies on one hand, and the urban environment, including malls, churches, the street, and public spaces in general on the other. In these contexts, slum residents interacted with the rich not as workers but as poor people and squatters. Their stigma, not their subordinate status, was at issue. They experienced class interaction in terms of discrimination rather than exploitation. Here the poor were likely to be treated with "contempt, ridicule, and patronizing sympathy" (Pinches 1991, 181): "This is often communicated in body language—for example, through the look that fails to recognize even a person's presence, a feature of *burgis* (bourgeois) behavior that people in Tatalon often simply refer to as 'no *pansin*' ('no recognition'). Alternatively, the behavior of the rich is often described as *matapobre*, meaning in general that they are snobbish, but more particularly, as the term suggests (*mata*—eye, *pobre*—poor), that they greet the poor with a mannered gaze of condescending scrutiny." Such experiences were limited, however, by class segregation. The rich and poor lived apart from each other, Pinches noted, and otherwise tended to avoid one another. Thus, employment remained the primary context for class interaction. I argue that today the situation has changed. The urban environment has become equally important as a source of class grievances. The experience of discrimination, much of it in the form of spatial exclusion, has become more salient.

## The Impact of Economic Restructuring

The Philippines underwent a transition to more open markets in the 1980s. The dictator Ferdinand Marcos secured a series of loans from the World Bank that were contingent on "structural adjustment"—reforms aimed at liberalizing trade and investment, privatizing government services and assets, and deregulating major economic sectors. The market orientation of the state was further entrenched in the post-Marcos period (since 1986). The Aquino and especially Ramos administrations reduced tariffs, acceded to a number of free-trade agreements, eliminated restrictions on foreign investment, deregulated key industries, and enlarged the role of the private sector in running utilities and building infrastructure. By some measures, these reforms succeeded. The inflow of foreign direct investment increased from an average of US$326 million annually between 1984 and 1989 to around $1.5 billion in the mid-1990s (Hong 2001). Much of this money went to Metro Manila: for example, 56 percent of it in 1993 (Lo and Marcotullio 2001). Neoliberal reforms led to a restructuring of the economy. By 2000, services overtook agriculture as the largest source of employment. In Manila today, 80 percent of the workforce is employed in services (see table 2.1).

The service economy merits further consideration given its importance in Manila. We can distinguish between its formal and informal sectors. Only the formal sector is reflected in official statistics. It includes traditional industries such as real estate, education, food, entertainment, transportation, and finance, as well as new banner industries, such as business process outsourcing. The informal sector in services includes microenterprises, such as vending, various forms of outsourced work, and some kinds of personal services. Perhaps the more relevant distinction is between decent and precarious work. What

Table 2.1 Share of employment by sector, 1970–2017

| Sector | Philippines | | | | | | | | | | Metro Manila |
|---|---|---|---|---|---|---|---|---|---|---|---|
| | 1970 | 1975 | 1980 | 1985 | 1990 | 1995 | 2000 | 2005 | 2010 | 2017 | 2015 |
| Agriculture | 53.7 | 53.5 | 51.8 | 49.6 | 45.2 | 44.1 | 37.1 | 26.0 | 33.2 | 25.5 | 0.5 |
| Industry | 16.5 | 15.2 | 15.4 | 13.8 | 15.0 | 15.6 | 16.2 | 15.6 | 15.0 | 17.4 | 19.7 |
| Services | 28.2 | 31.8 | 32.8 | 36.5 | 39.7 | 40.3 | 46.7 | 48.5 | 51.8 | 57.1 | 79.8 |

*Sources*: Ofreneo (2015); PSA (2016, 2017a).

the International Labor Organization calls decent work is fairly remunerated, legally protected, and relatively stable—actual occupations, if you will. Precarious work, in contrast, is merely a means to livelihood. It is distinguished, above all, by the insecurity of employment and income. Precarious workers are forced to move from job to job, to pursue various sidelines, and put their children to work in the effort to make ends meet. Liberalization of the service sector has heightened the disparity between decent and precarious work (Amoranto, Brooks, and Chun 2010). It has created more opportunities for high-skilled workers while the terms of work for low-skilled workers have generally worsened.

The problem is that service sector–led growth is not creating enough jobs. The World Bank (2013) figures that every year, only about a quarter of potential entrants to the labor force find decent jobs. Of the 1.15 million people attempting to enter the labor force every year, about half a million hold college degrees. Of that number, 240,000 find decent jobs in the formal sector, 200,000 find jobs abroad, and the remaining 60,000 end up unemployed or exiting the workforce. Meanwhile, the 650,000 potential entrants without college degrees must resort to low-paying, largely insecure jobs, predominantly in the informal sector. Part of the problem has to do with the capital-intensive and skills-biased nature of many of the new service industries. Take, for example, the business process outsourcing (BPO) industry in the Philippines. The industry offers voice services (i.e., call centers) and other high-value services such as software development, animation, and medical transcription. America Online (since renamed AOL) established the first call center at Clark Air Base in 1997. The BPO industry took off. In 2008, it contributed US$5.3 billion to the Philippine economy and accounted for 8.5 percent of the country's total exports of goods and services (Usui 2011). At the same time, however, it employed less than 1 percent of the country's labor force. These jobs, moreover, primarily went to young people from middle-class families in Metro Manila: college-educated, computer literate, and able to speak English with something like an American accent. It has become clear, in other words, that the BPO and other industries driven by information and communications technology will not, by themselves, solve the country's jobs problem.

The problem, restated, is that growth in output does not entirely translate into growth in employment and that growth in employment cannot keep pace with the growth of the labor force. The result is what Asian Development Bank economists Felipe and Lanzona (2006) call jobless growth. Consider this: the Philippine economy grew by 6.1 percent in 2004, and yet unemployment in Manila remained at 16 percent, and 20 percent among fifteen- to twenty-five-year-olds (370). In informal settlements, unemployment was 39 percent (Ragragio 2003). Indeed, the full extent of structural unemployment is masked by the exodus of workers overseas. There were 2.4 million overseas workers in 2016, 11 percent of them from Metro Manila (Philippine Statistics Authority 2015).

In general, economic restructuring has led to the expansion of precarious work. This expansion is manifest in the growth of the informal sector in Metro Manila. The sector has nearly doubled in size between 1995 and 2011, growing from 549,000 to 918,000 self-employed and unpaid family workers (Bureau of Labor and Employment Statistics 2011; Joshi 1997). Precarious work is not found only in the informal sector; it exists in the formal one as well. We see an increase in the proportion of nonregular workers—casual, contractual, and probationary—throughout the 1990s and 2000s. In 2004, the Bureau of Labor and Employment Statistics found that 26 percent of the labor force nationwide was nonregular (Sibal, Amante, and Tolentino 2008). Another survey drawn heavily from the Metro Manila area found that 74 percent of contractual workers had been working in the same company for at least one year, with some for more than five years (Daenekindt and Gonzales-Rosero 2003). This constitutes a flagrant violation of Philippine labor law, but it wasn't the only one they found. Most contractual workers did not sign a contract, earned significantly less than minimum wage, and did not receive employer-mandated benefits. The "flexibilization" of formal work, then, has made it hard to distinguish from informal work.

### Middle-Class Ascendance

Economic restructuring led to the growth of the middle class as both an economic group and a social group. A middle class preexisted economic liberalization, of course, but it lacked social power and a clear sense of identity. A class of white-collar workers emerged during the American colonial period. Doeppers (1984) puts the number of professionals, public servants, teachers, and clerks in Manila at 18 percent in 1939—more than double the number just thirty years prior. He attributes the increase to the expansion of public education and the colonial bureaucracy under the Americans. In the 1950s, following independence, import substitution industrialization created a new class of entrepreneurs. So-called new men entered into politics, their fortunes based not on landholdings but on professional and industrial success (Doronila 1992). The middle class in the 1960s was small and amorphous, but nevertheless it displayed some signs of distinction. Its members' lifestyles were modeled on those of their American counterparts, Carroll (1968) notes, rather than those of the landed elite. They were reluctant to take on traditional patronage roles. They participated in civic organizations such as the Jaycees, Lions, and Rotary. On the whole, however, the middle class tended to "amalgamate with either the upper class or the cosmopolitan lower class" (Fox and Lynch 1956). Writing about the Diliman community in Quezon City, Arcinas (1955, 37) observed that the major social cleavage appeared to run "between the small upper class with its closely allied middle class on the one hand, and the lower class group on the other."

The growth of the middle class as an economic group was mainly the result of new opportunities associated with liberalization and the influx of capital in the form of foreign investment and remittances. The expansion of producer services created new and better jobs for highly skilled workers. Remittances from overseas Filipino workers—a staggering US$20 billion a year throughout the 2010s—inflated consumption, particularly of real estate (Bangko Sentral ng Pilipinas 2017). The growth of the domestic market was good for entrepreneurs. Rising land values in Metro Manila were good for property owners and speculators. In general, the 1990s and 2000s were boom times for the middle class.

Virola and colleagues (2013) use income to classify 0.4 percent of Metro Manila's population as upper class, 54 percent as middle class, and 46 percent as lower class. This is a rarefied demography compared to the rest of the Philippines. Virtually everywhere else in the country, the lower class accounts for between 70 percent and 96 percent of the population. In other words, the middle (and upper) class is concentrated in and around Manila. The metro region contains 28 percent of the country's middle-income population (and 46 percent of its high-income population). If we include Central Luzon and Calabarzon, the regions to the north and south of Metro Manila, respectively, the proportion doubles to nearly 60 percent.

In terms of work, we see a shift in Manila's occupational distribution toward middle-class-type jobs (see table 2.2). The proportion of managers and professionals at the upper end of the spectrum and clerical and sales workers at the lower end increased from about one-quarter of registered jobs in 2001 to one-third in 2016. Meanwhile, the proportion

Table 2.2 Occupational distribution in Metro Manila, 2001 and 2016 (%)

| Occupation | 2001 | 2016 |
|---|---|---|
| Government officials and managers | 15.0 | 18.4 |
| Professionals | 7.0 | 7.8 |
| Technicians and associate professionals | 4.8 | 6.3 |
| *Subtotal* | *26.8* | *32.5* |
| Clerical workers | 9.7 | 12.4 |
| Service and sales workers | 12.8 | 21.0 |
| *Subtotal* | *22.5* | *33.4* |
| Farmers, fishermen, and forestry workers | 0.6 | 0.2 |
| Craft and trade workers | 13.5 | 8.8 |
| Plant and machine operators and assemblers | 11.7 | 8.8 |
| Laborers and unskilled workers | 24.4 | 16.0 |
| *Subtotal* | *50.2* | *33.8* |

*Sources*: NSCB (2002); PSA (2017b).
*Note*: Occupational groups were reclassified in 2001, making it hard to compare the occupational distributions before and after that point.

of lower-class-type jobs—agricultural, fishery, farmworkers, tradesmen, and laborers—decreased from one-half to one- third. (Note that these figures cover only those workers employed in the formal sector. The significant number of workers employed in the informal sector is not reflected in official statistics. The figures thus underrepresent the size of the lower class.)

Philippine scholars have noted the emergence of a remarkably coherent social identity among the middle class (e.g., Bautista, 1999, 2006; Clarke and Sison 2003; Pinches 1996, 1999, 2003, 2010; Rivera 2001). They acknowledge substantial heterogeneity within the group—distinguishing new, old, and marginal fractions; diverse allegiances (to the Catholic Church, the military, or the Left, for example); and politics ranging from conservative to revolutionary—yet they underscore members' common orientation to the project of modernization. Middle-class politics, writes Rivera (2001, 253), "may be considered to be an embodiment of some kind of modern consciousness acquired through higher education and standards of living and varying forms of contact and appreciation of Western modernity." We should be careful with the word *modernity*. Ray and Qayum (2009, 16) suggest that we consider it a folk category. To the middle class, *modernity* serves to capture the complex of meanings associated with a trajectory of progress modeled after Western, and increasingly East Asian, societies.

Beyond this orientation, the middle class has been described in the following terms: They define themselves against the traditional elite on the one hand and the *masa* on the other, both of which are considered backward, but in different ways. They reject "corruption" in various forms, including rent-seeking, cronyism, vote-buying, and the populism of local governments. They embrace the market and its logic, espousing the gospel of private enterprise and meritocracy. They adopt a paternalistic attitude toward the poor. They are unabashedly nationalist. What is new about the middle class, ultimately, is not just that their identity has acquired definition but also that they have acquired social power. If, before, the middle class had been incorporated into the traditional elite, the opposite is now the case. The new middle class sets the tone for the rest, old rich and poor, to follow.

### The Impact of Democratization

The dictator Ferdinand Marcos was deposed in 1986 by a massive, three-day "people power" demonstration held around the Shrine of Mary along Epifanio de los Santos Avenue. Edsa 1, as the demonstration came to be known, ushered in the presidency of Corazon Aquino, the widow of slain Marcos opponent Benigno "Noynoy" Aquino Jr. (For reference, I provide a list of the Philippine presidents since democratization in table 2.3.)

Democracy definitely affected class relations. A new constitution recognized the status of the urban poor as political actors. They were protected by legislation (the Urban Development and Housing Act of 1992), allotted representation in Congress through a party-list system,[2] and assigned a dedicated government agency (the Presidential Commission on the Urban Poor). In general, they were better equipped to pursue their claims through bureaucratic channels. At the same time, political decentralization following the Local Government Code passed in 1991 made local governments once again the locus of negotiation over tenure concerns. These developments had the effect of fragmenting urban poor political action. They encouraged the embrace of parochial identities (Karaos 1995).

To be sure, the urban poor organize beyond their immediate communities. Community organizations group into federations and even

---

2. The Philippines's party-list system makes it easier for disadvantaged sectors such as the urban poor to win representation in Congress. People vote for parties claiming to represent these sectors. The more votes the parties garner, the more candidates they are allowed to seat, up to three.

Table 2.3 Philippine presidents since democratization

| Years in office | President |
| --- | --- |
| *Before democratization* | |
| 1965–1986 | Ferdinand Marcos |
| *The democratic period* | |
| 1986–1992 | Corazon Aquino |
| 1992–1998 | Fidel Ramos |
| 1998–2001 | Joseph Estrada |
| 2001–2010 | Gloria Macapagal Arroyo |
| 2010–2016 | Benigno Aquino III |
| 2016–2022 | Rodrigo Duterte |

national coalitions. The structure of political opportunities is such, however, that urban poor groups are most effective when organized around local issues. At the supralocal level, solidarity begins to fray. Relations between different communities are strained by rivalry and competition. This situation led Berner (1997, 195) to conclude that "the urban poor, in general, are not one collective actor but a multitude of groups that are largely indifferent to each other."

The urban poor also became more fragmented as workers. The expansion of precarious work led to greater heterogeneity in their work situations, which undercut the already tenuous power of organized labor. Union membership declined precipitously between 2000 and 2010. At the same time, the number of unions ballooned. In 1985, there were about 2 million workers in fewer than two thousand unions. By 2010, according to Ofreneo (2013, 439), there were 1.7 million workers in 17,644 unions! Organized labor was further debilitated by ideological divisions, rivalries, and raiding (unions poaching members from one another).

The process of democratization, meanwhile, enhanced the power of the middle class as a political force. A middle-class political identity acquired definition through mobilization. It was clarified, Villegas and Yang (2013) argue, in the crucible of the anti-Marcos movement. It emerged as the product of political alliances between various factions, the identification of the protestors with white-collar workers (as opposed to laborers or activists), the appropriation of the class language deployed by the Left, and the narrative construction of the middle class as the protagonists of democracy. In 2001, I argue, dissensus over Estrada and the contrast between Edsa 2 and Edsa 3 threw into relief the divide between middle class and urban poor.

A middle-class political identity acquired definition, second, through associational activity. Since the advent of democracy, a middle-class-led civil society has expanded the scope of its activities considerably. Democratic conditions encouraged the proliferation of nongovernmental organizations. Between 1986 and 1996, the number of registered NGOs across the Philippines grew by 160 percent, from 27,100 to 70,200 (Clarke 1998). In 2007, Clarke (2013) counted 81,436 NGOs, 38 percent of which were based in Manila. In the Philippine context, the term *NGO* includes civic, religious, development, and charitable or welfare organizations. It excludes labor unions, cooperatives, political parties, and housing associations, including the community organizations of the urban poor. Clarke (1998) attributes the NGO boom to a hospitable political climate, a surge in overseas development assistance following democratic restoration, and the institutionalization of NGOs. Both the 1987 Constitution and the 1991 Local Government Code formalized their role in political processes.

The NGO sector is widely considered a middle-class field, which is to say, it is led, and its priorities defined, by middle-class actors. Even development work has become professionalized and a popular career option for college graduates (Encarnacion-Tadem 2008). Pinches (2010) views the local distinction between NGOs and POs, or "people's organizations" of popular sectors, as mirroring the class distinction between the middle class and the *masa*. NGOs are seen as ministering to POs, sponsoring, supporting, organizing, and sometimes speaking for them. They are seen as playing a largely tutelary role with respect to the urban poor. In the wake of Edsa 2, some scholars have come to regard the NGO sector as forming the vanguard of a "civil society" with hegemonic designs, one that claims to speak for the nation at large despite its narrow base in the urban middle class (Clarke 2013; Hedman 2005; Pinches 2010).

In sum, the urban poor grew more fragmented as workers and slum residents while the middle class grew more organized and assertive. In matters of politics, the urban poor are usually depicted as following the lead of political patrons or middle-class sponsors. Scholars point to their disaggregation on the one hand and to their integration in both clientelist networks and a middle-class-led civil society on the other hand. This view supports the popular reading of Edsa 3 as the product of manipulation and of the urban poor as mobilized from above by pro-Estrada politicians and organizations against their better interests. This cannot be the whole story. How would we explain the class divide exposed by Edsa 3? Or the urban poor's massive turnout for a demonstration largely opposed by the middle class in Manila? What about evidence that the poor were not just mobilized from above but moved from below by class grievances? Recall the urban poor's reaction to Estrada's mug shot presented in the introduction. Why did the image of Estrada looking like "a common criminal," as one informant put it, resonate so powerfully among them? Its publication, after all, was intended to have the opposite effect, to serve as an indictment of Estrada's venality, and yet it struck them differently and with enough force to push them into the streets in unprecedented numbers. Clearly, the urban poor can no longer be characterized as simply "audiences and followers."

In the chapters to follow, I argue that we need to look beyond the urban poor's social fragmentation at their *urban fragmentation*. I point to the urban environment having become more important as a source of class contention and the experience of spatial discrimination having become central to the urban poor's class identity. I set up this argument in the following section.

## Urban Fragmentation as Causal

Urban fragmentation in Manila takes the form of interspersion. By *interspersion*, I mean the proximity of slums and enclaves as a general pattern. My argument, in a nutshell, is that interspersion worsens class relations by facilitating categorically unequal interaction in the form of boundary imposition. I will elaborate, but let us first review two other accounts suggested by the literature on urban fragmentation.

Most scholars point to the role of enclaves in increasing the spatial segregation of the middle class and thus worsening class relations.[3] This focus has been informed, in particular, by Mike Davis's work (1990) on Los Angeles. Urban insecurity, Davis writes, has led middle- and upper-class homeowners to adopt a number of strategies designed to exclude, contain, and avoid stigmatized populations, including fortification, surveillance, private policing, and the abandonment of public spaces. According to this view, enclavization in developing world cities involves similar practices. The fortified enclaves of São Paulo, Caldeira (2000) writes, achieve segregation by design—that is, through the use of walls, the employment of private security services, and the bundling of facilities to better provide "a total way of life." These measures

3. The most influential account is probably Caldeira's (2000), but see also Coy and Pöhler (2002), Roitman (2005), Sandhu and Sandhu (2007), and UN-Habitat (2001).

reflect the security-conscious, "inward orientation" of residents. They promote an antisociability marked by suspicion of and discrimination against lower-class outsiders. Fortified enclaves, therefore, have the effect of foreclosing substantive class interaction and hardening class boundaries. "Cities segregated by walls and enclaves," Caldeira argues, "foster the sense that different groups belong to separate universes and have irreconcilable claims" (334).

The other view is that the propinquity of enclaves and poor areas has brought about a degree of social integration (Sabatini and Salcedo 2007; Salcedo and Rasse 2012; Salcedo and Torres 2004). Examining the case of a gated community located near a rural settlement in Santiago, Chile, Salcedo and Torres (2004) find that proximity allows for a functional integration—greater social interaction mainly in the context of employment—that works to soften class boundaries. This is not to say that a sense of shared community develops, only that interaction diminishes "segregation in the subjective realm" or social distance. In their case, the settlement's residents viewed the gated community in largely positive terms for having brought jobs and improvements to the physical environment. Walls, the authors observe, "have not precluded the creation of social links between groups" (40). These links translate into greater material benefits for the residents of poor communities. Thus proximity is viewed as improving class relations.

On the one hand, this conclusion is largely belied by the literature. On the other hand, Salcedo and colleagues point correctly to the extent of class interaction between the residents of enclaves and surrounding poor areas. Slums have never been as socially isolated as the American ghetto, a point made periodically from Perlman (1976) to Gilbert (2012). Regular interaction between slum and enclave residents in the context of employment and also benefaction, civic association, and routine encounters in the urban environment is "a fact of life for almost everyone" (Veloso 2010, 257). How do we reconcile this fact with widely held claims of worsening class relations?

Let me suggest that the two accounts—separate social worlds and social integration—appear contradictory only because they share a view of social interaction as invariably promoting social integration; hence either enclavization forecloses class interaction, thereby worsening class relations, or proximity facilitates class interaction, thereby improving class relations. What matters, I would argue, is not the presence or absence of class interaction but the particular form it takes. There is a good deal of class interaction in Metro Manila, all the more so with the greater proximity of class spaces, but much of the interaction is categorically unequal. It is not just that one side has more power than the other but that the two sides are seen as belonging to different and unequal groups.

It is not simply proximity driving categorically unequal interaction but proximity and strong social boundaries—so strong that the social group on one side of the boundary is stigmatized. If we understand interspersion as involving both elements, we see that the case examined by Salcedo and Torres (2004) is not really a case of interspersion. There is proximity but no strong social boundaries. The residents of the gated community and those of the rural settlement make a point of distinguishing the rural poor from the urban poor, the good poor from the bad. It is the urban poor who are seen as criminals; the walls are meant for them. Thus, the settlement's residents do not feel discriminated against. The absence of strong social boundaries explains why, in this case, the greater class interaction enabled by proximity works to reduce social distance. In contrast, conditions of proximity and strong social boundaries (i.e., interspersion) bring about a situation Veloso (2010) described as "compulsory closeness." For enclave residents in Rio de Janeiro, closeness is compulsory because they view the favela residents living nearby as potential criminals and morally polluting. Thus, they deal with proximity by imposing spatial boundaries, both physical and symbolic.

I argue that interspersion promotes categorically unequal interaction in the form of boundary imposition. Boundaries are imposed, Tilly (2004) writes, when the members of one relatively powerful group distinguish themselves from the members of another relatively less powerful one. As I use the term, *boundary imposition* involves the use of spatial boundaries to distinguish one group from another as categorically unequal. Boundary imposition is the mechanism connecting interspersion and class division. For enclave residents, the proximity of slums constitutes a source of insecurity. They feel besieged and thus compelled to impose spatial boundaries on slum residents. For slum residents, the proximity of enclaves constitutes a source of discrimination. They experience boundary imposition in the form of exclusion, circumscription (restrictions on movement within enclaves), and being made to feel out of place in certain public spaces—that is, as unequal treatment on the basis of their status as "squatters." Thus, we see the sharpening of class boundaries along the housing divide, as well as the class identities of the urban poor and middle class as squatters and villagers becoming salient.

This argument takes up the first half of the book. In chapter 3, I trace the emergence of interspersion as a spatial form characterizing Metro Manila, and in chapters 4 and 5 I show how interspersion affects relations between slum and enclave residents. In chapter 4, I discuss why and how enclave residents impose boundaries, and in chapter 5, I feature slum residents' experiences of boundary imposition. In the second half of the book, I argue that class identities defined by siege and discrimination shape the political thinking of the middle class and urban poor, respectively. Specifically, I trace the influence of these identities on how each group generally views Estrada. I properly introduce this argument at the beginning of part 2.

## Scope

My aim is not to explain the state of class relations exhaustively. Interspersion is not the only cause of worsening class relations. Nor is the urban environment the only context in which class relations play out. I focus on ecological relations because their role in shaping class interaction has been overlooked and because, with urban restructuring, this role has become more important than ever.

I caution against importing my analysis of Manila wholesale to other cities in the Global South. In Manila, interspersion is particularly pronounced, crosscutting social divisions relatively weak, and class division crystallized in the event of Edsa 3. Thus, the link between urban fragmentation and political contention may be clearer than elsewhere. The processes I identify in the Manila case may be obscured or absent in other cases, and it may not be possible to draw quite the same arc. In short, whether interspersion is affecting class relations and politics in other cities in the same way remains an empirical question.

This is not to say that my analysis does not have general value. It has value as a model. My account not only tells us something new about segregation, class relations, and democracy; it shows these things to be connected. It spells out how they are connected, and thus it helps us make similar connections in other cases. There is value, moreover, in my analytical approach. I focus not on the built form of enclaves but on relations between slum and enclave residents, not on the simple fact of interaction but on the form of interaction. I adopt a view of spatial relations as causal, of proximity as doing something, specifically, altering class relations for the worse. There is value in the concepts I develop along the way: interspersion and boundary imposition, and then the politics of electoral siege, the politics of recognition, and dissensus.

Even if disarticulated from the overarching argument, they provide new ways of thinking about space, class, and politics.

There is value, finally, in the thickness of my account. I do not expect that most readers will know much about the Philippines or care. Hopefully, they—you—will come to care. I hope to render the predicaments in which the urban poor and middle class find themselves with respect to one another sufficiently compelling that readers develop sympathy for both groups. Thick description not only illuminates social processes as they unfold (hence its power to explain), it invites readers to identify with the social actors involved and to imagine themselves enmeshed in their particular situations. Urban experiences that may be regarded as "foreign" are made scrutable. This is valuable in and of itself. These experiences, despite their prevalence, lack sufficient representation in urban scholarship—in sociology most of all. If the urban sociology produced in the United States is to become truly global, then it must be able to grasp these experiences and to incorporate them into its self-definition. This is not just a matter of making foreign experiences familiar to a domestic audience. These experiences must become foundational to American urban sociology. That is, they must inform how the very categories constituting the field are conceptualized.

# PART ONE

# From Urban Fragmentation to Class Division

# THREE

# Interspersion

There is nothing new about the proximity of rich and poor dwellings in Manila. In the postwar decades, stark contrasts in housing became more common thanks to rapid urbanization. Stone, writing in 1973, described "squatter areas nestle[d] against factories, alongside the high brick or stone walls of lavish family compounds, in vacant lots, or against a backdrop of modern skyscrapers" (34). What is new is the withdrawal of rich and poor into separate, clearly bounded spaces and the interspersion of those spaces as a general pattern. Urban fragmentation in Metro Manila is characterized by a patchwork quality. As I recount in this chapter, this pattern came about as the result of parallel streams of urban development by private actors: the urban poor on the one hand and the upper and middle class on the other.

## The Problem of Slums

Squatting came to be considered a social problem only after World War II. Before then, it was "an ephemeral and insignificant thing" (Arcinas 1955, 35). By the end of the war, however, provincial migrants came pouring into Manila. They were pushed by the physical devastation of the countryside, increasing population pressure on farmland, and rural insurgency. They were pulled by new job opportunities in the civil service and the prospect of jobs in industrial production. The big city had become a focus of aspiration, especially for young people with education, and the American colonial administration had instituted a system of widespread public education. For generations of young people growing up in provincial areas around the latter half of the twentieth century, social mobility required urban migration. "The soundest advice to give a barrio boy who wants to go up in the world," wrote the Jesuit sociologist Frank Lynch (1965, 173), "is simply, 'Get out' . . . preferably to the city, and to Manila if possible." Many migrants had no choice but to build their own housing, to squat, in available parts of the city. These parts included, ironically, areas the upper class had fled during the war: the walled city of Intramuros and surrounding districts (Ermita, Malate, Paco, Sampaloc, Tondo). The slum and squatter population multiplied forty times between 1946 and 1970. It went from constituting merely 2 percent of Manila's population to nearly 33 percent of it. Squatting on this scale represented a new phenomenon. By the 1970s, there was no mistaking it: slums had become a major urban form.

The problem was not the lack of urban land per se but its limited availability. A situation of "land dearth amid land plenty" prevailed in many Third World cities (Abrams 1964). The supply of land was mainly constricted by the concentration of land ownership. In 1938, only 4 percent of Manila's population owned land (Magno-Ballesteros 2000, 10). Concentration of ownership was compounded by land hoarding and speculation. Given high rates of urban growth, land prices increased exponentially. Those with means bought it up and held on to it as an investment, one that certainly paid better returns than an inchoate stock market. Administrative issues further affected the supply of urban land. The policies governing land titles were unclear, land taxes were too low, the transaction process was byzantine and rife with corruption, and controls on skyrocketing land prices were weak or nonexistent (Abrams 1964). Finally, the real estate industry was underdeveloped and focused on higher-end housing. On the demand side, the problem was clear: people lacked money and means of credit.

Politically, slums were largely tolerated. Indeed, they had to be. Self-built settlements provided an immediate solution to the housing problem. The government could certainly do no better. Although they were hardly recognized as such, squatters were city builders. They made significant swaths of urban space habitable according to their needs. Turner (1968) called attention to the fact that the focus of so many governments on building low-income housing up to "modern" standards was misplaced. The poor were better served by upgrading existing settlements. Second, slums came to be incorporated politically. Their residents formed clientelist relationships with local politicians, gaining a measure of protection from eviction in exchange for their political autonomy. Political tolerance, it is worth noting, coexisted with periodic drives to demolish slums.

The housing problem was inseparable from the problem of making a living in the city. It is not just that people cannot afford formal housing but also that they choose to live in slums in order to access work opportunities either close by or within the slums themselves. People are primarily concerned, after all, with making a living. Location—proximity to work—is a higher priority than the quality of housing. Of the slum residents Goss (1990, 190) surveyed, 78 percent worked within five kilometers of their residence, 67 percent within three kilometers, and 40 percent within one. Walking distance, he concluded, helps explain the location of informal settlements. Slums themselves provide various opportunities for making a living. They are residential as well as commercial centers, with an informal market for all sorts of goods and services. They contain barbershops, bodegas, and food stalls that serve everything from fish balls to popsicles. I saw billiard halls, cybercafés, and gyms in the slum areas I visited. There are carpenters, tailors, creditors, prostitutes, and "fixers."[1] You can buy toothpaste, shampoo, and coffee in sachets, cigarettes by the piece, and rice by weight (i.e., in affordable portions). As Laquian (1969, 178) observed, slums "make urban life possible at bargain basement rates." They are also places to come by work. Employers recruit workers directly from slums; slum residents are well situated to hear about jobs from neighbors; and in case work is scarce, slums offer residents opportunities for livelihood in the form of microentrepreneurial activities (Pinches 1987). Alcazaren, Ferrer, and Icamina (2011, 173) surveyed eight informal settlements in Metro Manila. Two-thirds of residents were employed informally, and of that number, three-fourths worked within or nearby the settlement where they lived.

Over the decades, the government has tried to solve the slum problem using different approaches, notably, slum clearance, slum upgrading, and the provision of social or government-subsidized housing. These approaches have been remedial. That is to say, they do not get at the root of the problem, which is the concentration of landownership and the inability of the poor to secure land legally. What is needed is thoroughgoing urban land reform, but the political power of the

---

1. Fixers are people who facilitate bureaucratic processes. For a fee, they use their connections in a government office to obtain licenses and permits usually in less time than it normally takes.

landed elite has made this impossible. Even during the martial law period, when state capacity was at its highest, land reform in Manila was ultimately confined to existing slum areas (Karaos 1995, 120–24). The government has focused instead on redressing the physical symptoms of the problem, that is, on erasing the spatial fact of slums.

In the immediate postwar period (1946–1971), the squatter problem was largely a local one (Poethig 1971). For the most part, local politicians dealt with squatters as clients, abiding them in return for electoral support. At the national level, the government sought both to accommodate the urban poor through public housing and to rid the city of slums. In the absence of a clear housing policy, however, it succeeded at neither. The People's Homesite and Housing Corporation (PHHC) created in 1947 built or administered nineteen housing projects (Ocampo 1978). These projects did little to benefit the urban poor, however. The price of units was based on their cost, not on the income of clients. As a result, the projects came to house middle-income residents, particularly government employees and the military. Other projects were simply ill conceived. One, funded by the US Agency for International Development, consisted of no more than four toilets built back-to-back (Abrams 1964, 179). Residents were expected to construct their dwellings around the toilets. The site came to be known, derisively, as Flushing Heights.

Mainly, however, the government tried to remove squatters through various schemes. One scheme involved returning them to the provinces via free one-way bus tickets (Hollnsteiner 1977). Another involved "retraining" them to farm and awarding them homesteads outside the city (Alcazaren et al. 2011, 65). These schemes failed, predictably, given their blatant disregard of the very reason squatters had come to Manila in the first place. Moreover, squatters were mostly relocated to the urban fringe. The efforts were often poorly planned, hampered by a lack of coordination among the relevant agencies and between local and national units. In 1963, ten thousand families were evicted from Intramuros and dumped—some were actually transported in garbage trucks—in Sapang Palay, some forty-odd kilometers away (Dwyer 1975, 79–85). The provincial site lacked services, infrastructure, and opportunities to make a living. The soil conditions precluded farming. As a result, most people sold their land rights and returned to squat in the city. After ten years, only about 20 percent of the people who had been brought there still remained (Karaos 1995, 104).

The use of demolition increased precipitously in the martial law period (1972–1981). Marcos approached the slum problem in other ways as well, including through upgrading,[2] but these approaches were eclipsed by an urban development strategy involving massive displacement of squatters. Slums were demolished to make way for large-scale infrastructure projects and in anticipation of international events. One hundred thousand people had their homes demolished for the Miss Universe Pageant in 1974, two hundred thousand for the visit of US president Gerald Ford in 1975, and sixty thousand for the International Monetary Fund–World Bank summit in 1976 (Pinches 1994, 31). Demolition also served political ends. It deprived communist insurgents of operations bases and asserted state control over urban land. Finally, demolition served an aesthetic vision of the modern city as a city without slums. This vision was espoused particularly by Imelda Marcos, who, by all accounts, found the sight of squatters deeply offensive (Naerssen 1993).

As governor of the newly formed metropolitan region of Manila and head of the Ministry of Human Settlements, the first lady engaged in various efforts to beautify Manila, to transform it, in her words, into the "Los Angeles of Southeast Asia." These efforts included ejecting vendors from exclusive areas of the city, concealing slums behind whitewashed fences (particularly along the route of foreign dignitaries' travel), and constructing architecturally ostentatious projects. Lico (2003) accused her of having an "edifice complex." Under the Bagong Lipunan (New Society) Integrated Sites and Services (BLISS) program, she constructed nine medium-rise housing projects, ostensibly for the urban poor. The projects were built as showpieces, however, and according to standards wholly incompatible with low-income housing. (Their roofs, for instance, were made of expensive terra-cotta tiles.) High construction costs put the price of units beyond the reach of the intended clientele, and the units fell, once again, into the hands of the middle class and favored government employees (Pinches 1994). Imelda Marcos's vision of the city was enacted most directly in the demolition of slum areas. By 1982, she had had enough. She launched the "Last Campaign against Squatting," which, of course, turned out to be just another attempt to expurgate Manila of slums. If anything, it had the effect of galvanizing the urban poor social movement (Naerssen 1989).

Evictions did not substantially abate with Marcos's ouster but rather

---

2. In 1977, Marcos implemented the Zonal Improvement Program in the Tondo foreshore area. The sites-and-services project was dependent on World Bank funding, however, and when this dried up, the project ran aground financially.

continued at high rates. In the post-Marcos period, the driving force was heightened developmental pressure on urban land throughout the 1990s and 2000s. The administration of Corazon Aquino (1986–1992) oversaw the demolition of 276 slum areas containing six hundred thousand residents, in most cases without any attempt at relocating them (Murphy 1993). This rate is remarkable given Aquino's image as an advocate for the urban poor. Moreover, squatters had won legal protection during this period. The Urban Development and Housing Act passed in 1992 regulated the conduct of evictions and mandated, among other things, that evicted families be provided with either a relocation site or compensation. In practice, many of these standards were simply ignored (Karaos 1996).

In 1975, Marcos created the National Housing Authority (NHA) to replace the PHHC and assorted housing agencies. The NHA continued to build social housing throughout the post-Marcos period. Its production was modest, however, and nowhere near the levels required to make an impact on the housing problem. In Manila, the NHA mostly built social housing along the urban fringe, where land was cheaper. This, of course, made it less attractive to the urban poor. In the 2000s, private developers such as Ayala Land got involved in building social housing. They saw social housing as an economic opportunity, a view encouraged, no doubt, by the government's raising the price ceiling on units (Habitat 2011). The problem with social housing, whether provided by the government or the private sector, has always been the same: high land prices, even along the urban fringe, drive up its cost. Social housing ends up being too expensive for the urban poor and going to the middle class. In terms of both cost and location, then, it proves no match for slum housing.

High land prices plagued a different approach to the slum problem. The Community Mortgage Program (CMP), established in 1988, enables squatters to purchase the land they occupy from its legal owners. The government helps them broker and finance the deal. (It gives them reduced interest rates with twenty-five years to pay). Although the CMP is a market mechanism, the land at issue has been depreciated by occupation, and the squatters are usually able to acquire it at well below—as much as 85 percent below—market price (Berner 2000). The program is popular, but its scope is limited. For one, the NHA lacks the institutional and financial capacity to meet existing demand. Second, high land prices have made the program infeasible in prime areas (Porio and Crisol 2004). By 2003, after fifteen years of operation, the CMP had benefited only a fraction of the informal settler population in Metro

Table 3.1 Slum population in Metro Manila, 1946–2020

| Year | Slum population (millions) | Metro population (millions) | Share of metro population in slums (%) |
|---|---|---|---|
| 1946 | .03 | 1.4 | 2 |
| 1956 | .09 | 1.87 | 5 |
| 1960 | .28 | 2.5 | 11 |
| 1970 | 1.2 | 3.9 | 31 |
| 1980 | 1.6 | 5.3 | 30 |
| 1990 | 2.8 | 7.4 | 38 |
| 2000 | 3.9 | 9.9 | 39 |
| 2010 | 4.6 | 11.6 | 40 |
| 2020 | 6.3 | 12.9 | 48 |

*Sources*: Ballesteros (2011); Karaos (1995); NHA (2000); PSA (various years).
*Notes*: Slums include informal or illegal settlements and blighted areas. The slum population figures for 2010 and 2020 are projected by Ballesteros (2011) on the basis of a figure of four million in 2006. The latest metro population figure is from 2018.

Manila: 514 areas and fewer than fifty thousand beneficiaries (NHMFC 2003)—not nothing, but hardly enough. There is another issue pertinent to this study: the CMP may confer tenure security, but it cannot be said to alleviate the stigma associated with slum residence. Slums that have been formalized—or upgraded, for that matter, as Pinches (1994, 34) notes—are no less slums in the eyes of the middle class.

Despite these various fixes, despite nearly seven decades of demolition displacing millions upon millions of slum residents, slums have become only more entrenched. The slum population today probably exceeds five million (table 3.1), or about 40 percent of the metro population. Further, slums are no longer populated mainly by provincial migrants. In 1972, only 27 percent of slum residents surveyed by Abueva, Guerrero, and Jurado were born in Metro Manila. In 2011, half the residents surveyed by Alcazaren and colleagues had relocated from within the metro area.[3] Thus, it may be the case that, today, slum growth has as much to do with natural increase as with provincial migration.

In the 1950s, slum residents were mostly poor. Juppenplatz (1970, 104) estimated that 81 percent of slum residents fell below the subsistence threshold. In 2010, only about 20 percent of the slum population in Manila fell below the national poverty line and merely 3.3 percent below the subsistence threshold (Ballesteros 2011). That threshold may be unrealistic, though, and most slum residents struggle economically.[4]

---

3. It is not clear from the study whether they were actually born in Metro Manila.
4. Indeed, the higher threshold of US$2 yields a poverty incidence of half the slum population in Metro Manila.

The point is simply that, on the whole, slum residents are no longer in such dire straits as they once were. They have become more secure, tenure status notwithstanding. In general, slums have become a common, even ubiquitous, feature of the urban landscape. Slum life has become a normal form of urban life.

## Slums as Stigmatized Places

Slums represent a discontinuity in urban space. They stand out physically. They have a pastiche quality owing less to the variety of materials used to construct dwellings than to the incremental manner in which dwellings are constructed: bits and pieces bit by bit. Pinches (1994) calls it "an architecture of improvisation." Infrastructure and services extend into them unevenly. Paved roads, electrical power, plumbing, and garbage pickup stop where some slums start. This was particularly true in Metro Manila during the immediate postwar years. Since that time most areas have acquired basic services, although not always legally. Slums manifest a different kind of order from middle-class housing. In formal subdivisions the houses are laid out on a grid. To find someone, you just need to know his or her "coordinates," or street name and house number. Slum colonies, in contrast, are largely a blank space on the map. To the outsider, their layout appears haphazard, even labyrinthine, making navigation a daunting prospect. Their order is apprehended as disorder. As Pinches observed, slums require local knowledge to decipher—knowledge, specifically, of distinctly social coordinates. "Particular openings, closures, rises, falls, twists and turns in the spaces between dwellings [are] associated with particular families, households or neighbors" (22).

The physical aspect of slums impressed early observers as representing something different and new. As Hollnsteiner (1977, 310) wrote, it was not the run-down quality of the housing that struck people—Manila already had plenty of slums—but "the unkempt surroundings and densely packed, irregular physical layout that jolted the passerby into this now vivid awareness" of squatter areas as "a new kind of slum."

Slums are socially distinct. Unemployment is rife, and most residents work as vendors or laborers of various kinds. Compare two occupational surveys of slum communities in Manila done forty years apart. In the first (Abueva et al. 1972), the top five jobs were, in order, vendor, driver, laborer, maid, and factory worker. In the second (Al-

Table 3.2 Selected outcomes for nonsquatter and squatter areas in Manila, 1977

| Outcome | Nonsquatter area | Squatter area |
|---|---|---|
| School dropouts before high school (%) | 20 | 35 |
| Ratio of hospital beds to population | 1:300 | 1:4,000 |
| Infant mortality rate (per 1,000 live births) | 76 | 210 |
| Birth rate (per 1,000 people) | 33 | 177 |
| Tuberculosis rate (per 100,000 people) | 800 | 7,000 |
| Gastroenteritis rate (per 100,000 people) | 780 | 1,352 |
| Typhoid rate (per 100,000 people) | 33 | 135 |
| Diphtheria rate (per 100,000 people) | 48 | 77 |
| Measles rate (per 100,000 people) | 130 | 160 |

Source: Basta (1977).

cazaren et al. 2011), they were vendor, driver, laborer, maid, and construction worker.[5] Life chances in slum areas, as indicated by levels of mortality, morbidity, and malnutrition, as well as school dropout rates and number of hospital beds per person, differ starkly from those in neighboring non–slum areas. Just look at the difference in outcomes between squatter and nonsquatter areas as tabulated by Basta in 1977 (table 3.2). Although the disparity is bound to have narrowed since then, it is unlikely to have been erased.

Slums form distinct communities. Scholars from Laquian (1969) to Shatkin (2007) have found them to be highly organized. Organizations form for defense against eviction, fire, and other disasters; for economic security (e.g., lending circles); for community life; and, crucially, to interface with political patrons. Shatkin (2007) estimates that there are more than two thousand slum-based community organizations in Metro Manila. In a survey of eighty informal settlements in the cities of Manila and Quezon City, he found that sixty (75 percent) had some sort of community organization. In addition to formal organizations, various informal networks inevitably develop, relations of kinship, compadrazgo (fictive kinship), friendship, and acquaintance. Strong patterns of "neighboring"—borrowing and lending, sharing news, and passing leisure time together—become established. Norms of mutual aid and support provide a measure of shelter from the rules of the market. Slums are not at all anomic or impersonal but are thickly, if sometimes oppressively, social environments. Strong ties furnish a

5. The category "driver" includes drivers of all kinds, from taxi to family drivers. "Vendor" includes both peddlers and sari-sari (variety) store owners. In the 1972 survey, "laborers" included cargadors (porters) and stevedores. Thus, in tabulating results from the 2011 survey, I added "warehouseman" and "pier porter" to the category of "laborer." "Maid" includes laundry women. I added "foreman" and "forklift operator" to the category of "construction worker."

means of social control particularly through gossip and jokes (Hollnsteiner 1972).

Slum life, moreover, has a distinctly public character. It takes place, in large part, on the street (Jocano 1975). Activities such as watching TV, playing video games, singing karaoke, gambling, and drinking happen out in the open. In formal subdivisions, in contrast, social life takes place indoors or in places designated for socializing—the community center, social club, or park. To paraphrase Bourdieu (1979, 89), in formal housing the outside world begins at the front door, but in informal settlements it begins outside the slum. These patterns of interaction breed "a closeness beyond mere sociability" (Hollnsteiner 1972, 32), a solidarity or "we consciousness" coincident with the slum's territorial boundaries.

This sense of community underlies the capacity of slum residents as political actors. Community organization has long been a requirement for obtaining the patronage of local politicians. In the post-Marcos period, community organization has become a route to greater political power in the form of institutional access and national-level patronage. The political agency of slum residents has become a function of their organizational "weight," with community organizations constituting the basic unit of larger agglomerations better able to pressure housing agencies and powerful political actors (Karaos 1998). Community organizations link with nongovernmental organizations and conglomerate into federations. They form coalitions around specific issues or political candidates. Slum residents, in other words, have gained a measure of political empowerment through community organization. To a significant extent, their political identities are rooted in their identities as residents of this or that particular community.

Slums, finally, represent a discontinuity in urban meaning. They are seen as ugly, unsanitary, unsafe, and obstructions to urban development. They have been described in pathological terms as an "urban sickness" in need of immediate remediation lest it spread (Juppenplatz 1970, 3). Further, the distinction between normal and abnormal housing underlies a moral valuation of the residents of each type. It may not always have been so. According to Abrams (1964, 16), the postwar squatters were seen as refugees fleeing the ravages of war and the Hukbalahap (the communist insurgency in Central Luzon) and were regarded sympathetically. As their numbers grew, however, sympathy gave way to hostility. Squatters came to be seen as willfully breaking the law and profiting by doing so. They were blamed for blighting the urban landscape. "A day rarely passes," Stone (1973, 35) observed, "without a story in the Manila press labeling squatting as a vicious disease impeding city and national development and breeding crime and corruption." The politician seen as "pampering" squatters incurred particular scorn. A columnist writing for a Manila newspaper in 1963 blasted "the disproportionate sense of social concern" shown squatters by public officials (cited in Lacquian 1966, 55). As he and others saw it, electoral interest masquerading as pity encouraged squatting and stood in the way of a real solution to the slum problem. That solution was eviction. Even the general manager of the PHHC, the agency in charge of housing the urban poor, saw it this way. Squatters must be relocated, he wrote, because they occupied property illegally, the areas they occupied were unsafe or intended for public use, and they were an "eyesore" to tourists (Santiago 1977, 45–46). A report by the Office of the President (1968, 92–94) linked the squatter problem to other social problems, such as crime, fire, disease, low property values, and a breakdown in morals (notably, "crimes against chastity"). Slum clearance was justified by the need to develop, beautify, secure, and sanitize the city. Squatters represented the antithesis of development. They did not just lack proper housing, jobs, and education. They were morally deficient as well.

## Enclavization

The influx of squatters in the 1950s hastened the exodus of Manila's elite to the suburbs (what are now Makati City and Quezon City). Around this time, the Ayala Corporation built a cluster of residential subdivisions in the boondocks of Makati according to an unprecedented standard of development (see Garrido 2013a). The subdivisions came with large lots and wide, fully paved streets, drainage, running water, streetlights, and, crucially, meticulous restrictions on building to preserve the order contained in the original plan. "New Makati" was explicitly developed in contradistinction to the haphazard growth of Manila. According to the official history, "The Ayalas saw in the shambles of overcrowded Manila an opportunity to create a new town," one that was finally "modern," finally "rational" in its use of space, and that could serve as a "model" for future development (Filipinas Foundation 1983, 38–45). The subdivisions were meant to accommodate residents of middle as well as high income, but demand drove up their cost, and New Makati was quickly priced beyond the reach of all but the elite. By the 1970s, land in Forbes Park, New Makati's premiere subdivision, returned initial investors an average yield of 967 percent *annually* (Keyes 1979, 222). New Makati's commercial district, meanwhile, had become the financial hub of the entire metropolitan region. The enclave came to possess its own gravity. Space reorganized around it, literally. Circumferential Road 4, for example, had originally been designed to bypass downtown Manila, but with Makati's centrality, it became the main arterial route to and from its central business district and, consequently, the most heavily utilized road in the metropolis (Corpuz 2000, 138). Today C4 is known as Epifanio de los Santos Avenue, or EDSA.

New Makati's success exacted a considerable toll on the rest of the city. The enclave distorted the surrounding land market, making it impossible for most workers employed in New Makati to afford housing in the area. It caused a traffic bottleneck that remains notorious to this day. According to Keyes (1979, 223), bus efficiency declined from 300 kilometers traveled per day to 220 kilometers as a direct result of New Makati's growth. The development constituted a drain on municipal resources disproportionate to the small size of its population. (In the six subdivisions of New Makati alone, Keyes counted 906 private swimming pools.) In sum, New Makati can be said to have transformed Manila, but not in the way its corporate planners had imagined. They had hoped that it would serve as a model for how, through planning, the disorder of Manila could be brought to heel. Instead, New Makati became a symbol of exclusivity. Moreover, the strategy of enclosing spaces for development, absent the pretension of inclusivity, came to be emulated widely in building specifically for the middle and upper class.

The middle class did not live in New Makati, however. In the 1950s through the 1970s, they lived in mixed neighborhoods and in subdivisions along the metropolitan outskirts. Hollnsteiner (1969) characterized the middle-class household as atomized and disconnected from its locality—a self-sufficiency enabled by its possession of a car and maids. Although middle-class subdivisions were generally not gated, each house constituted a "self-contained, independent unit," with "high walls with glass on top and an occasional ferocious watchdog below mark the middle-class block" (182). This changed in the post-Marcos period. Existing subdivisions put up gates and posted guards. New subdivisions were gated and guarded as a matter of course. What happened?

For one, the urban poor came to receive greater political consideration. Having played an active role in the anti-Marcos movement, they gained substantial concessions from the Aquino government. Early in her term, Aquino persuaded the mayors of Metro Manila to declare a moratorium on evictions and issued two presidential proclamations awarding large tracts of land to the occupants of the National Government Center area in Quezon City. These moves were taken as signaling an official tolerance of squatters and led to the second largest wave of squatting in Metro Manila since the postwar decades (Karaos 1995). In gating, the middle class were reacting to the greater presence of slums in the city. They were reacting to the urban poor's new political power, particularly in the form of the Urban Development and Housing Act. The law made it harder to dislodge squatters.

Gating was also a response to crime, or at least to the perception of crime. The crime rate spiked in the years following Marcos's ouster, but it declined sharply throughout the 1990s. In the 1980s the average crime rate was 183 per 100,000; in the 1990s it dropped to 109, then to 87 in the 2000s. Despite the falling crime rate, the gates stayed up. Moreover, by the 1990s, they had come to be seen as necessary. A new, darker view of the public city had gripped upper- and middle-class residents. They had long regarded Manila as disorderly, but now they portrayed the public city as repellant and treacherous and sought to insulate themselves from it. The prevalence of this view will be evident in the following chapter.

The pace of enclavization greatly accelerated in the 1990s. It was driven in large part by demand from a growing middle class and overseas Filipino workers (see Ortega 2016). The real estate industry focused on meeting this demand. It also helped create it by marketing gated communities and "closed" condominiums (heavily guarded high-rises) as the very definition of modern housing (Connell 1999). In 1976, according to Keyes, there were 750 subdivisions in all of Metro Manila registered with the now-defunct Department of Local Government and Community Development.[6] Between 1981 and 2013, according to data obtained from the Housing and Land Use Regulatory Board (HLURB) in 2014, 3,837 private residential subdivisions and condominiums were built.[7] Construction clustered around boom periods in 1989, 1997, and

---

6. This is likely an underestimate, Keyes (1976) notes. It may not include many older subdivisions.

7. These data consist of residential licenses to sell from 1981 to 2013, which furnish a count of all the residential housing projects in Metro Manila in the period. Mainly, projects were classified as "open market" or government subsidized. Government-subsidized housing comprises three categories: "socialized" and "economic" housing, distinguished by level of subsidy, and "compliance" housing, or projects built to satisfy the Balanced Housing Provision of the UDHA. The two classes of housing are covered by different laws. Presidential Decree No. 957 (1976) regulates subdivisions and condominiums sold at market rates, while Batas Pambansa 220 (1982) regulates socialized and economic housing. Because I am interested in upper- and middle-class

2012. The vast majority of residential construction during this period consisted of "open market" housing—housing constructed by the private sector and sold at prevailing market rates. Meanwhile, relatively little social housing was being built in the metro region because of high land prices. Between 1981 and 2013, only 14 percent of all residential construction in Manila received government support. Of this figure, 81 percent was classified as economic housing—the least subsidized type, supplied by the private sector and entailing full cost recovery. The HLURB data also tell us that the rate of condo building surpassed that of subdivision building in 1995. Between 2000 and 2013, twice as many condominiums were built.

The new subdivisions were built in the south of Metro Manila and in the "suburbs"—that is, the neighboring provinces of Laguna, Cavite, Rizal, and Bulacan (Reyes 1998). It was not just subdivisions being built but also corporate offices, call centers, export processing zones, and industrial parks. These areas were cheaper to build in, and they collected the developmental spillover from Manila's central districts. They have come to define the frontiers of an emerging megaregion. The new condominiums, meanwhile, were built around Manila's multiple central business districts. In the decades following World War II, new central business districts emerged in the cities of Makati (Ayala), Pasig (Ortigas), and Quezon City (Cubao). In the 1990s and 2000s, new central business districts were developed in Taguig (Bonifacio Global City) and Muntinlupa (Filinvest Corporate City). Currently, a new one is being developed in the North Triangle area of Quezon City (Vertis North). All in all, old subdivisions and new along with the mushrooming of condominiums in central areas, residential enclaves were no longer clustered in certain parts of Manila but spread across the metro region.

By the 2000s, enclavization had reached a point at which observers could speak of a "private city" having seceded from the public one (Muijzenberg and Naerssen 2005; Rimmer and Dick 2009; Shatkin 2008). Enclaves had not just become more numerous but larger in scale and increasingly connected through physical and social links. Corporate "cities" were being built, megaprojects bundling several facilities within the same complex, including office buildings, condominiums, malls, sports clubs, schools, hospitals, and even consulates. These spaces came equipped with premium, privately provisioned infrastruc-

---

residential enclaves, I include only open-market housing covered by PD 957 in my count of subdivisions and condominiums. This may be an undercount insofar as much social housing goes to the middle class.

ture and services. Bonifacio Global City, for example, is equipped with a dual piping system that allows one to distinguish water for drinking, cooking, and bathing from water meant for flushing, irrigation, and outdoor washing. Meanwhile, many of the neighborhoods surrounding the development cannot rely on a steady supply of water for any purpose. Further, different kinds of enclaves grew more connected. In the mid-1990s, the private sector came to exercise a greater role in urban planning through modalities such as Build-Operate-Transfer, the centerpiece of the government's program to privatize infrastructure (Corpuz 2000). Corporations could now enlist the government in service of their projects. The government would consolidate the land needed by the developer in return for a stake. Increasingly, real estate developers were partnering with the government to build transportation infrastructure (light rail and expressways). They were motivated, Shatkin (2008) writes, less by the profitability of these projects than by the opportunity to connect their various residential and commercial properties. He describes the resulting pattern of urban development led by the private sector as "bypass-implant urbanism." Private developers would implant new spaces for production and consumption—business districts, technology parks, commercial centers, and housing developments—and connect them through transportation projects, thereby "bypassing the congested arteries of the 'public city'" (388). This strategy helped shape the private city as a network of corporate, commercial, and residential enclaves.

Enclavization is worsening upper- and middle-class segmentation. On the one hand, the middle class is withdrawing from the public city. Its members are opting out of public services such as public schools and hospitals and shunning public spaces, including parks, walkways, and déclassé malls. On the other hand, upper- and middle-class social life is increasingly taking place in various kinds of enclaves having to do with nearly every aspect of their lives. Allow me to overstate the case to make this point: The upper and middle classes live in gated subdivisions and condominiums. They study in private schools. They work in office buildings in one of several central business districts around the metro. They shop in mid- to high-end malls (from SM to Greenbelt). They go out to clubs, cafés, and bars located inside commercial compounds. Sometimes they attend the churches within these compounds. They move in private cars from one enclave to another and travel through toll roads too expensive for the general public to use.

Residential enclavization, further, has led to a differentiation of administrative duties at the local level. Enclave residents primarily resort to their homeowners' or village association concerning matters of security and property. Meanwhile, the area's poorer population, particularly slum residents and the domestic workers living within subdivisions, turn to the *barangay*. The barangay is the smallest administrative division within cities and municipalities, akin to the barrio or neighborhood. It also refers to the administrative body at that level. The barangay and homeowners' association come to represent different constituencies whose interests, as we will see, often clash.

Slums are already stigmatized. With the proliferation of enclaves, the housing divide came into focus, and the social boundary it traced grew salient. Prescient observers warned that this would happen. "Metropolitan Manila's course today," Hollnsteiner (1969, 181) wrote in 1965, "threatens to transform her into a city of enclaves, each focused on its own needs and oblivious to those of the others." By 1988, Caoili (1999, 74–92) was able to discern the outlines of a "dual society" in Manila. Its two components were spatially distinct, yet functionally interdependent. The disparity between them—in terms of density, quality of life, sanitation, income, extent of services, and, of course, housing—was worsening. Caoili worried that the elite could afford to neglect Manila's problems because they lived apart and in vastly different conditions from the majority of its population. He worried that the problems of the public city would not be their problems. In 1997, Berner argued that the spatial division between slums and enclaves had become the most important social division in urban life. It subsumed other significant lines of differentiation, including provincial origin, ethnicity, and even class on the basis of work. "What is taking place," he wrote, "is the exhaustive emergence of enclaves, a de-differentiation of the city's population [into rich and poor] due to the social differentiation of urban space [into enclaves and slums]" (8). The spatial divide, in other words, is clarifying a class divide.

There has been at least one effort to correct course. The Urban Development and Housing Act contains a provision (article V, section 18) mandating that subdivision developers build social housing worth 20 percent of their project cost. According to one of the framers of the law, the provision was intended to encourage class integration, with "compliance housing" being built inside subdivisions.[8] In practice, however, this intent is routinely flouted. Land in Manila is simply too valuable to allot to social housing. Thus, developers meet their legal obligation by building compliance housing outside Metro Manila as

8. Interview with Jaime Cura, July 23, 2010.

part of separate, lower- to middle-income subdivisions, or they buy out of it altogether by funding NGOs that build housing for the poor at the outskirts of the metro area (Karaos 1996). As of 2013, compliance housing accounted for less than 1 percent of all residential construction in Metro Manila (HLURB 2014). Most of these projects were built following the passage of the UDHA in 1992. In the period between 2000 and 2013, a grand total of two compliance projects were built.

## Interspersion

Enclavization worsened the slum problem. The construction of commercial enclaves and the infrastructure projects connecting them entailed the massive displacement of informal settlers. Furthermore, enclavization led to the runaway inflation of land values. The price of land in central areas increased several thousandfold. Between 1987 and 1996, land values in the Makati and Ortigas central business districts appreciated by 6,000 percent and 8,000 percent, respectively (Shatkin 2004, 2474). The irony is that enclaves require labor to build and maintain them, and thus they attract the urban poor as workers. These workers, however, find it impossible to afford formal housing anywhere near where they work. Despite comparatively lower construction costs, housing prices in Metro Manila are some of the highest in Asia (Magno-Ballesteros 2000). Consequently, the poor, and even the lower middle class, are priced out of the housing market, including the market for government-subsidized housing within the metro area. To put the matter concretely: "A schoolteacher's salary is not enough to rent a simple apartment in the city; to buy a 100 square-meter lot (not to mention a house) in a medium-class residential area, he would need more than his lifetime income" (Berner 1998, 124).

The urban poor, therefore, are forced to trade off job opportunities closer to metropolitan hubs and opportunities for formal and better-quality housing farther away from them. They must choose between tenure insecurity and commutes lasting several hours each way that cost a significant fraction of their daily incomes (Shatkin 2009). Workers employ a number of strategies to deal with this trade-off. They board with family members, strangers, or at their workplace, they work fewer days but longer shifts, or they exit the scene entirely by going abroad for work. Their main resort, however, is slum and informal housing.

We know that the slum population has grown tremendously in the postwar decades. It probably exceeds five million today (see table 3.1).

Another, overlooked story is the explosion in the number of slum areas and their dispersal across Metro Manila. The reasons for their dispersal are various: the urban poor are chasing jobs around the city; urban land is becoming increasingly unavailable; existing settlements are filling to capacity; demolitions are proceeding apace; and natural disasters, particularly typhoons, are doing the work of demolition (Murphy 1993; Santiago 1992; Shatkin 2009). By the 2000s, hundreds of new slum areas had emerged in Manila, and many large colonies had broken up into smaller ones. In 1963, Juppenplatz (1970, 99) observed that the slum areas within greater Manila were few, well defined, and largely "contained in a wide band, approximately one kilometer in width, encircling the city." By 1981 the number of slum areas had grown to 405, and by 1990, 654 (Karaos 1987; Naerssen 1993). In 2011, the National Housing Authority identified 1,905 informal settlements across the metropolis. The settlements range in size from colonies with several thousand households to marginal locations with several dozen. They are largely found on private or government lots, but they are also found by the ocean (as well as in the ocean, in houses atop stilts); beside waterways and rail lines; under bridges; on dump sites, sidewalks, and easements; and even on the grass and concrete islands between the lanes of major roads. There is a logic to the location of settlements. They are built close to livelihood opportunities and transportation lines; where land is available, often in marginal or precarious locations; and in areas naturally equipped with sewerage (hence the clustering of settlements along Manila Bay and the Pasig River).

The number of slum areas grew almost five times between 1985 and 2011 (table 3.3). It grew in nearly every one of Metro Manila's sixteen cities and one municipality. To be sure, the distribution of informal settlers and slum areas is not uniform across cities. Quezon City contains the lion's share: 60 percent of the slum areas in Metro Manila and 40 percent of its informal settler population. This larger share, however, is not entirely out of proportion to its relative size, comprising 27 percent of Metro Manila's land area. The distribution of informal settlers has shifted over the years, in some cases dramatically (table 3.3). The city of Manila went from containing nearly one-third of the metro's informal settler population in 1985 to merely 5 percent in 2011. Quezon City's share increased from 23 percent to 40 percent over the same period. There are specific reasons for these shifts. In Manila City, the renovation of the Bay area, Intramuros, and other tourist sites entailed the massive relocation of squatters. Meanwhile, older settlements in Tondo

Table 3.3 Number of slum areas and distribution of informal settlers in Metro Manila

| City | Slum areas | | Distribution of informal settlers (%) | | | |
| | 1985 | 2011 | 1985 | 2000 | 2011 | City's share of land area |
| --- | --- | --- | --- | --- | --- | --- |
| Caloocan | 12 | 100 | 7.8 | 10.8 | 13.6 | 8.7 |
| Las Piñas | 8 | 30 | 2.4 | 5 | 2.4 | 5.2 |
| Makati | 19 | 103 | 3.3 | 1.5 | 1.7 | 3.5 |
| Malabon | 11 | 41 | 2.4 | 2.4 | 4.7 | 2.6 |
| Mandaluyong | 10 | 42 | 2.6 | 5 | 4.1 | 1.8 |
| Manila | 83 | 78 | 30.9 | 9.5 | 5.3 | 7 |
| Marikina | 17 | 25 | 3.7 | 5.5 | 1.7 | 3.7 |
| Muntinlupa | 17 | 29 | 2.6 | 6.8 | 3.5 | 6.8 |
| Navotas | 10 | 8 | 2.3 | 3.7 | 1.9 | 1.9 |
| Parañaque | 12 | 22 | 3.4 | 4.8 | 4.9 | 7.7 |
| Pasay | 36 | 113 | 4.8 | 6.5 | 5.9 | 3 |
| Pasig | 17 | 66 | 3.8 | 1.9 | 0.7 | 5.1 |
| Pateros | — | 14 | 0.7 | 0.7 | 0.3 | 0.3 |
| Quezon City | 142 | 1143 | 23.4 | 27.6 | 39.7 | 26.9 |
| San Juan | 7 | 23 | 0.4 | 2.9 | 2.5 | 1 |
| Taguig | — | 16 | 2.4 | 3.2 | 3.3 | 7.4 |
| Valenzuela | 4 | 52 | 3 | 2.2 | 3.7 | 7.5 |
| Total Metro Manila | 405 | 1905 | | | | |

Sources: Karaos (1987); NHA (2000, 2011).

and elsewhere have been upgraded and formalized. (Many of these areas, however, still qualify as slum areas.) Quezon City's increased share of informal settlers can be explained, in large part, by the Corazon Aquino–inspired wave of squatting in the late 1980s and the political tolerance—some would say encouragement—of successive mayors.

Distributional shifts notwithstanding, informal settlements have become a significant presence throughout the metropolis. In figure 3.1, I map the informal settler population in Metro Manila. As it shows, despite some clustering in the north, informal settlers can be found across the region as a whole. They can be found in every city and in multiple barangays or neighborhoods in every city. Indeed, zooming in to the city level, it becomes clear that in thirteen of the metro area's seventeen units there are informal settlements in the majority of barangays. In figures 3.2–3.4, I map the informal settler populations in the three cities where I did fieldwork: Quezon City, Parañaque, and Makati. I did this for all seventeen of Metro Manila's cities, in fact; the remaining fourteen are archived online, along with the data used to make the maps, at the website Patchwork City Archive (www.patchworkcityarchive.com). The maps illustrate just how wide-

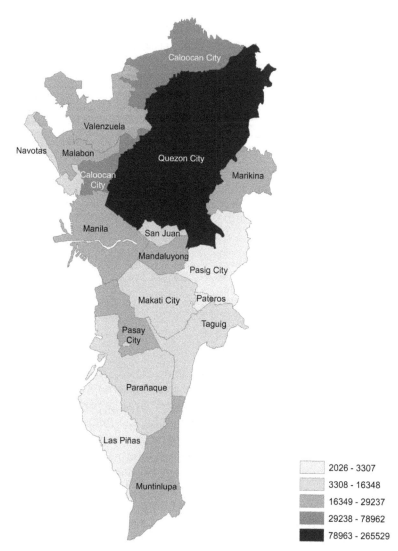

**FIGURE 3.1** Number of informal settler families in Metro Manila.
*Source*: NHA (2011).

spread the slum population is. In some cases, slum-free barangays are actually residential enclaves, and thus enclosed by physical boundaries. This is the case in Makati (fig. 3.4). The cluster of slum-free barangays at the center of the city covers an area comprising six residential enclaves and the central business district—that is, New Makati. In any case, the extent of informal settlement has informed the perception that slums are now everywhere.

The spread of slums and enclaves within the metro region has made their proximity inevitable. In figure 3.5, I map the enclaves and informal settlements in Quezon City. I rely on local government data listing 393 residential enclaves built between 1992 and 2011 (Quezon

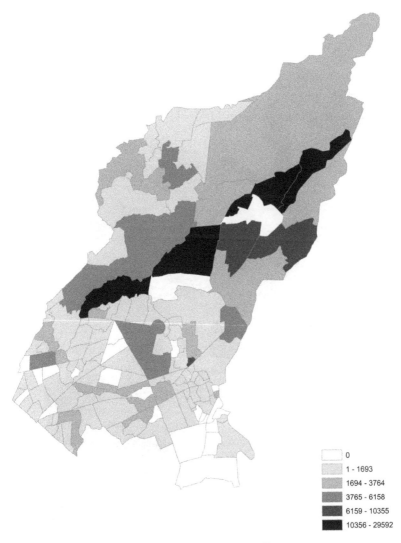

0
1 - 1693
1694 - 3764
3765 - 6158
6159 - 10355
10356 - 29592

**FIGURE 3.2** Number of informal settler families in Quezon City.
*Source*: NHA (2011).

**79**

City 2012) and counting 878 informal settlements around the city (Quezon City 2008). Figure 3.5 contains 344 of the enclaves and 721 of the settlements, or 88 percent and 82 percent, respectively. (Some points were too ambiguously defined to identify geographically.) Using the Near tool in ArcGIS, I calculated the median distance from an en-

0
1 - 323
324 - 834
835 - 1656
1657 - 3988

**FIGURE 3.3** Number of informal settler families in Parañaque City.
*Source:* NHA (2011).

FIGURE 3.4    Number of informal settler families in Makati City.
*Source*: NHA (2011).

clave to the nearest slum to be around 230 meters.[9] Although I would caution against reading from figure 3.5 the situation of the rest of the metropolis—the fragmentation of Quezon City is extreme compared to Manila's other cities—the map still serves to illustrate a situation that has become typical of the metro area overall: the general proximity of slums and enclaves. This situation has become so common that a neologism exists in Filipino describing the squatters who live just outside the walls of villages: *gilidgers*—a combination of *gilid*, meaning "on the edge," and villagers, as enclave residents are called.

I use the term *interspersion* to emphasize the general proximity of slums and enclaves. Take note: The proximity is *general* and not simply immediate. It is not the case that slums and enclaves are always right beside each other, but they do tend to be located in the same baran-

9. The distance is probably even shorter. For one, the map does not include all the slums and enclaves in Quezon City. It includes informal settlements not slums, and it includes only enclaves constructed between 1992 and 2011. Second, the map does not take into account the physical area actually taken up by enclaves and settlements. The Near tool calculates the distance only from one point to another.

**FIGURE 3.5** Interspersion in Quezon City.
*Sources:* Quezon City (2008, 2012).

▲ Enclaves
● Slums

gay. The spaces are close enough, in other words, for their residents to interact with one another in some way, even if only visually. This is to be distinguished from a situation of spatial polarization where the urban middle class and poor occupy different parts of the city. Second, interspersion describes a pattern of proximity and not just instances of it. Third, it is not just dwellings but classed spaces that are proximate. This is not the situation described at the beginning of the chapter, where high-walled houses abut more modest or dilapidated dwellings in mixed neighborhoods. It is one where bounded, mutually exclusive classed spaces are counterposed. Interspersion describes a patchwork of classed spaces. This pattern is new, as Berner (1997) recognized. It is distinguished by "the apartheid of contrasting elements—their segregation and mutual exclusion" (8).

## From Hodgepodge to Patchwork

In a recent book, Abdoumaliq Simone (2014) calls attention to the prevalence of so-called hodgepodge neighborhoods in Jakarta. These tend to be older districts in the central city occupied by the poor and lower middle class. The residents of these neighborhoods are distinguished by their socioeconomic and ethnic heterogeneity. The virtue of such places, Simone argues, is that different kinds of people must make an effort not just to get along but also to make a living. Interdependence forges an urban commons—a constant working together (out of necessity more than anything), an "orchestration"—and keeps differences from hardening. The stories throughout Simone's book illustrate "the willingness of residents to live amid differences as long as differences in kind do not connote differences in worth" (265).

It is true that slums in Manila are hodgepodge spaces, but it is equally true that in relation to enclaves they are stigmatized places. They may be hodgepodge internally, but they also form part of a patchwork of classed spaces. The focus of this patchwork view is on slums and enclaves. It is on the relations between their residents being categorically unequal, that is, very much connoting differences in worth. This may be a dualist reading of urban relations and, in this respect, only part of the story. It is an essential part, though. It tells us something important about how class relations have been changing in the wake of market reforms. Hodgepodge and patchwork are not just different ways of characterizing the urban environment of cities in the developing world. They also describe the trajectory of urban restructuring for many of these cities: the ongoing transformation of urban space from predominantly hodgepodge areas into a patchwork of classed spaces. In Manila, the urban poor and middle class are being increasingly sorted into slums and enclaves, and these spaces drawn closer together. Class boundaries, being spatialized, are more sharply drawn. They are also more extensive. In the following two chapters, we explore what this new spatial situation—interspersion—means for class relations.

# FOUR

# Imposing Boundaries: Villagers

My aim in this chapter and the next is to show how interspersion affects relations between slum and enclave residents. My focus is on enclave residents—"villagers," as they're called locally. I argue that the proximity of slum areas to enclaves fosters a sense of siege among enclave residents. They feel compelled to impose spatial boundaries on slum residents as a means of preventing crime and encroachment and of maintaining social distance. My data come from four cases of slums and enclaves in general proximity. The cases describe various spatial situations defined by interspersion. For reference, I list the cases in table 4.1.[1] My interest, to be clear, is not on the differences across cases—although I take these into account where I can—but on what the different cases tell us about how interspersion is affecting class relations.

## Cases

### Makati, New and Old

The slums and enclaves in Makati are located in different parts of the city (fig. 4.1). The enclaves are in New Makati,

---

1. I map their locations within Metro Manila in figure 1.1. I discuss case selection in the appendix. Photographs of each site are available in the online archive, at http://www.patchworkcityarchive.com.

Table 4.1 Cases and field sites

| City | Enclaves | Slums |
|------|----------|-------|
| Makati City | *New Makati* | *Old Makati* |
| | Forbes Park | D. Gomez St. in Tejeros |
| | Bel Air | La Peral Compound in Guadalupe Viejo |
| | Dasmariñas | Tripa de Gallena II in San Isidro |
| | San Lorenzo | Coryville in La Paz |
| | Urdaneta | McKinley Driver's Association in Cembo |
| Parañaque City | *BF Homes* | *De la Rama* |
| | Inner Circle | Target 1 |
| | | Target 2 |
| | | Clinicville |
| | | Ipilville |
| Quezon City | *Phil-Am Homes* | *San Roque* |
| | *Don Antonio Heights* | *Barangay Holy Spirit* |
| | | Kasiyahan, Samonte, and Zuzuarregui streets |

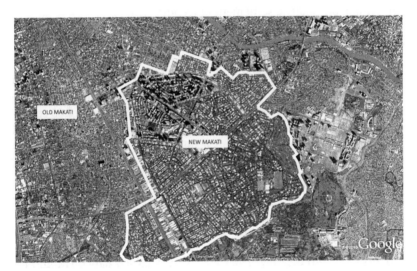

**FIGURE 4.1** New and Old Makati.
*Source*: Google Earth, 2010.

an exclusive area comprising six residential villages and the central business district. These enclaves are the oldest in Metro Manila, and perhaps some of the oldest gated communities in the developing world. They were built by the Ayala Company shortly after World War II as a haven for the upper class, and over time, they came to represent a model of residential enclosure. I interviewed residents from Forbes Park, Dasmariñas, San Lorenzo, and Urdaneta villages.

The slum areas are in Old Makati, which refers to the areas developed by Ayala before the war. Between 1924 and 1941, the company constructed twenty low-quality subdivisions. They had small lots, narrow streets, ill-defined blocks, inadequate sewerage, and neither running water nor electricity. These subdivisions were designed to sell quickly to the town's lower-middle-class residents, and they did. The division between Old and New Makati remains as stark as ever. The two areas are distinguished by housing quality, population density, and the socioeconomic status of residents. Unsurprisingly, most of the city's slum areas are found in Old Makati, whereas the villages of New Makati, being enclosed, are largely squatter-free. I interviewed residents from D. Gomez Street in Barangay Tejeros; La Peral Compound, a large colony in Guadalupe Viejo; Tripa de Gallena II, a row of shanties along the Pasig River; Coryville, a settlement built along the wall of an old factory building in La Paz; and McKinley Driver's Association (MCDA) in Cembo, originally a settlement of jeepney drivers.

### BF Homes and De la Rama

In this case, the slum is nestled beside a "supervillage": BF Homes is a complex of subdivisions so large that it spans three cities: Parañaque City mainly, as well as Las Piñas and Muntinlupa. It covers 7.65 square kilometers, contains 17,900 households (about 87,000 residents), and encompasses every kind of service imaginable, including preschools and a college, shopping centers, clinics, and a fire station. It has been called the biggest subdivision in Asia. It is not really one subdivision, however, but eighty-two clustered together, each one its own gated enclave. Don Tomás Aguirre, the founder of Banco Filipino, developed BF Homes in the late 1960s. He envisioned one large community loosely subdivided into four or five villages. By the 1980s, however, Aguirre's finances fell into disarray. The Central Bank closed Banco Filipino for insolvency, and Aguirre left for the United States. In 1989, the management of BF Homes transferred from developer to residents. The enclave was subdivided intensively. Clusters of streets were demarcated and walled off from one another. The new subdivisions put up their own homeowners' associations. I interviewed the residents of a subdivision called Inner Circle, so named for its location deep inside BF.

The De la Rama slum comprises four contiguous areas—Target 1, Target 2, Clinicville, and Ipilville—that, collectively, have come to be known for the street leading up to them. The slum is bound on one side by BF Homes and on the other by the cemetery Manila Memorial

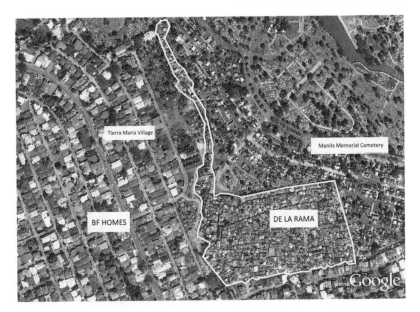

**FIGURE 4.2** BF Homes/De la Rama.
*Source*: Google Earth, 2010.

Park (fig. 4.2). Squatters began to settle in De la Rama as early as the mid-1970s. Target 1 and Target 2 had once served as Aguirre's shooting range, and the two areas together were supposed to have been developed into another subdivision. An empty guard post stands in front of the slum's entryway, a remnant of erstwhile plans. It faces the manned guard post of the subdivision across the street.

### Phil-Am Homes and San Roque

In this case the slum and enclave are separated by a highway (Epifanio de los Santos Avenue). Phil-Am Homes was developed in 1955 by the Philippine American Life Insurance Company. It was built to house mid-level executives and their families. At the time of my fieldwork, Phil-Am had about 650 households and upward of three thousand residents. Meanwhile, San Roque, the informal settlement across the street had around thirty thousand residents occupying half the land area of Phil-Am Homes (fig. 4.3).

San Roque's oldest residents arrived in the 1980s. The settlement once contained nearly ten thousand families. When I visited in 2009, only about six thousand remained. Today, San Roque is still in the

**FIGURE 4.3** Phil-Am Homes/San Roque.
*Source*: Google Earth, 2010.

process of being demolished. Ayala Land plans to build a new central business district on the land it occupies. Residents were given two options: relocate to a predisposed site in Rizal province or take a one-time payment—six thousand pesos (US$130) to leave or twenty-four thousand pesos (US$520) to return to one's home province. Many residents pressed for a third option, one in keeping with the spirit of the Urban Development and Housing Act: on-site accommodation. They wanted Ayala to build them a medium-rise housing development in the area. When I returned in 2014, San Roque had been reduced to half of its land area. Remaining residents had been offered a new relocation site in Bulacan and higher compensation for leaving, but the on-site option had been taken off the table.

### Don Antonio Heights in Barangay Holy Spirit

In this case, the slum areas surround the enclave (fig. 4.4). Barangay Holy Spirit in the National Government Center (NGC) area of Quezon City is predominantly poor, yet most of its land area is taken up by the gated subdivisions of the middle class. Although occupying little more than three square kilometers, Holy Spirit contains six or seven subdivisions amid several dense, slumlike neighborhoods. I interviewed the residents of Don Antonio Heights and the residents of the slum areas along Kasiyahan, Samonte, and Zuzuarregui Streets just outside the village's walls. Don Antonio was developed in the 1970s on land owned by the Zuzuarregui family. At the time, the Holy Spirit area was largely undeveloped, houses were few and far between, and the subdivision was parceled into several lots. According to the residents of Don Antonio, the caretakers of the lots brought in their relatives and rented out the land to squatters. The number of squatters multiplied in the late 1980s and 1990s, as presidents Cory Aquino and then Fidel Ramos issued land proclamations legalizing the tenure of settlers in the NGC area. Don Antonio had not been walled originally. It was only in the 1990s that the homeowners' association, lately organized—or organized "too late," as one resident put it—managed to erect walls. The problem is that the walls also enclosed the squatters who were already inside the village's perimeter.

The enclave and slum residents of Holy Spirit give different accounts

**FIGURE 4.4** Don Antonio/Kasiyahan, Samonte, and Zuzuarregui Streets. *Source*: Google Earth, 2010.

of informal settlement. These accounts ground opposing claims of the other side's illegitimacy. For example, Ava owned one of the first houses in Holy Spirit. She settled there with her new husband in 1967. The area was still largely grassland. "We even had to bulldoze our own roads," she said. After Marcos's ouster, squatters "of all sizes" started coming. They interpreted democracy as license to settle wherever they wanted. The Urban Development and Housing Act, or Lina Law, as it's known locally, only made things worse, Ava said, because it protected squatters. Now she lives inside a compound enclosed by high walls. Her story is familiar one: squatters overrun the property of hapless landowners, land values in the area plummet, crime rates soar, and the rightful residents retreat behind walls.

Many of Holy Spirit's slum residents have been around for a long time, though. They watched Don Antonio and the other subdivisions being constructed around them. They tell a different story, a story not of encroachment but of dispossession. In 1968, when Jose was born, Holy Spirit had a reputation as a forbidding place. In the 1970s, it was where Marcos dumped the bodies of "salvaged" political enemies. (During the Marcos era, the word *salvage* came to mean, perversely, the direct opposite of "to save.") "It used to be all trees here, not a lot of houses," Jose recounted. "The first settlers were people who just wanted to work the land. Eventually, people came and said, 'That's ours. This is ours.' There was nothing [the settlers] could do. Back then, all you had to do was measure the land, have it registered at the municipality, and that's it. It was yours so long as you paid the land tax."

"That's it?" I asked.

"Before."

"And today?"

"Today there are a lot of owners."

"So the people we call squatters just weren't able to have their land titled?"

"That's right."

Walter, another Holy Spirit resident, made a similar point. The NGC area used to be all government property, he said. The people who claim to own land here acquired their title simply by paying the *amilyar*, or property tax, for a certain number of years. The poor can't afford to do this, and thus, no matter how long they have lived on a plot of land, they cannot claim to own it. The rich can do this easily. Moreover, they can come in and make it look like they have been paying the *amilyar* for years. "And because they're rich," Walter concluded, "they're able to put up walls around their property to show that it's really theirs."

It should be clear even from these thumbnail descriptions that the cases admit various circumstances, and what I call slums and enclaves are, in fact, quite heterogeneous. The slums take various forms: a large colony, a section of a street, settlements along canals or beside old buildings—and here I'm just talking about the slum areas in Old Makati. Not all slum areas are informal settlements: Coryville in Old Makati has been formalized, and the slum areas in Holy Spirit are in the process of acquiring title under the Community Mortgage Program. Even the informal settlements differ in important ways. The residents of San Roque are being cleared out. The residents of De la Rama are able to squat relatively unperturbed by the threat of demolition. The residents of La Peral in Old Makati are squatting with the permission of the landowner (i.e., they enjoy usufructuary rights).

Furthermore, the residents of these areas are not homogeneously poor. Indeed, a few of them, it would seem, even possess the means to live in an enclave should they so choose. A woman whom De la Rama residents call "Mommy" owns a house and lot in a subdivision outside Manila. She lives in De la Rama because it is where she does business. Mommy owns an exceptionally well-stocked variety store in Target 1. She rents out about twenty dwellings in the area and supplies residents with electricity. As we spoke, she pointed to about a dozen or so power meters near the ceiling of her store, wires running to and fro. She showed me the lot where her several vehicles were parked: a jeepney, a jeep, a truck, and a Mitsubishi Pajero sport utility vehicle. I also met residents in desperate circumstances. Felipe, for instance, was so poor that he could not even cook the rice I gave him: he asked for ten pesos (US$0.20) to buy charcoal.

In general, however, most slum residents would be considered lower class and a few lower middle class. Most are laborers of some sort and/or engaged in some kind of microbusiness. Their limited means are reflected in the quality of their housing, most of which is self-built and exhibits an improvised or ramshackle quality (figs. 4.5 and 4.6). Dwellings are pieced together with various materials, particularly cement block, plywood, corrugated tin, aluminum sheets, and canvas. They are built immediately beside or on top of one another. I also, though, came upon one or two houses that would not look out of place in an enclave. One house along Kasiyahan Street in Holy Spirit was gated, with walls around it and guards at the door. Its owner is reputedly the barangay captain himself.

The enclaves, too, are different from one another in important respects. They differ, perhaps most importantly, in prestige. In Manila,

**FIGURE 4.5** Tripa de Gallena II (Old Makati).
*Source*: Author, 2009.

asking someone where they live has become a fairly reliable means of discovering their social standing. BF Homes, Phil-Am, and Don Antonio are, by reputation, middle-class enclaves. The enclaves in New Makati, meanwhile, have long been home to the Philippine elite.

Despite this heterogeneity, interaction among the residents of these spaces takes a common form. They tend to interact in terms of categorical inequality. Specifically, enclave residents impose spatial boundaries on slum residents. In the rest of this chapter, I explore why this is and illustrate how it occurs.

## A Sense of Siege

### The Blue Gardens

There are French gardens in low-income Holy Spirit. They include all the elements French formal gardens can be imagined to contain: fountains, flower-covered trellises, and a cobblestone area beneath a large gazebo of flowing white cloths. Beside the garden there is even a

**FIGURE 4.6**  La Peral Compound (Old Makati).
*Source*: Author, 2009.

chateau, with high ceilings, ornate chandeliers, and a grand, winding staircase. This place, the Blue Gardens, a venue for weddings and debuts that is now full of birds and butterflies, used to be full of squatters.

Felicia, a Don Antonio resident, bought the Gardens in 1990. She wanted it cleared of squatters. The seller was simply going to move them outside the perimeter, but Felicia planned to use that area, an easement, as a parking space. It was not small at about two thousand square meters. She made a deal with the seller: he would provide a relocation site in another part of the city, and she would pay the squatters to go. In addition to money, she gave them groceries and provided a truck for them to haul their belongings. Her easement was finally cleared, but after about a year people started to build on it again. This time she went to the barangay and requested one of the *kagawad* (councilors) to police the area. He asked her to construct an outpost for him along the easement, which she did. He spent a lot of time there, she noticed, "mostly sleeping." Soon he installed a toilet beside the outpost. Different people came by. Eventually, some of them began to construct their own dwellings there. "I was angry," Felicia said, giggling, perhaps because in recollection the whole affair seemed absurd. She demanded that the new settlers leave. They agreed to, for a price. What could she do but pay it? She couldn't turn to the barangay. The chief settler was a *kagawad* of the barangay! She paid them, they then wanted more, and so she paid them more. She had the toilet removed. Then she put up stilts all along the area. The stilts served both as a deterrent, preventing new construction, and as a boundary marking the area she claimed as her property. The stilts worked for a while, but soon after the Gardens were built, someone filed a complaint against her stilts. The people living in the area wanted to use her easement to park their jeeps and motorcycles. Was it not public space, after all? The barangay interceded for them, but Felicia stood firm. She had already spent several hundred thousand pesos clearing the area. This time the barangay captain took her side.

To think that the story of the Blue Gardens ends here, happily, would be to miss what a middle-class audience would take as the moral of the story: their property is constantly under threat from squatters. The only way to protect it is to enclose it behind walls. Felicia's story helps us understand why, for enclave residents, the proximity of squatters is a source of such insecurity and why they resort, compulsively, to imposing gates and other spatial boundaries on slum residents.

### The Importance of Gates

Keeping the village "secure" has become the paramount concern of homeowners' associations. Given their different circumstances, however, some villages are better able to maintain their boundaries than others.

New Makati

The gates of New Makati's villages are notoriously tight. Only the main gates are open to the public, and then entry is permitted only during certain windows. Visitors must pass through two checkpoints a few meters apart. Guards collect the visitor's driver's license and take down the license plate number. They call the person whom the visitor claims to be visiting. Without someone inside to vouch, attempts to enter, I quickly learned, are summarily rebuffed. As for domestics and other laborers who come on foot, they must obtain ID cards to enter. These cards are issued by the village association, pending the worker's obtaining police clearance, passing a drug test, and submitting "biodata" for review. Even then, workers' ability to move around the village is restricted. Recently, a similarly elite village, Ayala Alabang, banned construction workers from simply walking on the main roads in response to residents' complaints about seeing them in "droves."[2] New Makati's gates are tight because its guards are under strict orders to enforce security protocol. The guards of Dasmariñas village in New Makati even detained Makati's mayor and his four-car convoy for attempting to pass through the wrong gate after curfew. The mayor promptly had them and the village's security officer arrested.[3]

BF Homes

The security of the Inner Circle subdivision of BF Homes is enhanced by its interior location and enclosure behind a series of gates. To get to Inner Circle from the highway, one must pass through three different gates: one to enter the complex, one to drive through an adjacent subdivision, and one to enter the village itself. At the first gate, one's driver's license is taken in exchange for a pass card, which must be displayed at subsequent gates. This means that one must exit the complex the same way one entered to retrieve the driver's license. Residents are spared this inconvenience. They can affix official BF stickers on their cars. Guards, seeing the stickers, simply wave residents through. Nonresidents can purchase "friendship" stickers at a substantial markup: 2,200 pesos (US$44), whereas resident stickers cost only 200 pesos (US$4). This gives them the right to use BF's streets. The stickers are well worth the cost. Stickered cars gain access to a pretty extensive road network. BF is so large that one can travel internally a long way. Residents and "friends" often use these streets to bypass heavy traffic on public roads. Regulating the use of internal streets is an extension of

2. "New Rules for Construction Workers: Walking on Main Roads No Longer Allowed," *Alabang Bulletin*, June 2014.
3. "3 Dasma Guards who Stopped Binay Convoy Held, Freed," *Philippine Daily Inquirer*, December 19, 2013.

gating. It is a means of controlling access to private space and justified, primarily, as a security measure.

Phil-Am Homes

Phil-Am Homes contains a church, Santa Rita de Cascia, whose parish extends beyond the village and includes part of San Roque, the slum colony across Edsa. For this reason, it cannot close its gates completely. It must let in parishioners coming from the outside. It maintains its boundaries, then, by enforcing its gating selectively. Following a run of break-ins and "carnappings" (vehicle thefts) in the late 2000s, the Phil-Am Homeowners Association Inc. (PHAI)—called for the village's gates to be tightened all around. Church partisans objected. Half of Santa Rita's parishioners come from outside Phil-Am, from San Roque and the subdivisions along West Avenue. When the gates are tightened, church revenue dips. Attendance goes down, the weekly collection shrinks, and fewer people avail themselves of church services. A compromise measure was struck. PHAI decided to regulate the entry of San Roque's residents specifically. It did not bar them entirely but made it harder for them to enter the village. It closed the gate directly across the settlement. San Roque's residents were told to use a farther gate along West Avenue. The Edsa gate was reserved for homeowners (although I had little problem driving through it). San Roque's residents now had to walk more than a kilometer out of their way just to enter the village across the street. What used to be a five-minute walk now took twenty minutes.

Kevin, a parishioner of Santa Rita, expressed sympathy for their predicament. "They're already here and the guard tells them to go all the way around. They have to cross from Paramount to Gate 2. By the time they get here, the mass is already done, right? Some of them have children in tow."

"Why make them go all the way around if you're going to let them inside the village anyway?" I asked.

He seemed stunned by the obviousness of the question. "Yeah. I guess that's just common sense, right? As long as they leave their IDs, why not just let them in?" He thought some more and continued: "We're supposed to be this exclusive, posh subdivision. If you're exclusive, certain gates are just for you. Look at Dasmariñas. It's a matter of security."

Ramon, a former PHAI president, answered the question unequivocally. The board wants "to discourage [San Roque's residents] from entering Gate 1." "Look," he said, "some people want the gates to be tighter, some people want them to be looser, but everyone wants to keep Phil-Am exclusive."

Don Antonio

Gating effectively split Don Antonio into two parts. Holy Spirit Drive had once been the village's access road; it now divides Don Antonio North from Don Antonio South, with each subdivision separately enclosed. Don Antonio North is completely secured. One of its residents boasted that it has "only one entrance, one exit, and no squatters." Don Antonio South, however, has been "breached." Hundreds of squatters occupy vacant lots in the subdivision. Half of Don Vicente, the southern perimeter street, is virtually indistinguishable from the slum area outside the village walls. Houses made of plywood and concrete hollow blocks crowd close together on either side. The houses on the other half of Don Vicente can hardly be seen because of their high walls crowned with broken glass and arrow-tipped iron bars.

Don Vicente was not originally part of Don Antonio. It was part of a subdivision called Kaligtasan that was abandoned by its developers. Many of the area's well-heeled residents, lacking an association of their own, lobbied to join the Don Antonio Heights Homeowners Association (DAHHA). DAHHA has since incorporated the area; the problem is how to enclose it. Don Vicente is a public street, turned over to the local government by the developer. Blockading it is no simple matter. Some of Don Antonio's residents have tried to do so, to gate the "breaches" in Don Vicente, without going through political channels. The walls they put up are illegal, however, and thus vulnerable to public complaint. They are quickly taken down. Knowing this, Miguel took the trouble to prepare the political groundwork for walling off Don Vicente Street. He formally notified the barangay captain and *purok* (ward) leader and held a public hearing. In return for the barangay captain's support, he walled the captain's house, the big one on Kasiyahan Street, for free. Miguel succeeded in gating the intersection of Don Vicente and Doña Felicidad. At first he put up a steel gate and closed it only at night. When he found the gate punctured, he replaced it with a cement wall. For a while, the wall was being destroyed periodically. Miguel counted "at least four times" he had to patch it: "I poured the concrete in the morning only to find that someone had already busted through it the next evening." When I visited in 2010, the wall was intact. I asked Miguel about the intersection of Don Vicente and Zuzuarregui. "I've tried to close that too," he sighed, "but that's where the congressman lives."

The congressman remembers waking up to find that a steel gate had been erected overnight along Don Vicente. He was incensed. He serves a party list representing the urban poor and objected to his neighbors' efforts to "segregate themselves." He filed a formal complaint against the gate. For more than a year nothing happened. "These are influential people," he explained, referring to the DAHHA board. It turned out that the official responsible for overseeing the complaint had just been sitting on it: "I only found out because a guy I know saw my signature on the letter and told me what was happening." The Congressman went to city hall and threatened the official with legal action. Two weeks later the gate was taken down.

Securing the perimeter is one thing, but the fact remains that some three hundred squatter families already live inside Don Antonio South. Its "penetration" has heightened the siege mentality of its residents. Esme blamed her stratospheric electricity bill on squatters tapping the power lines. She pays thirteen thousand pesos a month (US$260), while the squatters down the street, "whom I see with all these electrical appliances," pay only fifty pesos (US$1) per room to the person in charge of the connection. The yard at Miguel's old house was ransacked. They scaled the walls. "Everything outside the doors was taken . . . *ultimo tsinelas* [even my slippers]." There were a lot of stories "in the air" of people being harassed or held up on the street and their houses broken into, many of them received second- or thirdhand, but enough to create an atmosphere of bone-deep insecurity. Elmer admitted to being more scared going around at night inside the village than outside it. A curfew prohibits tricycles from running after ten o'clock, and so Elmer, who leaves work late at night, must walk. "It's nerve-wracking," he said, "just walking from the gate of the subdivision to my house."

### Boundary Imposition inside the Gates

In situations when gates are not enough, enclave residents take it upon themselves to impose boundaries inside the gates. The gates of Phil-Am and Don Antonio are permeable for different reasons. Phil-Am is permeable not just because Santa Rita's parish extends beyond the village but also because its barangay undertakes outreach activities to San Roque. Although villagers cannot exclude San Roque's residents completely, their presence in the village is carefully circumscribed. Barangay Phil-Am came to "adopt" San Roque, I was told, out of a sense of pastoral obligation. Many of the *kagawad* are affiliated with Santa Rita or the Knights of Columbus and Caritas, two Catholic groups with a social service orientation. They continued to espouse this orientation as barangay councilors. The barangay offers various services to the residents of San Roque: eye exams, dental cleanings, vocational workshops, and so on. These services are held at the barangay hall and thus necessitate that San Roque's residents enter inside the village. Though admitted, their entry is controlled and their presence within the village circumscribed. They must obtain tickets from the coordinator hired to distribute them in San Roque, with the number of tickets limited by quota. They are allowed to enter only through a certain gate and during certain hours. Once inside, the coordinated efforts of Phil-Am's three separate security groups—barangay *tanods* (police), security guards hired by the village association, and the neighborhood watch[4]—keep them on path to their destination, with the rest of the village effectively off-limits to them.

A fire broke out in San Roque in 2004. Seeing the flames lapping at the shanties along Edsa, Phil-Am residents rushed to secure their main gate against looters, "but when we saw those people carrying months-old babies," Ernesto recalled. "When you see pregnant women and kids in slippers crossing Edsa." Despite some resistance, the PHAI and barangay mobilized to allow inside a certain number of "refugees": two hundred families in total, just enough to fit inside the village's covered basketball court. The families were sheltered and fed for four days. The whole undertaking involved extensive coordination, much of which over security. Pains were taken to keep the squatters "contained." Ernesto, the PHAI's security director at the time, recounted the precautions they took: "We had three shifts of security personnel, ten people each. They were confined to the basketball court. They weren't allowed to roam around. They weren't even allowed to go to the skating rink

---

4. The security guards staff the gates. The barangay *tanods* handle criminal incidents. They come from outside the village but are housed in barracks inside it. The Neighborhood Watch is composed of residents, volunteers, "all of us white-haired," one member cracked. They make the rounds at night. The watch group was formed in response to a spate of robberies in the early 2000s. The PHAI hired a security consultant to train the group in "information gathering, investigation, intelligence, counter-intelligence, surveillance, and the rules of engagement" (Phil-Am n.d.). Members took up *arnis*, a Philippine martial art involving stick fighting. According to its own material, the Neighborhood Watch has made a difference. Since it began patrolling the neighborhood, the number of criminal incidents declined from seven per month to once every two months.

and playground [right beside the court]. We explained to them, 'You have to stay here.' Some people wanted to leave, and we couldn't stop them, of course, but they had to be escorted out. If they wanted to leave, they had to be escorted." After a few days, some residents began to clamor for use of the basketball court, and eventually, the squatters were transferred to the care of the barangay actually responsible for them. Ernesto was proud to report that nothing happened during their stay—no burglary, petty theft, nothing. Other informants vaguely recalled an incident or two. "Snooty" residents came forward, Minggoy remembered, "claiming to have lost this and that" without any real evidence of theft. "And you know," Ernesto said, "the nice thing about it is that—before, you see, we had a lot of crime and most of it came from San Roque. But right after the fire, for about a year and a half, no one broke in. Zero crime. It's only been lately that things have been happening again."

In the case of Don Antonio, it is permeable because its gates have been breached. Consequently, its residents have resorted to more intensive forms of enclosure. Miguel grew alarmed when the empty lot beside his property began filling up with squatters, so he bought it. He had the squatters removed and then he walled the lot. Ava simply took the liberty of gating the abandoned lot next to her house, having been unable to locate its owner. When the steel gate she erected was destroyed, she had it replaced with barbed wire. "People still manage to sneak in and steal mangoes from the trees," she complained. She and her neighbor on the opposite side of the lot have made a ritual of patrolling their respective sides: "Every night flashlight here, flashlight there." Squatters have broken into another fenced lot nearby, but Ava is relieved that all they've done so far is put up a net and play basketball. Esme tried to get her neighbor to help her fence the alley in between their houses. The neighbor refused because it was illegal. "It's not illegal to me," she protested. "We're just protecting it." Her other neighbor was more cooperative. He extended his wall to cover the space in between their properties. She had warned him: "'Eugene, we had better fence this area otherwise they'll come.' He knew I was right." Esme even partitioned her own house by installing a gate between floors. Her house had been broken into a long time ago. The thief entered through a door on the first floor and hog-tied the maids using their own mosquito net. He ran off when they started screaming. Ever since then, Esme forbade anyone from sleeping downstairs. She locks the gate inside her house every night. It is as if Don Antonio's villagers were engaged with Don Antonio's squatters in a game of *go*: each parcel of space within the village must be defended. The question is no longer whether the property is yours but which side is claiming it.

### The Politics of Gating

Gating is inherently a political matter because it involves private citizens restricting public access. It pits homeowners against government bodies down the line: the barangay, city hall, and politicians. In their struggle against illegal squatting, homeowners may even find themselves falling afoul of the law. At issue is the conflict between private property interests and what is deemed the public interest. This conflict is especially fraught because the specific public being opposed—squatters—is considered illegitimate and lacking the same right to make political claims.

#### Homeowners' Associations versus the Barangay

The homeowners' association obviously represents the interests of enclave residents. The barangay, however, has a public mandate. Its constituents are the citizens within its jurisdiction, whether or not they are homeowners. In practice, the barangay tends to focus on the neediest of these. In cases where the jurisdiction of the barangay and village association overlap, the barangay may look outward. Phil-Am, for example, "adopts" needy communities outside the village's boundaries. More commonly, the barangay pays attention to underserved populations inside the village, especially domestic workers. In New Makati, "helpers"—including maids, drivers, gardeners, and guards—outnumber homeowners by four to one. The barangays of New Makati sponsor a number of programs for domestic workers: health services, vocational training, and "values formation" seminars for maids. As a result, the barangay in these places has developed a reputation as *pang-masa* (for the masses). Lorna, the *kagawad* in charge of health and sanitation in Dasmariñas village, takes issue with this reputation. "Residents have this idea that the barangay is only for the helpers," she said indignantly. "Can you believe they think we use recycled vaccines [i.e., donated by hospitals and potentially expired]!" She has made an effort to change this image by offering services on par with Manila's finest hospitals. In addition to the basic checkup that is offered for free, residents can pay for a more thorough "executive" checkup. Lorna also makes a point of being on hand when residents are seen, in order to reassure them that their treatment is first rate.

Although the barangay may focus on helpers or outreach in cases of overlap, it ultimately represents the villagers. Contention between the barangay and village association is thus an internal affair. It consists of negotiating the overlap—in practice, squabbling over who is supposed to do what. This can lead to very fine distinctions of authority. Allow me to illustrate. While snacking at the grocery store across the village park, Mel, the owner, sat down with us. He pointed across the street.

"You see the park?"

"Yes."

"The lamps around the perimeter, the barangay takes care of those."

"And the lamps inside?"

He taps the table triumphantly. "The association!"

The question of who has ultimate authority, the PHAI or Barangay Phil-Am, is constantly rehashed. PHAI officers say the homeowners' association because it subsidizes the barangay's programs and pays the salaries of its *tanods*. Barangay councilors say the barangay because its administrators, the captain and seven *kagawad*, are elected by the whole village, whereas the sixteen directors that make up the PHAI board are elected by different wards in the village. In any case, the biggest problem in the relationship is coordination, particularly over security.

This is different from the situation in Don Antonio, where the homeowners' association and barangay represent separate constituencies. DAHHA represents only the village, while the barangay represents all of Holy Spirit. When issues come up, Leo observed, "the IS [informal settlers] go straight to the barangay, while homeowners approach the association first." On the issue of gating Don Vicente, the interests of these constituencies are fundamentally at odds. Most villagers want Don Vicente closed, while the squatters living inside and just outside Don Antonio want it open. Contention between squatters and villagers ends up pitting the homeowners' association against the barangay.

Homeowners' Associations versus the City

Contention at the level of homeowners' associations and the city is usually over access through or into enclaves. To the city, access is a public good, but to enclave residents, it is an incursion on their property. There are two kinds of access at issue. The first is access through the village. Mayors want to open up village roads to public traffic in order to alleviate congestion. For example, in 1999 construction along Edsa made the Makati section of the highway an even worse bottleneck than it already was. The mayor of Makati sought to reroute traffic through Dasmariñas village. The homeowners' association agreed to open its gates during rush hour for a period of six months. Many of Dasmariñas's residents opposed the move, however. "Some even threatened me," said Gilberto, the association president at the time. "If something happens to my dogs," he said mockingly. The city has tried to get Dasmariñas to open its gates more permanently, but its residents fight every ordinance "tooth and nail" in the courts, he said.

The second kind of access is to the resources within the village, such as Santa Rita in Phil-Am or, more typically, the commercial strip along Aguirre Street in BF Homes. Business owners along the strip have lobbied the city to get the village to open up to the public. In 2005, it looked like the village would have to do so following a court order. The order was implemented but not for long. It was undermined by administrative difficulties—Aguirre Street runs through three cities, and their governments had trouble coordinating responsibility for the road—and the strenuous objection of BF residents.

Mel remembers a time when the barbeque in Phil-Am was famous across Manila. The barbeque stalls were set up around the park inside the village. Back then it used to be easier for people to enter. Over time, the PHAI sought to tighten Phil-Am's gates and kicked out the barbeque vendors. It cited fire hazard as an excuse. Mel owns the grocery store across the park. His business suffered as a result of the tightening. Around 2008, Quezon City made a move to open Phil-Am's main road (East Lawin) to traffic. Mel smelled an opportunity. His grocery store could once again be accessible to the public. Residents, predictably, resisted the move, citing concerns over security, traffic, and air and noise pollution—in that order. Mel himself felt conflicted. As a business owner he wanted the gates loosened, but as a homeowner he wanted to keep entry restricted. He was also mindful of his position as a *kagawad* in Barangay Phil-Am. "I'm an elected official," he said. "I can't just say 'Let's open the gates because it's good for my business.'" He wants people from outside Phil-Am to be able to patronize his grocery store, but at the same time he wants to preserve the distinction between inside and outside. "We can let people in," he stipulated, "but they'll have to leave their license with the guard. They can't just say, 'I'm headed to Mel's grocery.'"

Given the prospect of being made to open up, enclave residents underscore the importance of autonomy. Dasmariñas has been able to resist political pressure to open up on grounds that the village is private property. Don Antonio has been unable to gate Don Vicente because the area is public. Phil-Am remains private but has a harder time than

Dasmariñas shouldering all the expenses that come with exclusivity. "The roads are too expensive for the PHAI to maintain," Minggoy, a former PHAI president, told me, and so the association solicits assistance from local politicians on an ad hoc basis. The city has offered to take responsibility for Phil-Am's roads, but the PHAI has refused. Residents fear losing control of their gates.

"If our roads are donated to the city government," Mel said, "it has the right to tell us to open up to the public."

"Is that the issue?" I asked.

"That's the issue. That's why the association won't donate our roads."

Homeowners versus Politicians

Enclave residents see their property interests jeopardized by the electoral interests of politicians, whom they accuse of "coddling" squatters for votes. In Don Antonio, the congressman makes a lot of people angry. Clement, who sits on the DAHHA board, accused him of "taking up the cudgel" for squatters purely to garner votes. He accused him, further, of colluding with another politician on the board to shelter the squatters inside Don Antonio. "They're on the same frequency," he said, meaning that they participate in DAHHA as politicians and not as homeowners. For Clement, and for others, the two roles entail opposed interests. Enclave residents in general feel strongly about this. The residents of Phil-Am and Don Antonio accused the mayors of Quezon City, past and present, of encouraging informal settlement as a way of building up vote banks. The residents of Makati accused the mayor of showering the city's informal residents with services paid for by its formal ones. Enclave residents universally denounced the UDHA, or Lina Law (except, of course, for the congressperson, who actually helped pass it). Among other things, the law regulates the eviction of squatters. It stipulates that they must be given notice and either relocated or compensated for an amount equal to sixty days' minimum wage. The local government is responsible for fulfilling these provisions, but in practice, the financial burden often falls on the property owner. Enclave residents see the law as being anti–property rights and anti–middle class. It has deepened their sense that the government does not represent their interests.

In general, the conflict between property owners and politicians over squatters has become a rich source of grievance for the middle class. They see the government as favoring lawbreakers over taxpayers despite the greater right—many would say moral ascendancy—of the latter. "We pay the taxes," Clement fumed, "but they [squatters] get all the attention." This grievance has political ramifications, as we will see in chapter 6.

## A Sense of Social Responsibility

Along with a sense of siege, enclave residents manifested a sense of social responsibility. I would be remiss if I did not address it, because it clearly colors their relationship with the poor and slum residents. In every case, enclave residents made an effort to help, not just exclude, their poor neighbors. They did so individually and through organizations such as the barangay, church, or nonprofit organizations. This sense of social responsibility was more pronounced in cases where gates were permeable. This stands to reason. Where gates are permeable, enclave residents are more likely to interact with slum residents and form social ties across their separate spaces. These ties mainly concern employment and benefaction. The more permeable the gates, the more enclave residents hire and help slum residents. "We've gotten to know them," Tanya said. Outreach events provide a means for people from Phil-Am to find workers and for people from San Roque to find work. "Let's say you need a carpenter, you ask one of the people you meet from San Roque, and they find somebody for you. We're always in need of laundresses, gardeners, and carpenters. We get them from San Roque."

It is important to recognize that benefaction and boundary imposition are not mutually exclusive. Indeed, it would seem that permeability and greater social interaction lead to both a sharper sense of siege and social responsibility. Consider Felicia, of the Blue Gardens, who provides her employees, many of whom hail from the slum areas around Holy Spirit, with a line of credit. She subsidizes their livelihood purchases and bails them out when they run into financial trouble. Miguel, the wall builder of Don Antonio, took in one of the squatters living inside the village and made him his driver. He even put the man's son through school. The boy has grown up, gotten married, and found work in the States, Miguel recounted with evident pride. One would think he was talking about his own son. Esme proactively (and illegally) fenced the alleys beside her property, and yet she serves on the livelihood committee of DAHHA. The committee conducts medical missions in the slum areas around Holy Spirit and provides vocational training to the squatters living inside Don Antonio. Her Rotary club sponsors a microenterprise clinic for Holy Spirit's residents and distributes free milk to students in the public schools. She helps her employees save by matching whatever funds they are able to put away. She gives their children Christmas presents.

I asked Esme why she does so much to help the very squatters she considers a threat. "Our theory is let's befriend them," she said. "Let's try to help them improve their lives so they won't bother us anymore." This reasoning may figure into her motivation, but I don't think that it represents it fully. The evidence indicates that enclave residents' efforts to help are more than simply instrumental. They feel an obligation to help, whether born of Catholic teaching, noblesse oblige, or simple human charity in the face of deprivation. Thus, they tend to assume a paternalistic role in relation to the poor, even the squatters they otherwise denounce as a bane.

Benefaction and discrimination are not only compatible; the two kinds of interaction may take similar form. Even when helping, enclave residents may interact with slum residents as categorically unequal. They may treat them as disadvantaged and also as different, and even dishonorable. Benefaction, in short, does not necessarily negate the social boundary that distinguishes enclave from slum residents. It may even provide occasion to reinforce it.

When San Roque was ablaze, for example, Minggoy lobbied hard to allow its fleeing residents inside Phil-Am. That didn't stop him from disparaging the people coming in. He told me about a family hauling out their refrigerator and TV set. "They weren't really affected," he surmised, because they could bother with such things. "Their house may have been on fire, but they were coming in for the free ride." He sees the family as having taken advantage of the situation to avail themselves of free food and shelter. This view is consistent with a popular stereotype of poor people as vulgar opportunists. As we saw, even though San Roque's "refugees" were accommodated, their presence in the village was carefully contained, and their entry and egress policed. Though guests, they continued to be regarded as a security threat, as criminals. In the following chapter, I show that some San Roque residents actually experienced benefaction as discrimination.

I am certainly not saying that Phil-Am's residents shouldn't have helped San Roque's. Rather, I am using the case to make a larger point about class interaction: the form matters, not just the content. Interaction may be categorically unequal whether characterized by enmity or charity. Boundaries may be imposed even when helping.

## The Spatial Boundary as a Moral Boundary

Ava lives within sight of the squatter area along Don Vicente Street. Her house is one of two enclosed within the high walls of a two-thousand-square-meter compound. We talked in her yard over cucumber water. "This is my only consolation," she waved around, pointing out the fruit trees and all the birds. "But when I go outside, oh, my, I say to my husband. I just don't look anymore." She sees nothing but squalor, squalor everywhere and people accustomed to living in it. In the morning, kids line up to piss in the canal. Their mothers abandon them to the street and the mercy of passing cars. Squatters tap the village's water and electricity, then leave the water running. The men gamble at night, scandalous amounts. They sing karaoke well past the village's ten o'clock curfew, so loud, she complained, it keeps her granddaughter awake. She told me about one girl whose thirteen-year-old sister is pregnant: "Nobody gets married, they just—nothing. When they get tired of one person they find someone else. No semblance of a family unit. No husbands or wives, nothing. At least then you would be governed by laws. But with them, no. It's just fornication."

The rural poor are different. "They're respectful," she said. "They want to go to school and better their lives. But these ones here—" she cut herself off, disgusted. Still, there are exceptions. Ava heard about one child who came by at five every morning selling *pandesal* (bread rolls). Impressed, she got up early to talk to him. She asked him if he went to school. He responded that he did in the afternoons, and so she asked him to bring her bread every morning. She put a basket outside with money. The arrangement lasted for a few days, but eventually the money went missing, and then the bread. Someone had gotten wise to their arrangement and was robbing them both. Ava put the money in a locked mailbox and gave the boy a key. "He's graduating [grade school] in March," she said, obviously proud. "Sometimes you find stories like that."

For Ava, the slum area down the street is not just a different kind of space from the rest of the village. Its residents—"squatters"—are a different kind of people. They are different from villagers, different even from the rural poor. They are not all bad people, but in Ava's telling, exceptions have a way of proving the rule (the boy selling *pandesal* may have been honest, but Ava was robbed by squatters anyway). The difference at the core is a moral one.[5]

The twins Elmer and Emma learned this early. They grew up in Don Antonio and remember playing with the squatters who lived down their street. They remember the day their difference from them became apparent.

"Back when we were kids," Emma recounted, "we were told, 'Don't play with them. You'll catch their bad habits.'"

"Like what?" I asked.

"Noisy. The way they speak."

"I don't think we picked up any of that," Elmer assured me.

"Growing up," Emma continued, "I remember that someone stole our snack. So we stopped playing with him."

"Oh, yeah," Elmer recalled.

"Even back then, we knew that what he did was wrong, that it was something that *we* wouldn't do. After that, we didn't want to play with any of them anymore." She turned to her brother. "Remember Ronald?"

It is not just that Ronald took their food; he did something that, in their eyes, they would never do. The incident corroborated their parents' warnings about "catching" squatters' bad habits. The boy Ronald came to stand in for squatters as a group, and the twins learned to distinguish themselves from him and his ilk as morally different. Moreover, they learned to observe this difference by keeping their distance.

The distance separating villagers from squatters is not only spatial but social. Breaching it can feel like a moral affront. The permeability of Don Antonio led to a situation René found intolerable: her own maid living next door to her.

"We had a big fight with our maid and let her go. It's because she was so hardheaded. Then one day she came to our house and said, '*Te, te,*[6] I have my own place in Don Antonio.' We thought, 'What nerve! Where could she have ended up? What? Same street!' Turns out she was sold [the right to squat in] one of the lots. The caretaker, a squatter himself, sold it to her."

"The owner must be abroad," I conjectured.

"Well, the real owner found out about it and got rid of the squatters. But for a while—on our own street!—there were just so many of them, including our maid." She burst out laughing.

---

5. On moral boundaries, see Lamont (1992).

6. *Te* is short for *ate*, meaning "older sister," a term of deference.

René found the situation funny because it struck her as absurd. She can laugh now that it's over, but initially she reacted with indignation. The squatters living along her street made her feel unsafe, but what really upset her was the fact that her maid, someone she regards as socially beneath her, should live so close to her: "What? Same street!"

Enclave residents took for granted the moral difference separating them from slum residents. To them the difference was obvious, and when pressed, they were easily able to articulate its terms.

"The people who live in informal settlements?" Cecil began. "You would be surprised at their values: native, ethnic, pre-Hispanic Filipino values."

"Can you give me some examples?" I asked.

"OK. Macho, polygamous, love of gambling, love of drinking, and live-for-today-not-for-tomorrow [mentality]. So they don't mind Erap's [Joseph Estrada's] womanizing and gambling. They lack religious instruction, and so they're very superstitious. It's a distortion of Catholicism. It's like they're worshipping idols."

It is not just Cecil who felt this way but most middle-class informants, although most did not bother to account for the difference, as Cecil did. It struck them as obvious. The belief that squatters are morally backward had, for them, the quality of common sense. The perception of difference is so strong, in fact, that, for some, squatters are even imagined to *look* different. Rolf recounted visiting the slum where his carpenter lived: "A while ago my wife and I had a small business renovating houses. We got our workers from De la Rama. One time I went over there to talk to a carpenter. He had this small house, about a foot or so above the ground, made of wood. You know, it didn't look. . . . You could tell that he was a man of modest means. And then his wife stepped out of the room, no. She was wearing high heels. Her pants were those tight ones. What do you call them? She was really well dressed and made-up, too. And she was just walking [as opposed to taking a car]. Maybe she was going to Phase 1 [BF's commercial center]. But, man, was she dressed! Makeup, lipstick, no. And just walking. It's like she quickly made the adjustment from looking dowdy—like a frumpy old woman in a duster—to this!"

His surprise is the result of an incongruity between the woman before him and the picture in his head. He had such a definite idea of what the carpenter's wife should look like that he imagines her undergoing a transformation from "a frumpy old woman in a duster" to the fashionably dressed lady he observed leaving the slum. The transformation is unsettling. Once outside De la Rama, there would be no way to place the carpenter's wife as a squatter. She could be mistaken for a villager. She could even be someone to whom Rolf found himself attracted.

To be sure, slum residents draw moral boundaries, too. They hold stereotypes of the "rich" as selfish, condescending, and corrupt. The rich think only of themselves and merely pretend to help the poor. They worship money. They are also imagined to look different from them, smell differently, speak a different language (English), and move differently. Slum residents draw moral boundaries just like enclave residents do. The difference is that they lack the power to impose them.

## Conclusion

The walls give you, more than anything, a sense of order. The feeling that I can go home at night without being afraid. It's a feeling of security. The village is my oasis.

PAT, A RESIDENT OF BEL-AIR VILLAGE IN NEW MAKATI

A sense of siege is driving the rampant imposition of gates, walls, and other spatial boundaries. Although this seems to be a general consciousness among enclave residents, the data suggest that the more permeable the gates, the more acute the sense of siege, and hence the more intensive the imposition of boundaries. The insecurity that enclave residents feel is not unfounded. Yards have been ransacked, cars "napped," purses snatched, and houses broken into. Enclave residents have good reason to feel that their person and property are at risk. They feel that the government does more to compound than to allay this insecurity. At the same time, it is not just fear of crime and encroachment that drives gating, although those fears loom large. Enclave residents also desire their own spaces apart from those of the public city. They fear that opening up their village will lead to its environmental and moral pollution. Enclave residents derive a sense of identity as middle-class actors, as *not masa*, from spatial closure.

The four cases presented here have their peculiarities, it is true, but taken collectively they describe what has become a general situation. Berner described a similar situation in Manila back in 1997. In a short section of a book otherwise focused on the plight of slum residents, he wrote about the slum Marytown's "involuntary neighbor," the enclave Loyola Heights. Loyola Heights is enclosed by "an elaborate system of iron gates, roadblocks, and checkpoints" and "practically the whole of the association's impressive budget of P28,000 per month is used up on security measures." In their efforts to secure village boundaries, residents "have no doubt about their right to block a street that was built with public funds." They regard the barangay captain as a "foe" because he takes the squatters' welfare into consideration. For politicians, one resident said, "everybody is a voter regardless of whether he is a taxpaying citizen or a lawbreaker" (Berner 1997, 162–68). My account clearly lines up with Berner's. Since the time he wrote, however, gating has become even more prevalent, and the dynamics he describes more pronounced. It is now common to read in the newspapers about homeowners' associations fighting the courts to keep their gates closed. In this chapter, we saw enclave residents driven by a sense of siege regularly imposing spatial boundaries on slum residents. Let us now consider the other side of the coin: how slum residents experience boundary imposition.

# FIVE

# Boundary Imposition: Squatters

## A Taint of Place

The stigma of being a squatter is experienced primarily as shame. Nelly remembers the day when her son first became aware of the stigma attached to their circumstance as squatters: "My son asked me, 'Mama, are we squatters?' His classmate said we are. I said, we were but we're not anymore. That depressed me." Out of shame, Nelly parried the label "squatter" by equivocating, referring her son to their formal condition as technically no longer squatters, since they had recently acquired their land through the Community Mortgage Program. And yet she knows full well that her son's classmate was pointing out their territorial status, something that has not changed despite the change in their legal status.

Nida is an itinerant vendor from De la Rama. She would not talk about anything but her son with me for any length. Her son, Dodong, used to sell ice pops around the neighborhood. He did well in school, however, and won scholarships to attend Southridge, a private school for boys, and University of Asia and the Pacific. He graduated the year before with a bachelor of arts in management economics. When I spoke to Nida, Dodong was in the seminary studying to become a priest ("I can't tell him that it would be better if he gets a real job," she says). Nida radiates pride for her son, but in a flash of pique, she complains about having never met any of his friends, whom she supposes are "celebrities and rich people." He's too ashamed to bring them around, she says.

Being a squatter is conceived as a bodily condition, like a disease, and associated with various taboos, in order to prevent contamination. Informants described being met with disgust. "You do this to the rich," Myrna said, taking my palm and swiping it with a calloused finger—perhaps to see if I would recoil—"and they will say, 'Yuck!'" Evelyn recounted an incident that occurred at a party for the lay workers of Santa Rita church. The church serves both Phil-Am and San Roque, where Evelyn lives, and thus the party included residents from both places.

"You can't brush against one of them [an enclave resident]," she said obliquely.

"What do you mean?" I asked.

"They rub themselves with alcohol."

"In front of you?!"

"Yes."

"You're saying that someone at the party rubbed themselves with alcohol in front of you?"

"Yes!"

The stigma attached to living in a slum is inherently territorial, what Wacquant (2008) calls "a taint of place." In Wacquant's account, *banlieue* residents are able to temporarily shed their stigma by hiding their address. Similarly, the stigma of being a squatter can be concealed so long as person and place cannot be linked. This gives it the quality of a secret. The Manila Metro Rail flies over San Roque. For the four or five seconds the train takes to pass, passengers get a full view of the slum (fig. 5.1). While riding the metro, Elena overheard another passenger call her home San Roque "an eyesore." The word stung, she said. It felt like a personal reproach. But she felt powerless to speak up because doing so would mean revealing herself to be a squatter. She chose instead to "pass."

In some circumstances, the secret of one's territorial status may be revealed deliberately to expose the other party's prejudice. Pilar attended a seminar hosted by a Catholic social services organization. The topic was an outreach project in San Roque. She was scandalized by how the seminar's participants talked about the residents: "They said, 'Those people, really! Why do they act like that? Maybe it's because they lack schooling. Maybe it's because they're starving.' When I couldn't take it anymore, I stood up and said, 'Don't you know! I'm one of those people you're talking about!' They grew quiet. One man

**FIGURE 5.1** A view of San Roque from the Manila's Metro Rail Transit.
*Source*: Author, 2009.

was so nervous that he couldn't look at me. I could see the sweat growing under his arm." The seminar's participants had assumed, given the setting, that Pilar was one of them. By "outing" herself, she made them feel ashamed—a meager consolation. Most of the time, however, slum residents cannot hide. Interspersion has entrenched discrimination into the urban ecology. Proximity, a source of insecurity for enclave residents, becomes, for slum residents, a source of discrimination. The spatial boundaries imposed by enclave residents are imposed on them.

## Boundary Imposition

### Exclusion

San Roque

San Roque residents resent being barred from entering Phil-Am through the Edsa gate. They had gotten used to just crossing the street. Now they have to go all the way around and up an overpass, stalked by purse snatchers. "It used to be so simple," Evelyn sighed. I asked her what happened. "All these things had gone missing [from Santa Rita church].

Their fruits, their flowers, the air con, the microphone, statues of saints." San Roque's residents were automatically blamed. "I told them you have to investigate, to see whether those things were really lost or if someone from inside the village had set them aside. They said no; this [San Roque] is where all the thieves and drug addicts come from."

"It's true that thieves run through here," Myrna admitted, but she took issue with all of San Roque being smeared. Even the priests objected to the closure. A priest told Evelyn that the collection at mass "broke down" when the gate was closed: "I thought we only gave a few pesos here and there, but I guess it adds up."

"I just don't feel comfortable at Phil-Am," Didi said. "We attend mass there, but they still don't accept us. They question why we have to go all the way over there just to attend mass."

"They say it's because they've been burglarized," Jolene offered.

"Is that the reason?" I asked.

"I don't understand why though," Jolene continued. "Don't they have security guards? We give them our IDs when we enter and collect them on the way out. That's how they keep track of us."

"So why do you think—"

"I think we disgust them [nandidiri]."

"Yeah," Didi added, "especially if you're dressed shabbily. That's how they think. Well, we may be poor but we're still people."

Discrimination continues inside the gates. Residents used to attend the prayer group at Santa Rita in greater numbers, but they were gradually driven away. The problem, Evelyn said, was that participants from Phil-Am would say bad things about the people from San Roque. They would deride their political opinions: "Our views were opposite. They used to like Gloria [Macapagal Arroyo]. They said that she was smart and knew how to handle the economy." Meanwhile, they made fun of Estrada. The participants from Phil-Am were given to lecturing those from San Roque. They even made a couple of them cry. "Not me," Evelyn asserted. "I wouldn't cry in front of them, not when I knew that I hadn't done anything wrong." Evelyn would stand up for herself and for Estrada. She would give them as good as she got. Thus she developed a reputation for being siga, or a tough guy. She also ended up as the only person from San Roque left in the prayer group.

Once Evelyn was asked to serve as a lector at mass. The readings were in English, and people criticized her assignment. "'Why did you get Evelyn?'" she mimicked her critics. "'Wrong grammar! Wrong intonation!'" The priest took her side, reprimanding her detractors. "'Your English may be fluent,'" he told them, "'but when it's time to do your job, you're always absent!' I just laughed at them," Evelyn said, delighted by the story.

Because of her job at the church, Evelyn's interaction with Phil-Am residents has been particularly extensive. They rely on her to run their errands, find them workers, and round up beneficiaries for their programs. She has even made friends with a few of them, including one who lets her borrow her car, driver included, on occasion. Given these ties, Evelyn hesitates to paint all the villagers with the same brush. She tells me that Phil-Am is full of good people. And yet despite these ties—or, rather, because of them—Evelyn told more stories of discrimination than anyone else in San Roque. Although these stories may not fully account for her relations with Phil-Am residents, she remembers them vividly.

De la Rama

De la Rama is bounded on one side by BF Homes and on the other by Manila Memorial Park, a cemetery. On the one hand, the location is opportune. De la Rama residents find work as tricycle drivers and domestics within BF and are hired to maintain the burial plots and mausoleums of the cemetery. On the other hand, residents find themselves enclosed on both sides.

On the BF side, one of the subdivisions abutting De la Rama, Tierra Maria, closed its gate with a part of the settlement called Target 1. The board of Tierra Maria's homeowners' association invited the officers of Target 1's community organization (CO) to the meeting at which it announced the closure. The CO's officers refused to accept the news and pleaded with the board to reconsider. Target 1's drinking water and construction materials were delivered through the gate, they argued. If it were closed, the residents would suffer. "What, would you have us die in here?" Target 1's president demanded. The officers walked out of the meeting in protest. One of Tierra Maria's board members, an older man and soldier, followed them out. He wore a gun on either side of his hip. He pursued them until the gate, cursing them all the while, and threatened to shoot them. Target 1's president stopped to remonstrate with him. It was at this point that Leonisa, the Target 1 CO's secretary, began to panic: "'Artemio, let's go!' I told him. I had my eyes on the guy's guns. I was pulling him already. 'Leave him. Let's just go!'" Following the incident, the CO appealed to the mayor of Parañaque but succeeded in being allowed use of the gate only in emergencies. As it stands, to enter Tierra Maria, Target 1 residents must obtain a permit from Leonisa. The permit must be signed by the president of Tierra Maria's homeowners' association and two copies of the document made, one for each organization. This process is contingent on the availability of the officials involved and may take several days.

The cemetery on the other side of De la Rama, Manila Memorial Park, is also gated and guarded. Residents are allowed through the gate from five o'clock to ten in the morning. Many of them plan their day around this window. They enter the cemetery to dispatch their caretaking duties or pass through it to reach the highway beyond (figs. 5.2 and 5.3). There is another way out of the slum, through De la Rama Street, but it involves taking a circuitous route through BF Homes simply to exit the complex. This would be easier with wheels, of course, and several residents do own motorcycles. But even these are proscribed: both BF and Memorial require that motor vehicles passing through their roads display stickers. The Memorial sticker costs about a day's wage at 300 pesos (US$6) and the BF sticker over a week's at 2,200 pesos (US$44).

So, the Tierra Maria gate is closed, the Memorial Park gate is open for only a few hours in the morning, the De la Rama Street exit is highly inconvenient, and the stickers needed to drive out are prohibitively expensive. Although De la Rama is located inside BF, a series of bound-

**FIGURE 5.2** The wall separating Manila Memorial Cemetery from De la Rama. *Source*: Author, 2009.

**FIGURE 5.3** A caretaker tending a mausoleum in the cemetery.
*Source*: Author, 2009.

aries exclude the slum from both the enclave and cemetery bordering it. De la Rama residents regard their containment with frustration: "We're banned from BF. When they close off Memorial, where are we supposed to pass?" Manuel complained. "It's like we're imprisoned here."

"Sure, we're part of BF," Juvy remarked bitterly: "*B*ack of the *F*ence!"

De la Rama's residents fare no better within BF. Their presence inside the village must be warranted by their function as laborers. They are personae non gratae otherwise. "When they need you, they'll call for you," George said. "If they see you inside, they'll call your attention and say, '*Hoy*, you can't just walk around here!'"

"How do they know that you don't belong?"

"The way you're dressed. That's another thing. If you don't look decent, they'll think you come from the squatter area with bad intentions. But if they see you holding a hammer or something . . . 'Well, that's just a construction boy. It's OK that he's here.' Because these days you're not free unless you're walking on the highway."

George is one of De la Rama's earliest residents. He arrived in 1976 as a young man. A carpenter by trade, he now runs an illegal gambling game called *jueteng*. George talked my ear off about the electricity situation in Target 1. The connection was "legal but illegal." He meant that one of the area's "big men"—"Mommy," the proprietor of the area's general store—had been able to obtain the connection by producing the necessary documents but was distributing the current illegally. Moreover, she was wildly overcharging Target 1 residents for the tap. George figured he was paying double what he should be. He went on to complain about the trash and water problems in De la Rama. The trash wasn't being collected regularly, and the water being piped in wasn't potable. He had taken to collecting rainwater, mixing in a tablet of chlorine or *tawas* (alum), and boiling it to improve the taste. Eventually, George got around to the subject of gates. He remembered a time before all the gates went up and the residents living "here" and "there" used to interact more freely. "It didn't use to be like this," he said, waving around. "Back in the day, Mommy Orbe [apparently a BF resident] would bring a pig around for us to sell. The missus was an auctioneer during the time of Marcos. We would only have to pay [Mommy Orbe] back the cost of the pig. No one does that anymore." Then, wistfully: "I have a mind to walk over there [BF Homes] with a bucket full of goods to sell. But I already know what will happen. I'll get as far as the gate and then the guard will stop me. He'll tell me to talk to the president of the homeowners' association first to see if he'll allow it."

## Holy Spirit

Residents of the slum areas just outside the walls of Don Antonio, like slum residents elsewhere, complained about their restricted access to the village. "There used to be a way through here," Sandra said, "but they [Don Antonio residents] blocked it off." Residents along Samonte Street who work inside the village can no longer pass through Don Vicente, the next street over. They have to go around to Holy Spirit Drive and enter through the village's main gate. "It's because they think we're thieves," she surmised.

Jenine on Kasiyahan Street said the same thing: "When there's a burglary [in Don Antonio], the burglars run through here, so that's how they [Don Antonio residents] see us." "But we're homeowners too," she protested, referring to the area's semiformal status under the Community Mortgage Program. "It's just that we live in a poor area."

We've seen this before, of course. What stands out in this case, however, is the level of enmity between neighbors. Slum residents feel aggrieved not just by their exclusion but also by past, extraordinarily grave incidents of boundary enforcement. Clara recounted the time that a seven-year-old boy was shot in the back by a villager. He and his friends were trying to pick the fruit off a guava tree inside one of the compounds in Don Antonio. She emphasized that the boys were standing outside the walls of the compound. They were using a rod with a hook on one end to fish the fruit from the branches that were overhanging the wall. The homeowner got wind of their activities and ran outside with a gun. He accosted the children. They fled. He fired at them and hit one in the back, killing him. I asked Clara if the man was apprehended. "He was a retired soldier," she said by way of explanation. "There are more stories like that." In a different instance, another purported thief was shot and killed, but what Clara found most offensive was the fact that the perpetrator took the trouble to dump the body in the slum outside the village gate, presumably where he thought it belonged. Stories of crime on one side and stories of discrimination on the other have created a gulf of resentment and mistrust. Being neighbors despite this gulf has made the boundary between these spaces the focus of contention.

Old Makati

The slum areas in Old Makati where I interviewed residents were relatively far away from the enclaves in New Makati. Their distance as well as the impermeability of the enclaves themselves seem to have inhibited interactions among slum and enclave residents. This does not mean, however, that slum residents do not experience boundary imposition—on the contrary. They told stories of being policed in public spaces, particularly upscale malls and other commercial areas associated with the "rich." Their stories involved being harassed by security guards, shadowed by sales clerks, and most of all, scrutinized "head to foot" by other patrons. Ella, for example, recounted the terrible unease she felt simply walking around Rockwell, an upscale mall in Makati.

"It's like we're maids there," she told me.

"What do you mean?" I asked.

"The people that go there [regularly] are different from us. I went with my family. I couldn't . . . 'Let's leave!' Why? Just look at the people who come in."

"Did people look at you?"

"Head to foot. They look at what you buy. Can you afford it? The sales ladies especially. Sometimes you just want to take a look, for the kids, like at toys, but . . ."

"You feel embarrassed?"

"Yes! Yes, of course."

"Did the sales lady say anything to you?"

"No, of course not. You just feel it. You feel like you don't belong."

Notably, it is not clear from Ella's account that she was actually mistreated. We cannot say whether people judge her, only that she feels judged to be socially unworthy. She became overwhelmed by the sense that someone like her had no right to be in a place like Rockwell, and thus she left the mall. This sense of place, or more specifically, the sense of being out of place, may as well be a form of boundary imposition. It leads slum residents to exclude themselves from places where they expect to be excluded. Informants in Old Makati were able to identify a set of exclusive spaces from the general down to the specific, naming parts of the city (Ayala or New Makati), malls and commercial areas (Greenbelt; Glorietta; Rockwell; the "Fort," or Bonifacio Global City), and specific establishments (Starbucks). Moreover, they were able to distinguish, with virtual consensus, the class character of these places. The Glorietta mall is sufficiently *masa* for them to patronize comfortably. Likewise, Market Market has become "adulterated" by the poor. Rockwell, meanwhile, remains upscale and so off-limits.

My informants from slum areas in all cases, not just the ones from Makati, expressed an acute boundary consciousness—and not just with regard to malls. They felt out of place in a range of exclusive public spaces. Manuel would have to drive his boss to Shangri-La, a five-star hotel. Once inside, "I would look at what other people were looking at, and it felt like they were all looking at me." Renato stopped attending mass at Santa Rita in Phil-Am: "People look at you like you're suspicious. They know we're squatters but no one says anything. You just feel it. Even the members of our [prayer group], the ones from the village, you feel it from them, too." I asked Natividad, Was there anywhere both rich and poor felt comfortable? She thought for a moment. "There were such places in Mindanao," she said. "But here the rich stay in places for the rich and the poor in places for the poor." She said it more succinctly in Filipino—*dito mayaman mayaman, mahirap mahirap* (literally, "here rich rich, poor poor")—and in a way that conveyed how neatly class ordered urban space. This sense of place, then, endows symbolic boundaries with nearly the same power to exclude as physical boundaries have. It has brought about the partitioning of Metro Manila beyond just slums and enclaves.[1]

---

1. I develop the notion of a sense of place—drawing on Bourdieu, Herbert Blumer, and the literature on cognitive maps and symbolic boundaries—in Garrido (2013b).

## *Eviction and Ejection*

San Roque has been undergoing demolition for the better part of the twenty-first century. A large segment was dismantled in the mid-2000s to make way for the Trinoma mall. The rest of the colony remains slated for demolition. In its place, Ayala Land is building Vertis North, a twenty-nine-hectare mixed-use space. Reportedly, forty-five new buildings are going up, about half of them office buildings and half residential condos. Two hectares have been set aside for a garden or park area. The idea of this much land deliberately being left open must strike San Roque's residents as obscene. Some of the evicted residents, rather than leave for good, have retreated deeper inside the remaining settlement. The part of San Roque where Victor once lived was razed by fire in 2005. Quezon City officials took the opportunity to demolish the rest of it the following year. Vic had nowhere to go. As a renter, he was not granted relocation assistance. The area that had been demolished was walled and guarded to prevent its former residents from returning. Vic made his living in San Roque as a carpenter. As he saw it, he had a right to stay, and so, over the objection of the National Housing Authority (but with the blessing of the barangay captain), he found accommodation in another part of the settlement.

"We're demolished and the very next day we put something else up. Then that's demolished and we put it up again," he said.

"For how long?" I asked.

"Until, perhaps, they take pity on us. We're not animals. We just want to live in the city because there's work here for people like us. We live where we work because it saves us the cost of commuting."

As the advertisement for Vertis North reads: "Everything you need is within reach." The ad, of course, is targeted at potential condo residents; it appeared in the glossy pages of the lifestyle magazine *Real Living*. The observation, nonetheless, applies just as well to San Roque's residents.

In addition to livelihood, residents base their right to stay on two further claims. One, they contribute to the local economy as workers and consumers. Their eviction, Didi reasoned, would create a vacuum. Two, many of them have lived in San Roque for a considerable period of time, some for more than twenty-five years. Their personal histories are tied to the place. Didi's history is especially bitter, but in her eyes, it has tied her to San Roque all the more: "My husband died here. My mother died here. My child died here around the same time as my mother. To cope [with all my losses], I've devoted myself to community organizing. I would rather cut my own neck than leave."

The fact that residents' claims are summarily ignored and their welfare almost completely disregarded feels to them like a kind of discrimination. As poor people and squatters, they feel powerless. "We speak and they remain stone cold [*dedma lang sila*]," Myrna said. "We have no voice because they don't have to listen to us." Residents complained, further, about the price they pay in lost livelihood, the disruption of their children's schooling, and the difficulty and expense of having to start over periodically. Marivic owned a welding shop in a part of San Roque that had been demolished. She used to make good money, sometimes a thousand pesos a week, she boasted. As a longtime resident, she was compensated exactly 11,228.96 pesos (US$225). This was barely enough money to move to another part of San Roque. Since being evicted, Marivic has had to learn "how to do five-sixths," that is, she has had to avail herself of small, high-interest loans just to make it through the week.[2]

A few residents cited evidence of dirty tricks. Didi counted five fires in the previous five years (2005–2009) but couldn't recall a single one in the twenty years before that. The story used as cover is always the same. A husband and wife are fighting in the early morning hours when one of them knocks over a gas lamp, or they forget to turn off the stove. The source of the fire is never definitively established. Alberto claimed that a local boy overheard two men discussing which homes to set alight. Didi claimed to have uncovered gas canisters after one blaze. Regardless of their veracity, stories like these have made residents feel like walls are closing in on them (and they are, of course, in the form of new enclaves being built around them). In 2009, the atmosphere of insecurity was already corroding their resolve, but residents still held out hope of being accommodated on-site. The organization Didi works for, the San Roque Community Council (SRCC)—a federation of several dozen community organizations from the area—had proposed a land-sharing arrangement. It wanted Ayala Land to build them a medium-rise residential building. By 2014, this hope had evaporated. The colony's land area had been reduced by half, and the SRCC had all but declared defeat, having shifted its focus to improving the terms of relocation. Whatever moral claims residents had once made to the land were rendered moot by the settlement's progressive disappearance.

2. "Five-sixths" are small, short-term loans with a 20 percent interest rate. They are collected on a daily or weekly basis.

Finally, slum residents experience boundary imposition in the form of their ejection from public walkways as part of the Metro Manila Development Authority's (MMDA) beautification campaign. The Metro Gwapo (*gwapo* means "handsome") campaign launched in 2006 represented yet another attempt to bring Manila in line with an image of urban modernity. It proved hugely popular among the middle class and accounted, in part, for the MMDA chairman Bayani Fernando's support when he ran for vice president in 2010. MMDA officers were ordered to round up vagrants, beggars, and street children and to clear sidewalks and footbridges of vendors. The wares of recalcitrant vendors were allegedly doused with gasoline. Didi found these tactics heartless. The wares were probably purchased on credit through five-sixths, she noted. Destroying them did not "discipline" vendors, as intended; it ruined them financially. The campaign left slum residents feeling squeezed out even from the public city. "It's like they want to throw us all away to the boondocks so that only the rich remain," Marietta lamented.

I discuss eviction and ejection here because they form an indispensable part of slum residents' urban experience and undoubtedly deepen their sense of discrimination. These forms of boundary imposition, however, have more to do with the pace and direction of urban development than with interspersion. Exclusion, in contrast—boundary imposition by enclave residents and the rich in public spaces—follows directly from the proximity of slums and enclaves.

### The Institutionalization of Boundary Imposition

Boundary imposition is not the only source of discrimination. Discrimination also happens in the contexts of employment and institutions. Informants told stories of being mistreated in their capacity as workers, particularly as domestics and drivers. They told stories of being discounted in courts, schools, hospitals, and government agencies. I could write another chapter about these experiences, but they are beside the point I am trying to make. My focus is on the effects of interspersion, and discrimination in these contexts does not result from interspersion. Even if the middle class and urban poor were concentrated in different parts of the city—that is, absent interspersion—they would still be bound to interact unequally in the context of employment and institutions. Boundary imposition, though, results specifically from sharply distinguished class spaces being drawn closer together. It is their prox-

Table 5.1 Varieties of boundary imposition

| Case | Configuration | Boundary imposition |
|------|---------------|---------------------|
| Phil-Am/San Roque | Slum across the street from enclave | Slum residents are "locked out" or excluded from resources inside the enclave. Their presence within the enclave is circumscribed or heavily surveilled. |
| BF Homes/De la Rama | Slum inside a complex of enclaves | Slum residents are "locked in" by neighboring enclaves. Their presence within the enclave is circumscribed. |
| Don Antonio/Holy Spirit | Slum just outside enclave | Severe incidents of boundary enforcement, collectively remembered, have hardened slum residents against their neighbors. |
| New Makati/Old Makati | Slum in a different part of the city | Slum residents experience boundary imposition not by enclave residents but by the "rich" in public spaces. |

imity that necessitates the imposition of boundaries. My argument is that interspersion has made boundary imposition prevalent.[3]

We have seen boundary imposition take different forms (see table 5.1). San Roque's residents were locked out or excluded from the resources in Phil-Am, while De la Rama's residents were locked in by neighboring enclaves, the cemetery included. When slum residents were allowed inside enclaves as workers, parishioners, or guests, their presence was circumscribed or heavily surveilled. Grave incidents of boundary imposition have hardened Holy Spirit's slum residents against their neighbors in Don Antonio. Boundaries were imposed not just by enclave residents but also by the rich, in what Connell (1999) has called "pseudo-public" spaces. In such spaces, slum residents felt policed or out of place. The prospect of exclusion led them to avoid such places altogether. In general, they navigated the city according to a well-developed sense of place, observing not just physical but also symbolic boundaries.

We saw a sharp boundary consciousness among slum residents in every case. Slum residents do not seem to be more boundary conscious in Quezon City, which is extremely fragmented. There may be a dif-

3. We know that boundary imposition is important because it comes up in every case and clearly weighs on the minds of many informants. We can infer that it has become more important than ever based on the spread of interspersion (assuming that greater interspersion means more boundary imposition). What I cannot say with any precision, however, is how important boundary imposition is relative to other sources of discrimination. This is partly a consequence of method. As George and Bennett (2005) observed, case study methods are good at uncovering social mechanisms but not so good at determining their relative significance or causal weight. And so it is in this case. We can establish whether and how boundary imposition matters but have difficulty establishing *how much*.

ference I have been unable to parse that further research will detect. For now, the data suggest that we can treat the metro region as a single context despite the uneven distribution of slum areas. On the whole, Metro Manila is sufficiently fragmented to make boundary imposition a common experience and boundary consciousness a general consciousness among slum residents.

We might say that interspersion has institutionalized boundary imposition. By this, I mean that given the patchwork quality of urban space, slum residents encounter boundaries wherever they turn. Discrimination has become entrenched ecologically. Although it may be true that the urban poor have always been excluded, what is new is how frequently this now happens and the intensity of exclusion—gates, walls, guards, and other spatial boundaries are a constant feature of the urban landscape, and for slum residents, they are a fact of urban life. As a result, slum residents have become acutely boundary conscious and also highly sensitive to discrimination.

## A Sense of Discrimination

### Antonio

When I first met him, Antonio was lifting weights in an open lot in Target 1, De la Rama. He was doing bench presses. The bench in this case was an actual wooden bench, and the barbell a metal pipe with concrete blocks on either end. Antonio was a big man in his thirties with a big, smiling face. He surprised me by calling out to me in English. "Hey, man," he said, sitting up on the bench. His whole aspect—it made me wonder if this was a BF resident "slumming it" in De la Rama. "Do you live here?" I asked him reflexively. He seemed delighted that I mistook him for a villager. "Almost twenty-five years," he said. I sat down on the bench next to him and introduced myself. Antonio worked as a salesman. At one point he sold these yogurt-like, bacteria-laced health drinks. Now it was magnetic bracelets to improve circulation. Not even his mother knew that he spoke English this well (well enough at least to keep it up for stretches at a time). He had finished only high school but learned to speak English in the course of his work. His clients, he said, worked inside office buildings in Makati and Ortigas, where English was part of the atmosphere.

"I'm not expecting anything from this place," he said, waving around. "Neighbors yelling at each other, couples always fighting, people drunk every weekend. That guy over there is a construction worker. He gets paid on Saturday, blows it all on booze on Sunday, and has to borrow money on Monday just to get something to eat. Do you know why I stay here?" He paused, waiting for me to ask. "Because I love it. It's happy here. Everybody knows everyone else. They greet you. 'Hey, Ton, what's up? You're getting fat, huh?' We hang out, play basketball, make fun of each other. 'Pare [buddy], let's put on a DVD. I'll go make noodles.'"

"I used to live with my girlfriend in Westmont Village—the condominiums," he clarified. "Four months. Check it out, man. My girlfriend was forty-four years old, a beautiful woman and the general manager of [a Filipino manufacturing company]. We were going to get married, but we broke up."

"Why," I asked, indelicately.

"Because they're rich," he said. He had my attention. "When we went to meet her family [pamanhikan, a Filipino tradition where families of the engaged couple meet over a meal], I was"—he used the English word here—"underestimated."

Both the mother and sister of Antonio's "old rich" girlfriend, Fe, lived in "a mansion, no, a palace" in New Manila, an neighborhood of the "old rich" in Quezon City. He brought his own mother to the pamanhikan, as well as a bag filled with milkfish and shrimp. "I spent fifteen thousand," he said sadly, "and they didn't even open the bag." After arriving at their place, by the time he had remembered the bag, it was too late to retrieve it.

It is unclear from the story whether the slight that undid his relationship was intended or imagined. In any case, a simple question did it, cut him to the quick, unleashing all the self-doubt that comes with marrying above one's station.

"Her mother said, and her sister, 'Anton, why are you in such a hurry to get married?' What does that mean? We just want their support, right? We're asking for their permission to get married. I wasn't there to be interrogated or investigated, right? You know what that means? 'What are you after? Fe's inheritance? Her money or what? Her land, her work?' I said, 'Ate [older sister], maybe Fe and I should talk about it some more. Maybe we're not yet ready.' We're old enough to be ready!"

He shifted registers. "I was dismissed out of hand [parang tinapon ako, 'it's like I was thrown away']. They wanted someone else [for Fe]."

"But that's not how your girlfriend felt," I offered.

"No, that's right. But of course she was affected. "'Fe, you're old enough, why did you pick someone from the squatter area?' [he imagined them telling her]. See? We were going to be married November 21 last year. The papers were done. The reception was paid for." He wouldn't let go of the question. "'Anton, why the rush?' Then: 'What are your plans?' She rephrased the question, you see. I was *struck*." He kept going. "*That* meant, 'What are you after from our sister? Her *this*, or *that*, or *that*?!' No. We love each other, but I'm not fighting anymore because I know what will happen."

"Your girlfriend didn't try to fix things?"

"No, she did. I was the one who didn't want to go on. How could I? Those people would be my in-laws."

### An Expectation of Discrimination

In general, informants approached class interaction on guard against slights, as if they expected to be discriminated against. Their stories and actions suggest a tendency to interpret certain, otherwise ambiguous situations in terms of discrimination. Marivic, a San Roque resident working as a *tanod* for Barangay Bagong Pagasa in Quezon City, described an incident at the birthday party of the barangay administrator: "He was really rich. It was his birthday, so of course, all of us [the barangay staff] had to be invited. When we were introduced, he said to me, 'Did you bring a plastic bag [for taking food home]?' If he wasn't standing beside Cap [the barangay captain] . . . ! I wanted to spit on him and say 'Even if we're squatters, we know how to respect ourselves! We know where to bring a plastic bag!'" She laughed.

"Did you?" I asked.

"Only in her head," said Victor, sitting nearby, with a smirk.

"I left. I didn't even eat," she said.

Given the facts of her story and keeping in mind that, in the Philippines, hosts traditionally distribute food from the party to departing guests, it is possible to interpret the administrator's question as a feckless attempt to be considerate rather than snide. Marivic took it as insulting. In her eyes, the question reduced her to being poor and hungry—*patay-gutom*, someone dying of hunger, a common class putdown—and therefore interested in the party only as an opportunity to eat.

I found myself on the receiving end of such ire while doing fieldwork in De la Rama. I was interviewing Randy when Mila, whom I had just interviewed, interrupted to offer me a plate of spaghetti. She was having a small party and saw us sitting on stools outside Randy's house. I made the mistake of telling her that I had already eaten. She winced and said, "You just don't want to eat it because I made it." Unwilling to abort my interview with Randy, I asked her to bag it so I could take it home. "Don't just throw it away," she implored. Mila assumed that I refused her food because I found it dirty and that I found it dirty because of where she lived. She imagined a slight where none was intended. Ordinarily, the actions behind these perceived slights—offering a plastic bag, refusing a plate of food, asking about future plans, as in the case of Antonio—would be interpreted in a way that is consistent with situational cues, that is, without malice intended. Informants, however, interpreted them tendentiously.

Some informants distinguished themselves from other slum residents they deemed more deserving of the label "squatter." Recounting an incident when a neighborhood drunkard pelted his house with stones, Manuel ruefully observed, "The way people are here [in De la Rama], it's like they're really squatters." Annie was invited to attend a ceremony at the presidential palace for people who had been jailed for participating in Edsa 3. Guests were told to "dress up, so it's not obvious that you're a squatter," but some people, in her words, still behaved like squatters. "They didn't comb their hair. Some didn't bathe. Some even brought their children, even though they were told not to." These examples indicate not only the power of the label "squatter" as a slur but also the extent to which slum residents have accepted its terms. I interviewed Annie and her neighbor Wilma while eating at Annie's food stall. She felt the need to reassure me that her food was not only tasty but clean.

"Aling Amy often buys noodles from me," Annie began. "One day she went into my kitchen and asked to see my sink. Then she asked to see my bathroom. 'Here, pull aside the curtain.' When she saw how clean it was, she went back to her seat and ordered another plate of noodles. Maybe she thought that if where I lived was dirty, then my food would be dirty, too."

"I'll admit it, Annie," Wilma copped. "When I first bought food from you, I checked out your bathroom and kitchen, too. Ah!" They laughed together.

"Like my utensils, I boil them. When people are finished eating, I replace the hot water. Sometimes people reach for a spoon"—she wags her hand in pretend pain—"Ay! It's still hot!" Another round of laughter.

Despite the lighthearted banter, the stakes of the exchange are clear. Annie wants to persuade us that she prepared her food hygienically. It would be hard to understand why she is making the effort without an appreciation for just how salient a view of the squatter as unsanitary is, not least in the minds of Annie and Wilma, "squatters" both.

I want to be careful not to overstate the case. Interaction between slum and enclave residents cannot be reduced to discrimination. It is more complex, and on the whole, slum residents expressed ambivalence about their relations with the "rich." Many informants tempered their accounts of discrimination by citing exceptions or appending qualifications ("but not all, of course"). Nevertheless, the data suggest that discrimination is a powerful experience. Discriminatory incidents loom large in slum residents' imaginations. They are remembered and recounted. Compared with positive and neutral or unremarkable experiences of class interaction (which probably comprise the bulk), negative experiences stand out.[4] They seem to play a disproportionate role in shaping how slum residents approach class relations. As the examples attest, the sense of discrimination among slum residents is palpable. It undoubtedly accounts in large part for just how fraught class relations have become.

A sense of discrimination may even color interactions that, on their face, are the very opposite of discriminatory. Consider Myrna's account of a charity event held at Phil-Am: "They give us a kilo of rice, a can of noodles, sardines, and you line up behind a long, long line, waiting half the day while they're taking your picture. It hurts. It stings. That's why we avoid the rich, because they see us as trash." She cited the event—the kind that Phil-Am residents pointed to as an example of how well they treat their neighbors in San Roque—as an instance of discrimination. Phil-Am took in the residents of San Roque fleeing fire in their slum but treated them as would-be criminals, limiting their movement within the village to policed areas. They let them inside the village, but only as objects of charity. They were made to wait for hours, Myrna said, all the while being photographed for the barangay newsletter. She found the experience humiliating. To be clear, I am not indicting the outreach efforts of Phil-Am residents. They are only trying to help. Their actions are beneficial to and generally appreciated by San Roque's residents. The problem has to do with the form that class interaction, whether excluding or helping, generally takes. Benefaction in the face of categorical inequality ends up reinforcing the social boundaries that keep each group in its place.

---

4. There is support for this claim in the literature on intergroup contact. Paolini, Harwood, and Rubin (2010) have found that negative contact is more salient than positive contact. Indeed, relatively infrequent negative encounters may outweigh the effects of numerous positive encounters (Barlow et al. 2012).

## *Exceptions*

Slum residents held up as exceptions "rich" people who actively disregarded class boundaries. After recounting her humiliation at the hands of one boss, Marivic recalled being uplifted by another: "I had this other boss, Sir Popoy. When he sees me, 'Hello! Marivic, come here' and gives me a kiss. I don't feel uneasy with him at all. Even if he's rich, he kisses me. I even kiss him back! It makes me happy, that even if he's rich that's the way he sees me." She described being treated without disgust or condescension. Other informants described being treated with consideration. Lita followed up her story of a bad boss with a story of a good one. "They're not all the same," she said. "I had this one boss who would eat along with us. It's like she didn't consider us maids. She didn't even make us wear uniforms. It was all the same to her. We could use the same glass she had used. We could use the same plate." These small acts of equality made Lita feel seen as more than just a servant, as a person. This kind of treatment made Fely, another maid, feel "free" or able to let down her guard with her employer. "I'm able to be honest with them," she said of the Ochoa family. "I told them that if they make a mess I'm not going to clean it up. The old guy really makes a mess, but I just ignore it. I said to him, 'Don't test me, because if I really needed the money I could just borrow it.' It's a great thing when they trust you. Then you can really get along with them. That's the most important thing: trust."

The first thing I heard about Sister Tess was that she's a millionaire. She owns a local supermarket in Quezon City. She lives in Phil-Am and volunteers with the Santa Rita church. San Roque's residents have gotten to know her well. They call her sister not because she's a nun but out of affection. Jolene and Didi regard her as a cherished friend. She hangs out with them, jokes with them, and even visits them on special occasions even though she's rich—a point they take pains to underscore. "Even if she's rich, you won't see her wearing any jewelry. Even me," Jolene admitted, "I put some on when I see her. But she's such a simple person. You wouldn't even think she's rich. These clothes we're wearing are nicer than [what she wears]. Really. She just wears a white T-shirt and black pants, sometimes jeans."

Jolene and Didi value Sister Tess, above all, for her sincerity (*totoong tao*). Her benevolence is not forced or affected but a reflection of her true disposition toward the poor. They know this by the way she treats them. "She'll tell me, 'C'mon, have something to eat.' Or 'you haven't slept yet,'" Didi said. "One time I was sick. Can you believe that she wanted to take me to the hospital! When you're with her you don't feel uneasy at all."

"You don't feel the same way around other rich people?" I asked.

"*Naku!*" Jolene interjected. "The person always with Sister Tess, Beloy? When she leans in to hug you, you can see in her face how disgusted she is. Who does she think she is!"

In general, informants describe as exceptions rich people who treat them in a way that negates their stigma as poor people and squatters. This treatment changes them. Customary feelings of uneasiness dissipate. They describe feeling light and happy and able to relax in the relationship. Acts of consideration from above derive their power from being exceptional and thus can be understood only in relation to slum residents' sense of discrimination. The exceptional status of the individuals involved is conveyed rhetorically through the use of qualification—"Sister Tess treats me kindly even if she's rich"—and foil. Exceptional individuals are contrasted to more typical—indeed, stereotypical—examples of rich people. Sir Popoy stands out against the barangay administrator, the Ochoa family against a series of bad bosses, and Sister Tess against Beloy.

These exceptions deserve our attention because they describe how slum residents would like to be treated. They provide a model of moral behavior. This model is politically consequential. It applies beyond the rich to other people with power over the poor, namely, political leaders. Jolene and Didi described Corazon "Cory" Aquino as exceptional in the same way as Sister Tess was. They characterized her as simple and sincere. They cited seemingly trivial acts of consideration from some twenty-five years earlier, when Aquino was still a housewife and used to attend mass at Santa Rita.

"Cory's number one with me," Jolene declared. "At mass, she would scoot over to make room for you [on the pew]."

"They would serve food after mass and she would be one of the people serving," Didi continued. "What other president would do that? Gloria [Arroyo]? When she smiles, it's so fake [*ngiting aso*, 'a dog's smile']." In chapter 7, I develop the argument linking slum residents' sense of discrimination to their evaluation of Joseph Estrada—like Cory, an icon of sincerity, although one significantly harder for the middle class to appreciate.

# From Class Division to Political Dissensus

# Introduction to Part Two

In part 1 of the book, I focused on the influence of class on urban space and class interaction; here I trace its influence on politics. In part 1, I emphasized the role of boundary imposition in defining class groups—in making class "real," Bourdieu would say. We saw the middle class impose spatial boundaries out of a sense of siege and the urban poor experience boundary imposition as discrimination. In part 2, I focus on the politicization of these identities. I show the figure of Joseph Estrada doing symbolic work. Estrada's appeal largely cut along class lines, hence identification with or against him served to clarify class identities. Bourdieu portrays the process of representation through a spokesperson as a top-down one. Political agents craft appeals that hail certain people and, in the process, construct them as groups. I describe a bottom-up process, showing the middle class and urban poor taking political positions based on their experience of class relations. Specifically, I show a sense of siege and discrimination predisposing, respectively, aversion and reception to Estrada.

The middle class feel besieged not just territorially but electorally. They see themselves as a moral minority, knowing better than the poor, yet outnumbered and, specifically, outvoted by them. In chapter 6, I show how this sense of electoral siege has shaped their political thinking with respect to Estrada and his successor, Gloria Macapagal Arroyo. By focusing on the urban poor's sense of discrimination, we're better able to explain why they responded so strongly to Estrada's populist appeals. In chapter 7, I

Table I.1 Timeline of Joseph Estrada's political career

| 1969–1986 | Mayor of San Juan |
|---|---|
| 1987–1992 | Senator |
| 1992–1998 | Vice President |
| 1998–2001 | President |
| January 17–20, 2001 | Ousted by protest (Edsa 2) |
| April 27–May 1, 2001 | A second protest (Edsa 3) unsuccessfully attempted to reinstall him |
| 2001–2007 | Under house arrest |
| September 12, 2007 | Tried and convicted of plunder and sentenced to life imprisonment |
| October 25, 2007 | Pardoned by President Arroyo |
| 2010 | Ran for president and came in second |
| 2013–present (2019) | Mayor of Manila City |

argue that the poor judge Estrada to be sincere on the basis of a political performance distinguished by the negation of their sense of stigma as poor people and squatters. My data speak to the importance of a politics of recognition among the urban poor. In chapter 8, I show that the different views of the urban poor and middle class with respect to Estrada led them to interpret Edsa 3, the demonstration following Estrada's arrest, in antithetical ways: as a product of political manipulation or as an expression of people power. This dissensus is politically significant because it makes class division visible.

The focus of part 2, then, is on the experience of class relations shaping political subjectivity and contentious politics. The data mainly consist of conversations on class and politics. These conversations presuppose a knowledge of context (as do all conversations), specifically, Philippine politics between 2001 and 2010. I summarize the necessary context here to help the reader situate the conversations to follow.

## The Political Context, 2001–2010

Joseph Estrada was a movie star in the 1960s and 1970s. He served as mayor of San Juan, a city in Metro Manila, in the 1970s and 1980s and went on to become a senator and then vice president. He ran for president in 1998. The archbishop of Manila, Jaime Cardinal Sin, opposed Estrada even as a candidate. Sin objected to Estrada's "immoral" lifestyle and criticized him in statements read from the pulpit by clergy across the country. On the eve of the presidential election in 1998, Catholic bishops urged their flocks to vote for "anybody but Erap." (Erap is Estrada's nickname. Tellingly, it's a palindrome for *pare*, the Filipino word for "buddy.") Estrada won anyway, with 40 percent of the vote. The bulk of this support came from the lower classes. Indeed, Estrada's election marked the first time that social class played a significant role—more significant than geography, gender, or age—in determining the presidential vote (Mangahas 1998). Not long after his election, though, whatever support Estrada had among the middle and upper classes largely evaporated amid reports of cronyism, serial indiscretions involving women and alcohol, and lavish expenditures.

Just two and a half years into his term, Estrada was accused of receiving kickbacks from the illegal lottery game *jueteng*. The accusation precipitated a string of resignations and defections from the administration. Hundreds of civil society groups joined forces in the effort to remove Estrada from office. Contending leftist camps, organized labor, business clubs, civic and lay religious organizations, student groups, and even some nongovernmental organizations working for the urban poor united around the message "Resign, Impeach, Ouster," or RIO (Arugay 2004). These various groups staged a series of mass actions involving hundreds of thousands of people. In October 2000, an impeachment case was filed against Estrada. People followed his trial like a telenovela. "Dinner parties now start at 9 p.m.," a columnist for the *Philippine Daily Inquirer* noted, "as most guests can't leave their homes until the televised impeachment hearings are over. And once at dinner, they talk of nothing else but the case."[1] On January 16, 2001, Estrada's allies in the Senate voted to block the opening of a crucial piece of evidence: an envelope allegedly containing documents showing Estrada to be the owner of a bank account into which ill-gotten funds had been deposited. The prosecution resigned en masse, the trial was suspended, and people took to the streets.

Edsa 2, as the demonstration was called, lasted from January 17 to January 20, 2001. Nearly a million people, mainly of the middle and upper classes, gathered around the shrine located along Epifanio de los Santos Avenue. On the third day of the demonstration, the military leadership defected. On the fourth, Estrada's vice president, Gloria Macapagal Arroyo, took the stage at the Edsa shrine and was sworn in as president. At the time, there were a few scattered protests against Estrada's ouster in parts of Manila, but nothing substantial. It seemed as if his supporters had accepted the development. Three months later, on April 25, Arroyo moved to arrest Estrada. The move precipitated a gigantic protest, largely comprising Estrada's supporters among the

---

1. Rina Jimenez-David, "The Chicken at the Trial," *Philippine Daily Inquirer*, January 13, 2001.

urban poor. In chapter 8, I depict Edsa 3 from the perspectives of both the mainstream media and its urban poor participants. In the years following, Estrada was convicted of plunder and sentenced to life imprisonment. Shortly thereafter, Arroyo pardoned him.

Gloria Arroyo was never very popular from the start. Given the circumstances surrounding her assumption of the presidency, her government lacked legitimacy. Early into her administration, facing criticism from all sides, she promised not to run for election in 2004. The gesture won her goodwill and a stay from criticism. Less than a year later, she reversed course and threw her hat in the electoral ring. Her chief rival was Fernando Poe Jr. (known as FPJ), Estrada's good friend and an even bigger movie star than he had been. Arroyo won the election by about a million votes. The following year a recording surfaced of Arroyo phoning the election commissioner Virgilio Garcillano and asking him to secure her lead by one million votes. The "Hello Garci" scandal prompted calls for Arroyo's resignation. Although she weathered the crisis, others followed. Indeed, her presidential term, lasting from 2004 to 2010, came to be defined by a series of corruption scandals, including senior officials in her administration taking bribes from a Chinese telecommunications company. Informants referred to the scandal as NBN-ZTE, in reference to the national broadband network plus the name of the company, Zhongxing Telecommunications Equipment Corporation. At different points in her term, Arroyo was accused of bribing election officials, party members, and congressional representatives. Her husband was accused of receiving kickbacks from *jueteng* operators (the same charge that had led to Estrada's ouster). She managed to finish her term despite three coup attempts and five impeachment attempts.[2]

In chapter 6, I discuss why many in the middle class felt bound to support Arroyo despite mounting evidence of corruption. They felt they needed to prevent "*masa* candidates" from taking power, including FPJ in the 2004 election and Arroyo's vice president, the popular news broadcaster Noli de Castro, thereafter. To the middle class, Arroyo represented "the lesser evil."

Estrada ran for president once again in 2010. He lost to Benigno "Noynoy" Aquino, who was riding a wave of popular support follow-

---

2. In 2011 and 2012, under the Aquino administration, Arroyo was charged with electoral fraud and corruption, then arrested. She was cleared of the corruption charges in 2016. She now serves as the congresswoman for her district in the province of Pampanga.

ing the death of his mother, Cory Aquino. What's remarkable is that Estrada came in second despite having joined the race late, running a relatively underfunded campaign, and having been ousted, convicted of plunder, and imprisoned. In chapter 7, I unravel the puzzle of the urban poor's support for Estrada.

# SIX

# The Politics of Electoral Siege

In this chapter, I argue that the middle class see themselves as besieged not just territorially but electorally. On the one hand, they see the poor as political dupes, able to be fooled and bought by unscrupulous politicians. On the other hand, they see themselves as possessing moral authority over the poor by virtue of their greater education and autonomy from political inducements. They see themselves, in short, as possessing a greater right to govern. The problem is, they're outnumbered, and thus, in the electoral system, outvoted in cases of candidates whose appeal cuts along class lines. I show here how a situation of electoral siege has informed their political calculations with respect to both the populist president Joseph Estrada and his successor, Gloria Macapagal Arroyo. Informants discounted the urban poor's support for Estrada as misguided. They rejected Estrada not just because he was corrupt but also because he was vulgar. His political persona embodied the very qualities that they, as class actors, identified themselves against, and thus they deemed him morally unfit to represent them. Meanwhile, in the wake of evidence that Arroyo had cheated in the election, informants abided Arroyo despite overwhelming evidence of malfeasance, partly because she represented "the lesser evil" in comparison to *masa* candidates Fernando Poe Jr., in the 2004 presidential election, and Noli de Castro, Arroyo's vice president. Informants' sense of electoral siege has bred frustration with Philippine democracy. It has led some of them to call for a new kind of boundary to be drawn against the urban poor: disenfranchisement. To make sense of these positions, we need to understand how profoundly a durable inequality has shaped the situation of the middle class in Manila.

## The Poor as Political Dupes

### *The Poor Don't Know Any Better*

I am talking to Allan and Marlene, an upper-middle-class couple who live in BF Homes. We are sitting around the patio table in their backyard, drinking coffee from beans that have been ingested by a civet. Allan is raving about it. He purchased the beans on a recent trip to Vietnam. In theory, enzymes enhance the taste of the coffee during the civet's digestion of them. I agree politely, imagining the beans of the coffee I am drinking being culled from civet dung. We end up talking, perhaps inevitably, about inequality. The conversation is long and wide-ranging and impossible to summarize with any justice. Instead, let me highlight two "scenes" that, taken together, suggest the thorny ambivalence Allan and Marlene feel about living in a deeply unequal society.

The first scene: "Just tonight," Marlene began. "I was watching that program, did you see *TV Patrol*? It was about that boy who was being eaten up by wounds all over his—"

"Oh, my," came out of my mouth.

"He's six years old but he's as big as what . . . a three-year-old? On Ted Failon's show?" Ted Failon hosts a popular radio and TV news show.

"Yes."

"There was a woman that passed his house every day. She's a street sweeper. She said, 'Every time I see him, I feel really bad but I can't do anything about it because I can hardly make ends meet myself, but I couldn't stand it anymore.' So she asked Ted Failon for help, and Ted Failon found the boy. He's been sick for three years now."

"Oh, no."

"He doesn't have a nose anymore. And he can't even close his eyes because . . . I don't know what kind of sickness."

"Something triggered by malnutrition," Allan suggested.

"Malnutrition. If you see the boy—"

"And here's our president having a meal in New York for a million pesos!" Allan interjected angrily. He was referring to the news report that Gloria Macapagal Arroyo and her entourage had spent almost US$20,000 dining at a fancy restaurant in New York while visiting on state business.

"I know," Marlene said. "When you see those things, you really . . . you know . . ." Her voice trailed off.

The second scene: "Even the guys that work on my garden or the guy that comes and cleans the pool," Allan said. "I mean, how can you compare your life to theirs?"

"There's just no comparison," Marlene agreed.

"What he makes in a week, and I pay legal wages," Allan huffed, "I don't, you know, underpay. But what he makes in a week is what I spend on one meal when we all go out."

"Not even," Marlene added.

"What we spend on one lunch, ha, will take him a month and a half to make working eight hours a day."

"But then it makes your life easier," I suggested. "You know, in terms of being able to afford these services."

Allan paused and looked straight at me. "Why do you think I'm still in this country?" We laugh.

"It's comfortable," I conjectured.

"Ah, yes," Marlene said.

"Oh, yes," Allan said. "You know, I had a house in New Mexico. I sold it. I refuse to live in America."

"Too much trouble?" I ventured.

"The only reason why I made my own coffee today is because this coffee has to be made a certain way."

"Otherwise . . ." Marlene chuckled.

"I can't ask the maid to make it. Otherwise, you're in America, you want a cup of coffee, you have to make it yourself. But here, you know, I just sit around and say *kape* [coffee], and it comes out. My mother-in-law and I always argued about it. She lived over there. She's passed away now, but she would tell me, 'Allan, it's so easy. Everything is automatic—'"

"You just press the button," Marlene continued.

"You press the button and it works."

"And then he says, 'But I still have to press the button!'"

We laugh.

"'I don't like to press the button,'" she says, aping her husband with a put-on whine.

More laughter.

Allan continued: "I said, 'Are you kidding me?' I said 'You know when I go there—'"

"That's the only consolation being here," Marlene sighed.

"I have to take my pants off and put them inside the washing machine. I have to put in the detergent and turn on the switch. I have to turn on the water. Hell! In my house, I walk in the front door, I take off my pants, I throw it in one corner, I take off my shirt, I throw it on the stairs."

"The next day it's ironed," I said.

"Yeah. It's in the closet already," Marlene said.

He continued: "And I take off my socks in the bathroom, I take a shower, I come out, I put on fresh clothes, I go out. The next morning, everything I've thrown away is back in my closet, washed, pressed . . . you know, just hanging there. I mean, what the hell do you mean, 'automatic'? *I* have automatic; you don't."


On the one hand, Allan and Marlene are scandalized by the level of inequality they see. On the other hand, they knowingly exploit it. It enables them to enjoy a comfortable lifestyle—even a decadent one, by their admission—one that would be out of reach if they lived in the United States. They live this contradiction every day, such that it constitutes a source of moral discomfort, an insistent pea underneath all those mattresses. "Sometimes you just close your eyes," said Millie, an informant from New Makati. But it's not so easy to turn a blind eye. The scale of inequality has an impact on the state of politics, and that's something that members of the middle class cannot escape unless they leave the country (as, indeed, many of them—mostly people less well-off than Allan and Marlene—have been doing). In the view of my middle-class informants, the *masa* are so far backward that they are unable to properly participate in the political process. They don't know enough or don't know any better, and thus are liable to being misled or mesmerized by demagogues. The problem, in their diagnosis, is that a lack of education and consistent cultivation has impaired the *masa's* power of political discernment.

"They're stupid," Allan said. Referring to the 2009 movie *Ang panday*—in which the actor Bong Revilla plays a blacksmith (*panday*) who defeats an evil wizard with a magical sword—he continued: "They vote for the guy because he's Bong Revilla. And they think that if they put him there [in the Senate], he'll turn into *Panday*! Look, I know. I've been in the movie business for a while now. When you show a movie of FPJ's in the provinces, in the boonies, and the bad guy, he's about to ambush him from the back, someone from the audience will pull out his gun and start shooting the screen!" Allan went on, "You know, Marco, these guys are high school, even grade school, dropouts. What do they know? I actually know a guy that when you're talking about a sanitary napkin, he thinks you're talking about this [he holds up a table napkin]." Everybody laughs. Our laughter is telling. Allan's napkin remark belongs to a class of "*masa* jokes" that turns on such misunderstandings. The single punch line is the gulf between them and us. Kevin tried to make the point more scientifically: "You're sociology right?" he asked me.

"Uh-huh," I said, meaning "uh-oh."

"So, you know Maslow's hierarchy of needs?"

I knew where this was going. This was not the first time one of my informants had brought up Maslow, and it wouldn't be the last.

"OK, so most of the people in San Roque, they're still in the physiological stage and concerned with their physical and security needs. That's what they're thinking about when they go for certain candidates . . ."

"OK."

"That I need this guy to meet my basic needs."

"OK."

"But for those of us in the higher stages, we're already in the achievement stage, the esteem stage, whatever. We're more educated and we look for other things. We're able to see the bigger picture."

However dressed up, the belief is that the disparity in education and other means of refinement has created a difference in the political values of the middle class and *masa*. That they, the middle class, know better is simply taken for granted. Members of the middle class see themselves as a moral minority—a conceit predicated on two assumptions: their social difference from the *masa* and their moral authority over them.

### The Poor Can Be Bought

The poor are further discounted by the middle class because they are seen as selling their vote. "They're hungry," Pat reasoned. "This guy is going to give me [meaning "them," the poor] five hundred pesos to vote for him. I'll vote for him!" "It's sad," Minggoy said. "A candidate will go to San Roque and pass out envelopes. It's SOP [standard operating procedure]. You give. Candidate 1 gives, then candidate 2 comes along and his envelopes are fatter. Now they're voting for candidate 2." Vote buying, however, gets at only one side of a reciprocal relationship. It's not just that politicians corrupt poor voters; the politician himself is constrained by the expectations of the people. Rolf explained by way of personal experience. He grew up in the province of Tarlac, where his father was often thrust into the position of acting governor: "I'd remember waking up and the house would be full of visitors. I'd want to have breakfast in my sleeping clothes, but there were all these people downstairs."

"Asking for money?" I asked.

"Asking for money. Their carabao [water buffalo] had died or their child was getting married. And they would stay for breakfast, lunch, and dinner."

"Because your father was a politician, people felt that they could impose themselves upon him?"

"Oh, yes. All the time. Any time. By the way, that's how they [politicians] justify stealing."

"Because they have to give at weddings and funerals?"

"Not just. The basketball team for the neighborhood kids. You put up a court, you buy them a ball. Where do you think that money comes from? It has to come from somewhere, right?"

Santi described a similar dynamic in Makati: "When the Filipino gets sick or has to return to the province, he goes to the politician and asks for money to pay for the trip or hospital bill. That's why Binay wins elections here. It's because people know they can go to him when they get into trouble." Santi was referring to Jejomar Binay, the long-time mayor of Makati City who ran with Estrada in 2010 and won the vice presidency. At issue is the "dole-out mentality" of the poor, their "sense of entitlement." As Pat put it, reasoning on behalf of the poor: "I'm poor; it's your job [as a politician] to help me." To be sure, most informants recognize that this attitude is born of poverty and takes hold in a highly unequal society. They can see its basis as a moral claim. Whatever the circumstances, the fact remains that the poor lack autonomy as political actors and so pursue a politics that middle-class informants judge to be shortsighted, regressive, and ultimately detrimental even to the poor themselves.

Middle-class informants see their own situation as different. They enjoy a measure of economic security; thus, in contrast to the poor, they act relatively independently of political mediation. "We're not looking for handouts," Rolf said. "A small bag of rice with sidings [meat or fish] and noodles. We don't need it. The five hundred pesos Gloria is giving out for her Pangtawid or whatever [Arroyo's poverty-relief program]. We don't think of those things." He went on: "We think more in terms of services." And even with respect to services the middle class have become more independent. As discussed in chapter 4, the middle class has become increasingly segmented administratively and socially. The middle class look to the homeowners' association for the security and maintenance of their neighborhood. They avail themselves of private schools and hospitals. They socialize in private clubs and other exclusive spaces. I asked Rolf about this. "You're saying that you expect different things from the barangay?"

"I don't even *think* of the barangay." He pauses for a moment: "I don't even know where the barangay is." Another pause. "Or even which barangay I'm part of." He thinks, then continues: "Do you know?"

Middle-class informants, moreover, were jealous of their autonomy and displayed a wariness of becoming entangled in clientelist relationships. Minggoy, for instance, pointed out all the officials living in Phil-Am. "Two houses down the road is a close aide of Joe de Venecia [the former Speaker of the House]. Across from her is Congressman Milo [a pseudonym]. Beside Milo is Mr. Muñoz, who used to head the DPWH [Department of Public Works and Highways] under Cory. As long as we can live with—around—them, it works out fine."

"As long as politics doesn't enter the village?"

"Sure. And actually nobody would ever—well, except for Milo. He's a young guy and every once in a while he takes me aside [as president of the village association], 'Ming, what can I do for Phil-Am?' I'll do dental, medical missions.' I said, 'Fine, I'll let you know.' But what he's asking, that's tantamount to saying, 'Hey, you better vote for me.' I won't go for that. I'll help you to an extent, but I don't want you dictating my politics."

Indeed, middle-class informants were likely to characterize their interactions with politicians and bureaucrats in terms of corruption. Many complained about being shaken down by officials at various levels, from *kotong* (bribe-seeking) traffic cops to fault-finding auditors with the Bureau of Internal Revenue. Consequently, they had taken to avoiding or insulating themselves from such interactions as much as possible. Miguel, a contractor, described the process of acquiring a building permit: "It starts with the barangay."

"They ask for SOP [a bribe]?"

"Oh, yeah. Terrible. It happens so many times too. Just to get the permit you need thirty-eight signatures."

"Thirty-eight!"

"Yeah. Want me to list them all out for you?"

"You need to give each one?"

"No, not all. Of the thirty-eight, I'd say probably twenty."

"So, then how do you manage as a businessman?"

"I don't deal with government contracts. Just private ones."

"But you still have to deal with the government."

"I still have to get permits."

"What do you do?"

"Well, I try to minimize . . . you see, we know that's how it is—"

"Minimize your exposure?"

"My exposure to government."

The poor, then, in the view of my middle-class informants, are compromised as political actors. They can be fooled and they can be bought. The middle class, meanwhile, possess the right values and the requisite autonomy to choose appropriate leaders. Here's the rub: despite their qualifications, they are outnumbered and hence periodically outvoted. As they see it, theirs is a situation of electoral siege.

## Electoral Siege

Informants' sense of electoral siege reflects their sense of being besieged territorially. "Go around Holy Spirit and you'll see," Miguel said. "Although we're full of subdivisions, the squatters are everywhere. In BF they're there, in Mapayapa they're there, in Don Enrique they're there, and you already know that in Don Antonio they're here. The subdivisions take up most of the land area but in terms of population . . ."

"There's more of them."

"Probably 80 percent more."

I nodded.

Miguel continued: "In Don Antonio, there are about 700 homes. An average family of five, let's say, that's only 3,500. Go down to Samonte Street. There's your 3,500."

Informants brandished the ratios of 80 to 20, sometimes 70 to 30—meaning 80 percent "them," 20 percent "us"—to make the point of their minority status. This status, again, is premised on their difference, as a class, from the *masa*. This difference translates into different political values and their political choices sometimes being at odds as a result. In these cases, the greater numbers of the *masa* result in the middle class being outvoted. This situation can lead to a feeling of futility and can prompt some to withdraw from the political process altogether.

"It's painfully obvious that we're a minority when it comes to voting," Marianne said. "Ours don't count for much."

"I can vote for whomever I want," Nani said, "but it's the *masa* that dictates."

Agnes concurred: "What can we do if it's the *masa* that elects?"

"You're Don Quixote," Allan concluded.

Santi threw up his hands: "Our votes won't be enough to offset the votes of the *masa* anyway, so why bother?"

Len, upon reviewing his political choices since 1986, exclaimed, as if just realizing it, "I've never voted for anyone that's won!"

Informants' sense of being an electoral minority informs their approach to voting. They feel compelled to take into account a candidate's winnability, a quality seen as directly proportional to his or her "*masa* appeal." If a candidate is thought to lack *masa* appeal, the question becomes whether to stick with the candidate or to vote "pragmatically," that is, for someone else—not their first choice, but at least not their last. At the time of my fieldwork, informants were thinking about the 2010 presidential election, mere months away. Allan spoke at length about the merits of Dick Gordon as a candidate. He thought that Gordon displayed "executive ability" during his tenure as chairman of the Subic Bay Metropolitan Authority and the Red Cross. "But do I think he's going to win?" he asked, a question put to himself as much as to me.

"Do you?"

"He has the chance of an ice cube in hell."

Carla also liked Gordon, but as soon as she told me, she dismissed him. "He's not going to win," she said, "so what's the use of voting for him?" In fact, she reasoned, voting for Gordon would only take votes away from Noynoy Aquino, a candidate with crossover appeal, and it was better that he win than Estrada or Villar, the two populist candidates. She emphasized the need to be pragmatic, the need specifically to avert the "danger" of the *masa* winning.

In contrast to pragmatic voters, so-called conscience voters prioritize their political values. They point out that winnability is a self-fulfilling prophecy and a cynical standard besides. Millie recounted sitting down with her friends and family and discussing the matter. She concluded that it was more important to vote her values and leave the rest in God's hands. This, by the way, is the position taken by the influential Catholic Bishops' Conference of the Philippines. The organization issued a statement preceding the May elections counseling voters to "follow the dictates of your conscience after a prayerful and collective period of discernment." "'Winnability,'" it cautioned, "is not at all a criterion for voting!"[1]

Informants resorted to something like fieldwork to gauge the will of the *masa*. They interviewed the various laborers they encountered in daily life. It was their way of reading the political tea leaves. "I've been talking to taxi drivers," Alana told me. "I like talking to them and, you would be surprised, they're very intelligent. Most of the time I talk to them, you know, they talk sense. This time they don't. . . . Well, I got to talk to three of them. They don't want a celebrity. They don't want someone who is 'accomplished and intelligent' [*magaling at matalino*, the campaign slogan of candidate Gilberto Teodoro]. And I guess that's why Noynoy will win."

I spoke with Tess about her fieldwork. She volunteers with her church catechizing the maids and contract workers around her village. In the process, she gets to ask them about their politics: "What I discovered was, yes, their politics are different. They prefer popular politicians. People they think will make their lives a little better. The reality is they need money. So they vote for the person . . ."

"Who pays them," I said.

"Yes. But I asked them, 'Does that mean you'll always vote for the person who pays you?' And they said no. They will take the money because they need it but will still vote for—"

"Ah, okay," Tess's friend Agnes interjected, relieved.

"The person they want. A majority of them said that. 'Because they will never know whom we voted for anyway,' they said."

"Exactly!" Agnes said.

"So we'll vote for the people we want."

"Are the people they want the same as the people you want?" I asked.

"No!" Tess laughed. "I mean, they're going for Erap!"

"Oh, my God!" Agnes interjected, horrified.

Finally, informants felt it incumbent upon them, being better-off and better educated, to "conscientize," or raise the political consciousness of, the *masa* around them. It was a matter of social obligation. They used their influence as employers and benefactors. They spoke to their maids. Phil-Am residents spoke to the people in San Roque they hired or helped. "Our maids, our washerwomen, our cleaning ladies,

---

1. Catholic Bishops' Conference of the Philippines, "A Call for Vigilance and Involvement," January 24, 2010.

they all come from [San Roque]," Ernesto pointed out. "Medical missions, gift-giving, Halloween, a hundred kids come over to trick-or-treat," he went on. "So when we whisper, 'Hey, let's go for Noynoy,' they listen." Felicia sought to enlist me in the effort. She asked me about my interviews with slum residents. I explained to her that I engaged them in conversations about politics. "That's not enough," she said disapprovingly. Her rebuke caught me off guard.

"Should I be telling them whom to vote for?"

"You should be direct, I think, in order to improve our chances in this country." She told me that she made a point of sitting down with her employees during break time and talking with them about the upcoming elections. She even provided them with a short list of acceptable candidates. She suggested that I do the same. Just look at the front-runners in the senatorial election, she said. "Bong Revilla."

"Jinggoy Estrada," I added. Jinggoy is Joseph Estrada's son, also an actor, and a senator since 2004.

"Jinggoy Estrada. You need to make time to discuss the election with the settlers. I think they may listen to reason. If you just leave it to them, they'll go to the voting booth without any kind of preparation."

I felt scolded.

"And who will they vote for?" Felicia needled. "The likes of Bong Revilla."

I mumbled something sheepishly.

"There needs to be some sort of intervention." She thought for a moment: "You should hold teach-ins for the informal settlers."

Such interventions are not meant to be prescriptive but to initiate a process of deliberation. The goal is to get the *masa* to make informed choices. Deliberation has limits, however. Lena makes an effort to get her household helpers on the same page: "I sit down with my five angels and say, 'Come, let's decide whom to vote for.' I try to find out who they like and why they like them. For example, my maid. She's been with me a long time. She likes Gordon. I ask her why. In the end, we come to a consensus."

"That's nice," I said.

"For now, it's Noynoy."

"You vote as a bloc."

"Not really. For all I know, she may vote for Gordon anyway. Fine. If you insist on voting for Gordon, go ahead. Just not. . . . If I have one maid that says, 'I'm for Erap,' I might tell her, 'Get out of here. You don't belong here.'"

These conscientization efforts are premised on the faith that deliberation will lead the *masa* to make choices similar to those of the middle class—not necessarily that they will end up choosing the same candidates but that, upon reflection, they will at least be unable to justify choosing the worst ones. I don't share this faith. My research suggests that the middle class and urban poor hold different political values—not completely, but to a meaningful extent. These values have been molded by their different social and political situations and reflect their different class and political identities. For this reason, there is a limit to which the political views of the poor can be "rectified" by educational initiatives. The experience of poor voters orients them otherwise. I have more to say about this experience in the following chapter. For now, the question is, What happens when the *masa* cannot be enlightened, persuaded, or browbeaten? What happens in cases of dissensus? The case of Estrada provides one answer. The middle class came to find him morally objectionable—intolerably so—and yet he remained popular among the urban poor. In Estrada's case, the middle class claimed the right to exercise its moral authority even if doing so meant acting extraconstitutionally.

In the following two sections, I illustrate how a sense of electoral siege has shaped the political thinking of my middle-class informants with regard to two Philippine presidents. It has led them to reject Estrada as vulgar and to abide Arroyo as the lesser evil.

### Estrada's Vulgarity

Most of my middle-class informants opposed Estrada. Forty-six percent participated in the demonstration to remove him (table 6.1). Speaking with them, it became apparent that their rejection of Estrada had a lot to do with their perception of why the poor supported him.

Table 6.1 Middle-class informants' positions on Estrada and Edsa 2 (%)

|  | Yes | No | Not sure or response ambiguous |
| --- | --- | --- | --- |
| Opposed Estrada | 85 | 5 | 10 |
| Supported Edsa 2 | 65 | 12 | 22 |
| Participated in Edsa 2 | 46 | 54 | — |

Notes: *N* = 81. The high number of ambiguous responses with respect to support for Edsa 2 reflects informants' assessment of the demonstration in hindsight. For some informants, it had come to be associated less with the removal of one bad president (Estrada) than with the ushering into office of another bad president (Arroyo). Thus, they had come to feel ambivalent about Edsa 2. They probably supported it at the time it was happening.

## *Why the Poor Support Estrada*

Screen Persona

My informants gave two main reasons for why the poor support Estrada. The first reason is because of his screen persona as "defender of the oppressed."[2] Early in his film career, Estrada played the role of lower-class hero—squatter, jeepney driver, tenant farmer, rebel—so often and so memorably that movies featuring the actor in that role became an identifiable genre: "Joseph Estrada proletarian potboilers" (Lacaba 1983). Some people saw in this identity the source of Estrada's political appeal. There are two versions of this argument. The crude version is that the poor confuse Estrada's movies for reality. The *masa* "go to the movies and see Estrada beating the shit out of the bad guys," Allan said. "They actually believe the same thing will happen in real life." The more sophisticated version emphasizes a process of identification. The claim is that the poor recognize themselves in Estrada's movie roles. The argument was articulated most forcefully for me, ironically, by one of Estrada's most prominent supporters.

Ronald Lumbao is the leader of the activist organization People's Movement against Poverty (PMAP). I happened upon Lumbao entirely by chance. I knew who he was, of course, but I had no idea how to reach him. I was visiting the city hall in San Juan hoping to interview J. V. Ejercito, Estrada's son and San Juan's mayor, when a secretary, perhaps wishing to spare his boss my pestering, suggested I speak to Lumbao instead. He directed me to an office off to one corner of the municipal compound. I found him with nothing to do, legs up on an empty desk. We made plans to meet that evening at the Gerry's Grill in Quezon City. He arrived nearly an hour late with four of his PMAP deputies.

We spoke for almost four hours. Lumbao was delirious and inspired at times (often the same times), helped along, no doubt, by the dozen or so beers he imbibed throughout the evening. It quickly became clear that the topic of Estrada and Edsa 3 caused him pain and anger. I could see why. In the aftermath of Edsa 3, Lumbao and nine others, all senators, were charged with rebellion for instigating the march on Malacañang. Lumbao ended up the fall guy for the bunch. He was the only one imprisoned, serving fifteen months before being released on bail.

"Why Erap?" I asked him.

---

2. The phrase comes from Abinales and Amoroso (2005, 270).

"Why Erap?" he repeated. "Because we believed that we could use him. [It would save us from] having to do the painstaking work of re-orienting the people towards [a better understanding] of Philippine politics. Because when you invoke Erap's name, the *masa* have no problem believing what you tell them."

"Actually, we just wanted to use him for one thing," Ronald Coronado, PMAP's treasurer, started to say.

Lumbao cut him off: "Wait, wait, wait. When I speak, and I'm a good speaker, the *masa* won't just believe me. The things I say, it will take them a year, six months, no, ten years, to believe it. The things Erap says, they'll believe it that very minute and for the rest of their lives."

"Why is that?" I persisted.

He stared at me for what felt like several minutes. Perhaps my questions had upset him.

"I'm going to hit you now," he said. He put down his beer, got up, and walked over to my side of the table. He stood over me. Everyone just watched him. I remained seated but braced for something terrible to happen.

"I'm the goon and you're Erap," he said, and he drummed my head with his palms. "You survive [my beating]. The next time around you beat *me* up."

I considered obliging him.

"Every day the *masa* sees this. You're playing a driver. He's a driver, too."

"Ah, yeah, that's Estrada's role in the movies," Coronado interjected, relieved. He could see where this was going.

Lumbao's associates tried to return him to his seat. In an effort to occupy me, Coronado asked me whether I had seen the Erap movie *Bankang papel sa dagat ng apoy* (*Paper Boat in a Sea of Fire*). I hadn't.

"No, it's like this!" Lumbao asserted. He was standing up but back on his side of the table now. He still looked angry: "The simplest way I can put it. Quite simple. You talk of theories, you talk of Marxism, you talk of whatever ism there is to it, but there's only one Erapism and you see it in his movies. He always plays the role of the poor: a driver."

"A labor leader!" "A tough guy!" The others chimed in.

"All of that! And everything he tells you, that you're poor, that other people are the ones making you poor, that you should do something about it. Everything in Marx is in an Erap movie. And not just one of them, all of them, decades' worth. So you're Joseph Estrada. What do we think of you? You're higher than Mao Zedong. Higher than Lenin.

Higher than anyone! You know why? Because every day we see you getting beaten up. You should be dead, but wait! You're not dead!" We laughed, mostly out of relief. "You're a symbol of hope and when we see you we know there's still hope," he continued. He slumped back into his chair.

Lumbao's associates changed the subject. We talked about the election, Edsa 1, the prospect of revolution in the Philippines, recession in the United States, China's designs on Southeast Asia, back to Estrada's movies, back to Erap.

"Do you understand now?" Lumbao, rousing, asked me.

"Do I understand why Estrada became a symbol of the poor?"

"Years and years of watching Erap movies," Coronado said.

"Which one?"

"Doesn't matter!" Lumbao interrupted. "Even the corniest one!" Conciliatory now, he offered something of a recapitulation. "If we had a *Little Red Book*, it was Estrada's movies. There's only one story to them. I beat you up, but in the end you kill me. You're the hero. Over and over again. See? How can you not believe in him? [The people who dismiss him] as merely an actor don't get it. They don't see how *real* he is in his movies."

In both the crude and the sophisticated versions of this argument, the basis of Estrada's political appeal lies in his screen persona. Lumbao's version is able to tell us why this persona is so compelling, but the poor still come off as lacking in discernment. They may be able to distinguish between movies and reality, but they still mistake Estrada's on-screen prowess for political prowess. They misrecognize the source of Estrada's appeal. This makes them susceptible to manipulation, not just by politicians but also by political activists such as Lumbao and company. The PMAP officers don't take the poor's support for Estrada at face value. They approach it as a means of organizing them for higher ends. They see themselves as working toward a nationalist revolution. The poor are to be brought along for the ride, whether they know it or not.

Estrada's Populism

Informants also say that the poor support Estrada because they have been fooled. They point to his populist line. Estrada made allegiance to the *masa* the keynote of his political performance. His campaign slogan unequivocally staked his position: *Erap para sa masa* (Erap is for the poor). He presented himself as unaffected, approachable, and singularly devoted to the poor. The poor swallowed his performance hook, line, and sinker. They failed to see Estrada's populism for what it was: a stratagem. To illustrate this point of view, let's pick up where we left off with Agnes and Tess. Tess had just told us, to Agnes's dismay, that the people whom she catechizes support Estrada. She explained: "They like him because their perception, it's been influenced by the media. They think Erap is for the *masa* even if he hasn't done anything for them."

"OK," I said.

"I asked them, I said, 'Tell me frankly, What has Erap done for you? Why do you like him when he's only enriched himself?'"

"And what do they say?"

"They say, 'No, ma'am. We're still for Erap because he likes us.'"

"That's also why Binay is popular," Agnes added. "They [politicians] feed on the mentality of poor people that it's popularity that matters."

"Yeah," Tess said. "Plus rapport."

"Rapport," Agnes agreed. "That the poor can talk with them anytime."

"They're approachable," I suggested.

"Yeah, yeah," Agnes said.

"In short," Tess concluded, "they're bamboozled [*nabobola sila*]."

Informants pointed, further, to Estrada's repudiation of polite society. He comes off as brusque, consistently informal, and brazenly indulgent in unseemly conduct—notably, gambling, drinking, and womanizing. Early in his presidential term, the media had already characterized him as "a boor" given to a "*kanto* [street-corner] boy kind of vulgar wit and coarse behavior" (David 2001, 155): "Whenever he speaks without a prepared speech, whether in English or Tagalog, he slides into a familiar grunt, a patented way of talking tough that immediately connects him with the *masa*, but which sharply alienates him from the intelligentsia and the middle classes, who expect more decorum from the highest official of the land." Estrada's persona became the subject of an entire class of Erap jokes having to do with his alleged dim-wittedness, infidelities, and inarticulacy. These very qualities, informants say, endeared him to the poor. Lena went further and argued that the poor saw in Estrada's bad behavior a validation of their own uncouth lifestyle: "He flaunted it, his three or four wives [mistresses], and tried to justify it. And the *masa* loved it. Why? Because it became easy to justify their own behavior. The macho image of the Filipino really. He struck a chord there. Any Pinoy [Filipino guy] with no shirt hanging out on the street could just look at the president [and say] 'He's just like me!'"

In the view of my upper- and middle-class informants, then, the poor supported Estrada for bad reasons. They were mesmerized, misled, and manipulated. Now a few informants also voted for Estrada in 1998. They supported him, however, for perfectly good reasons. They were impressed by his record as mayor of San Juan and encouraged by his having surrounded himself with capable people. Santi used to live in North Greenhills, Estrada's subdivision. "I voted for him," he admitted sheepishly, as if confessing a crime. "I'm ashamed to admit it, but I did vote for him. Why? Because he was our mayor for a long time in San Juan and he ran the town very well, or we thought he did. . . . But yeah, Estrada turned out to be a big fraud."[3] Sid was a year behind Estrada at the Ateneo de Manila University. When he saw his classmates at an alumni function, he asked them, "'*Pare* [buddy], who are we going for?' 'We're going for Erap.' Because they knew that they'd be able to benefit from being close to him." This wasn't a reason Sid condoned, but it was one that he could understand.

### Why the Middle Class Rejected Estrada

I asked BF Homes resident Rolf about Estrada: "Well, Erap became known for wine, women, and song. And *jueteng*. And you can't make do with someone like that. Right? It's immoral. My God, it goes against all norms . . . not just in government but in personal conduct, no? I mean, one of the problems in Philippine culture is that when you reach a certain level, it's kind of assumed that you have a girlfriend, no?"

"And the more money you have . . ."

"The more women, no? All right, it's your life, it's his life. I'm not gonna—but don't display it in front of everyone! And don't support them [your mistresses] with money that you steal from me!"

He returned to the question of why not Estrada: "Womanizer, number one. Drunk. There was a lot of talk about his 'midnight cabinet,' no? They would get together, drink, play mah-jongg, et cetera. Oh my God!" he said, disgusted. He recalled Estrada's former chief of staff, a respectable academic, "who just couldn't keep up with [Estrada's antics] and had to be fired." Rolf was referring to Aprodicio Laquian, an early scholar of the urban poor in Manila. Laquian later wrote a book about the experience, subtitled *Tales from the Snake Pit*.

---

3. Santi goes on to say that, behind the scenes, San Juan was really run by Estrada's brother-in-law, Raul de Guzman, dean of the College of Public Administration at the University of the Philippines.

I asked if his views on Estrada had changed in the nine years since Edsa 2, the demonstration leading to Estrada's ouster: "No, I don't regret [having participated in Edsa 2] because the guy had to be kicked out. Nobody, no country, deserves a leader like Erap. He wasn't even a leader, no? I think the problem is how come the people haven't mustered the same level of anger towards Gloria [Arroyo]. She's a thief, too, that damn [woman]!"

"Isn't she more corrupt than Estrada?"

"That's what everybody says."

"So how is it that she's lasted, what, nine years now?"

"Yeah. Estrada was just too vulgar."

"Vulgar?"

"Did you see that video? One time he was getting out of his car to attend a diplomatic event, no? As soon as he stepped out he threw up, no, because he was so drunk." Rolf started laughing, a deep belly laugh. "Yeah, he did!" He suddenly became indignant. "You see that—pardon my French, but what the fuck? That's the president of the Philippines!"

"It's too much!"

"So now this GMA [Gloria Macapagal Arroyo]. Well, at least there's nothing like that, right? She's just quietly stealing and having people killed."

"In a not-so-vulgar way."

"Yeah, right?"

Informants also described Estrada as corrupt, incompetent, and immoral, yet none of these qualities by itself quite captures the peculiar object of animus. Estrada was impeached on grounds of corruption, but compared to his predecessor, and certainly his successor, his corruption was small-time. Estrada was called incompetent, but incompetence alone is not particularly reprehensible. Cory Aquino was also described as incompetent in the sense of being inadequate to the task of being president, but people appreciated her anyway. The label "immoral," finally, needs to be unpacked. I think Rolf's word, *vulgar*, gets at the source of offense more exactly. I would argue that it's not the quality of being vulgar itself that is offensive. After all, the current president, Rodrigo Duterte, is also unmistakably vulgar and yet enjoys enormous popularity among the middle class. At issue is vulgarity as articulated within a particular moral discourse, one centered on the notion of civility. Vulgarity must be understood in relation to civility as a standard of conduct associated with and promoted by the middle class.

Civility owes more to cultural than economic capital. It reflects education, cultivation, and taste, not simply wealth. Indeed, displaying wealth ostentatiously is considered vulgar. Harms (2016, 92) describes a resident of the Vietnamese enclave Phú My Hung where he did field-work driving around the neighborhood in a yellow Lamborghini. He drove slowly, slower even than Harms was walking, to show off his car. So indelicate a display of wealth had the effect of irritating, not impress-ing, the man's neighbors. People display civility in how they speak, how they dress, how they eat, how they treat other people, how they drive, but also in how they behave as political subjects. Civility describes a mode of citizenship. For the enclave residents Harms interviewed, the notion of *civitas* conjures "a social order based on the rule of law, on carefully delineated rights and responsibilities, and on disciplined self-conduct and treatment of others" (84). They believe that the behavior exhibited within their enclave provides a model of citizenship for the rest of the country.

I would situate the notion of civility in the context of what Norbert Elias ([1939] 2000) called the civilizing process. Elias argued that the es-tablishment of political order led to greater social coordination and self-regulation, such that norms of socially acceptable conduct developed and became institutionalized. Civility entailed bodily discipline and a heightened regard for others in interaction. "Proper" conduct became a mark of distinction and an important basis of social status. The civilizing process was, of course, at the center of the colonial project. It did not end with the departure of the colonial powers, but was carried on by leading groups in postcolonial nations. It lives on in the development project, with the upper classes on the front lines in the war against bad manners. Such is the case in the Philippines and in Manila society especially, as it would appear to be in urban societies across the Global South.[4]

Civility, Elias tells us, manifests affectively. Vulgarity is encountered by "civil society" with feelings of shame and repugnance reflecting its fear of social degradation. Consider de la Torre's depiction (2010, 49) of the Ecuadorian populist Abdalá Bucaram. Like Estrada, Bucaram was formerly president, accused of corruption, and removed from office: "Seeing Abdalá on TV, sweaty and overweight, with his shirt unbut-toned and showing his gold chains and glitter, climbing on a horse to leave the stage as a cowboy. . . . Bucaram eating with a spoon, gulping Pepsi directly from the bottle, or dancing with bleach blond models." To a middle-class audience, Bucaram was vulgarity incarnate. I would suggest that Estrada made the same impression on the Philippine mid-

---

4. I mentioned Harms (2016). See also Anjaria (2016); Liechty (2003); and Zhang (2010).

dle class. His behavior was not just crude; it was lowbrow, conduct associated with the poor. Lena made the connection between his behavior and the *masa*'s supposed lifestyle explicit: the *masa* see themselves in Estrada. Members of the middle class define themselves against this kind of behavior. They found it especially unbefitting for the president of the country, the figure of the nation. Thus, it's not just that Estrada did not represent them; he also embarrassed them.

Even Estrada's corruption was vulgar. "You know what caused his downfall, right?" Len asked me. "*Jueteng* money brought to his house. By the bundle! [Estrada reportedly had bags full of money delivered directly to his house.] My God. By the bundle! You're the president and that's how you're receiving money? There's the impeachment case against him right there. Plunder." He thought for a moment. "That's actually a good thing," he figured. "Estrada was a goon." He didn't have the brains to make money on "foreign projects," that is, on a larger scale, like Ramos did and like Arroyo was doing. His corruption was limited by his stupidity, and his stupidity was galling.

Lena recited the same litany of transgressions I had heard from Rolf and others: Estrada's womanizing, his gambling, his middle-of-the-night bacchanals, even his stumbling over polysyllabic English words. She concluded remorsefully: "The values he had didn't really mirror the values that we had. I mean, that's a big deal."

"We had heard so many stories already," Marianne said. "He would appear with his cabinet at three o'clock in the afternoon. In his pajamas. Drunk." They had had enough, and so when the opportunity to get rid of Estrada presented itself, groups led by the middle class snapped to action.

The informants who participated in Edsa 2 reported being moved by outrage. "I was just so angry!" said Rex.

Marianne recalled leaving her subdivision in Makati to find "a solid line of citizens" stretching all the way to the Edsa shrine (a distance of some seven to eight kilometers). These informants portrayed their participation as a moral imperative. It was something they had to do. The media characterized Estrada's ouster as an expression of the popular will. The ouster may have bypassed democratic institutions, but institutions had failed, and because Edsa 2 represented the will of the people, it was in keeping with the spirit of democracy.

A survey conducted a week after the demonstration estimated that 13 percent of Metro Manila's residents participated in Edsa 2 (SWS 2001a), or more than a million people. Levels of participation, however, skewed toward upper- and middle-class households. Another survey of Manila's residents found that 65 percent of protestors belonged to the upper and middle classes (Pulse Asia 2001).[5] The proportion rises to 74 percent when including, as Bautista (2001, 8) suggests, members of the lower class with middle-class jobs and at least some college education—that is, survey respondents "sharing the work orientation and values of their educated counterparts in the upper and middle class." Meanwhile, only 4 percent of the lowest class, essentially the urban poor, participated in Edsa 2.

The conceit that Estrada's ouster reflected the people's will became harder to maintain with Edsa 3 (for more on this, see chapter 8). Edsa 2 partisans were forced to shift the basis of their justification for Estrada's ouster from "the people" to their moral authority as a class. This line of reasoning was never very far from view to begin with. As people began to mass around the Edsa shrine, one *Inquirer* columnist reminded Estrada that the demonstrators represented a moral minority: "Yes, Mr. President, the people holding protests against you are not members of the ignorant *masa* and therefore are in the minority. But, remember"—here he cited the example of Edsa 1—"the poor, ignorant Filipinos, just like their counterparts in other countries, are like herded cattle that follow the dictates of their intellectual superiors."[6]

To sum up, as my middle-class informants saw it, the poor had supported Estrada for bad reasons. It was up to them, knowing better, to "correct" their mistake. As a leading observer put it, Edsa 2 "corrected the error of having elected Estrada on a populist platform."[7] Furthermore, informants saw it as up to them to keep such mistakes from happening in the future, no matter the cost. This is the topic of the following section.

## The Logic of the Lesser Evil

How did Arroyo survive her term after it had been revealed that she meddled with the results of the 2004 election (known as the "Hello

---

5. An A-through-E classification scheme is widely used as an indicator of social class, with AB equivalent to the upper and upper middle, C the middle, and D and E the lower classes. The categories are based on the household head's occupation, household income, housing quality, and the presence of certain commodities (e.g., flushing toilet, cell phone, car) in a household (Roberto 2002).

6. Ramon Tulfo, "Mindanaons are Proud of Nene," *Philippine Daily Inquirer*, January 18, 2001.

7. Amando Doronila, "People's Coup: Bloodless, Constitutional, Democratic," *Philippine Daily Inquirer*, January 22, 2001.

Garci" scandal)? How did she survive the cascade of corruption allegations that followed? There are several reasons. One is her political skill in neutralizing the opposition.[8] Another is luck: her electoral rival, Fernando Poe Jr. (FPJ), passed away months after the election. Had he been alive when the Hello Garci scandal broke, he would probably have become the figure of the opposition. Finally, Arroyo survived because the coalition that had worked to depose Estrada was deeply divided over the question of how to deal with her. My data shed light on this last reason in revealing a middle class that was reluctant to remove Arroyo because of a lack of acceptable alternatives.

Informants found themselves in a bind. They felt constrained to support Arroyo—even if all that meant was abiding her—by the need to reject *"masa* candidates," first, FPJ in the 2004 election and then Arroyo's vice president, Noli de Castro, in the wake of the Hello Garci scandal. In each case, informants considered Arroyo the lesser evil. In the 2004 election, Arroyo was not the first choice of many informants. They would have preferred Roco or Lacson, one of the other "middle class" candidates. She was, however, seen as the only candidate who could win against FPJ, and the prospect of an FPJ presidency was sufficiently daunting that it brought most informants into line. When Poe announced his candidacy in December 2004, Arroyo lagged well behind in the surveys. By May, election month, she had managed to inch just ahead of him. I was in the country at the time and remember the sense of urgency within middle-class circles. The need to avert "the looming disaster of an FPJ presidency" had become an imperative overriding ideological and factional divisions.[9] Civil society figures on the Left, in the Catholic Church, and in the business and nonprofit sectors called for a closing of ranks around Arroyo. She won, of course, but soon after, she was discovered to have meddled in the process. Even so, the outrage over the Hello Garci incident failed to translate into concerted action. Why?

When the scandal broke, Agnes and Tess didn't believe that Arroyo had committed electoral fraud. They came to, eventually, but figured that she would probably have won anyway. In any case, even if she had cheated, the outcome was still better than FPJ winning.

8. Unpopular in Manila, she rallied her supporters in the provinces. She cultivated the support of popular civil society groups (e.g., the charismatic sect El Shaddai). She mobilized her allies in Congress to scuttle the impeachment complaints against her and secured the loyalty of the military brass.

9. Joel Rocamora, "Can FPJ Translate Reel into Real?" *Philippine Daily Inquirer*, February 22, 2004.

"Didn't you want her out?" I asked them.

"When we heard the tape?" Tess clarified. "Yes, I wanted her out but there was no, no . . . replacement for her, you know? At the time, the question was, Who would take over?"

"Well, there was Noli de Castro. Before that it was FPJ."

"There was no choice," Agnes insisted.

"If you knew that Gloria would cheat would you still have voted for her?"

"Yes, of course," Agnes said, without hesitation.

I turned to Tess: "Oh, yeah, yeah."

At the time of the scandal, Poe was no longer the issue. It was Arroyo's vice president, Noli de Castro. De Castro had been the anchor of popular news shows *Magandang gabi bayan* (*Good Evening, Countrymen*) and *TV Patrol*. He was seen as a political lightweight. For many informants, a de Castro presidency was simply off the table. This hard line limited what they could do about Arroyo.

"It's very lucky [for Arroyo] that her vice president is Noli de Castro," Sid said. "That's my reading of the situation. If it had been someone else, she would have been gone."

"You mean someone more qualified?"

"Yeah. She would have been gone. But then everybody was thinking, 'What do we do with Noli? What does he know?'"

Sebastian heads an influential business association that helped spearhead the organization of Edsa 2. He called de Castro Arroyo's "best insurance." He continued: "The public perception was that Noli wasn't up to it and that he would have made a lousy president for the balance of Arroyo's term. He would have been president for five years, and that would have been too long. We would have suffered in the end." He began to wonder: "I mean, he might have muddled through, but would people have been more vigilant? Would there have been less corruption?"

Sebastian took stock, counting the scandals associated with Arroyo. "There was the Bolante fertilizer scam, then NBN-ZTE. That's all post-2005 [i.e., after the Hello Garci scandal]. There was the fortified noodles thing and other big deals, all post-2005. The attempts at cha-cha,[10] the payola to congressmen, and the bags of money given to Among Ed and others. NBN-ZTE led to more [malfeasance], including the two

10. *Cha-cha* is short for "charter change." It refers to discussions afoot at the time to amend the Constitution to change the Philippines from a presidential to a parliamentary system.

hundred billion pesos offered to Romulo Neri. All that is post-2005. So I guess her staying on [following the Hello Garci scandal] set the tone. They must have thought, 'We dodged the bullet on that one. Anything goes. We can get away with anything.'"

Finally, Sebastian ventured, "I think it might have been better if Estrada had been fully impeached [i.e., found guilty and forced to resign] rather than thrown out in Edsa 2." This is remarkable coming from one of the chief organizers of Edsa 2. Elsewhere in the interview he revisited the topic, more poignantly: "I would count myself as one of those people who say 'I regret Edsa 2.' But as soon as I say that my friends jump in and say, 'Oh, don't tell me you wish we still had Estrada!' I tell them, 'No, it's not that.' But look at what's happened since then. It's so far from what we all expected."

I would hesitate to say that Sebastian's regret was widespread, though. Lena's sentiments better captured the majority opinion of my middle-class informants. I found her complaining about Arroyo. "You can't defend her anymore," she said. "It's just coming out left and right"—evidence of her corruption, that is. I took the opportunity to prod her about the events leading to Arroyo's accession.

"Do you think that Edsa 2 was a mistake?"

"No, no, no," she said firmly. "No, we're still better off with her. I'm not justifying her stealing, OK? But no, we would have been worse off."

"Erap was—"

"Gutter. Gutter, I say."

In short, for many middle-class informants, Arroyo, as bad as she was, was still better than the alternatives: Erap, FPJ, and Noli.

There was a palpable feeling of "Edsa fatigue" among informants: disillusion with people power as a means of bringing about political change, disappointment in Arroyo, and a general sense of impotence regarding politics. The siblings Elmer and Emma were activists in college for a few years, and they had participated enthusiastically in Edsa 2. By the time I interviewed them, they had all but sworn off "politics." They were busy with work, for one. Emma taught kindergarten, and Elmer worked in a bank. But more than that, they had come to view political involvement as a dead end.

"I just don't see why I should put effort into [politics] when in the end nothing comes of it," Elmer said.

"What would make you take to the streets?" I asked.

"It's not that we're lacking reasons," Emma said quickly. "There are plenty of reasons. If it's not NBN-ZTE, it could be . . ."

"Hello Garci."

"Yeah, Hello Garci. . . . The streets don't really appeal to us anymore. Fine, go rally, but what's the point? It just goes down the drain."

I nodded.

"Fine, go to Edsa, say for ZTE," she repeated. "Get rid of Gloria. Then what? Who would you get to replace her?"

For some informants, the feelings of constraint associated with electoral siege have bred frustration with democracy as a political system.

## Too Much Democracy

Informants complained of there being "too much democracy." This was not the majority opinion, but I can testify to its currency in the late 2000s. Perhaps as never before since democratic restoration in 1986, people talked openly about their frustrations with democracy, waxed nostalgic about the Marcos period, and seriously entertained the idea of restricting the electoral franchise. One powerful group, the Chamber of Real Estate Builders' Association (CREBA 2003), called for the disenfranchisement of squatters. Their argument should be familiar by now. Squatters are susceptible to vote-buying, vote-buying distorts elections, and so squatters should be deprived of the vote. The CREBA position paper reads:

Squatters—comprising some one-half of the population in urban centers and capable of delivering some ten million votes, which is more than sufficient to considerably influence election results—are the most susceptible to vote-buying, and, having no legal residency, form the bulk of flying voters [people brought in by politicians expressly to vote].

As laws penalizing these acts have been ineffective, Government should immediately push . . . to disqualify squatters from voting.

Several middle-class informants proposed the idea of restricting the franchise to taxpayers. "I pay taxes," Cary said. "I mean, I'm an *investor* in the country. But we have a lot of poor people."

"And they outnumber you."

"See. That's the problem. What's more, [the urban poor] don't have any investment in the country. They steal power. They steal water. They steal land. You have to make a contribution. Without a contribution, you shouldn't be able to vote. Why can't it be like that? Why does everybody get to vote? The people who pay taxes, they're the ones who want to see things change but nothing happens because the majority, well, they elect people like Erap."

Ned offered a variation on the proposal. "Me, I subscribe to what the Constitution says: one man, one vote."

"You believe that?" I asked.

"No, not exactly. What I believe in is that every person should be entitled to *at least* one vote."

"At least?"

"At least one vote. And correspondingly more—this is revolutionary—depending on the amount of income tax you pay."

"I see."

"Like a corporation."

"In other words, sir, you think there should be limits to democracy, the way it is now?"

"I wouldn't call it limits."

"No?"

"I would call it an *enrichment* of democracy."

In effect, Ned sees the country as a corporation and its citizens as shareholders. I heard this view repeatedly. The metaphor probably reflects the business background of many informants. The metaphor is useful because it allows informants to argue, by analogy, against political equality—that is, as citizens, their say in the country should be proportionate to their "investment" in the form of taxes.

"Take San Miguel," said Ging, referring to the Filipino conglomerate. "There are probably only ten to fifteen people who run the whole thing. Now, do all the shareholders get to vote on who's going to be the new president of the company? No, right?"

He saw that I assented and continued: "A small group of people decides who's going to run it. Should be the same with the Philippines. The other portion, the urban poor, they should not really get involved because . . ." He searched for the thought.

I ventured a guess: "It doesn't make sense from a management perspective?"

"Exactly! I think of the Philippines as a company. Philippines Inc."

The most popular proposal of all, however, was simply the wish for a "benevolent dictatorship," a leader in the mold of the late Lee Kuan Yew, Singapore's longtime ruler.

"We need someone like Lee Kuan Yew," Agnes said.

"Yes!" Tess agreed.

"I wish we had someone like Lee Kuan Yew," Agnes repeated.

"Personally," Tess said, "I would welcome martial law if we had someone like him."

These views do not go unchallenged; they form only one side of an increasingly lively debate among the upper and middle class about whether democracy is right for the Philippines. Informants on the other side of the debate favored democracy on principle. "Dictatorship is never enlightened," Felipe said. Some, like Sebastian, rejected dictatorship out of hand: "We've tried it before, and it didn't work." Notably, Sebastian accepts the basic premise of the other side, that Philippines-level inequality compromises democracy. I told him that several informants had called for limiting or even abolishing democracy. He wasn't surprised: "There are many people who say that. One of the main proponents of this school of thinking is [a prominent businessman], and we've had a nice argument about it. He says that we need a benevolent dictatorship. And I guess . . . it kind of makes sense. As long as there's great poverty, you can't really have democracy because you don't have economic freedom. The poor will just be manipulated by politicians. I think that's absolutely correct." Nonetheless, he argued, it was better to muddle through, political freedom being valuable in and of itself.

The question at the core of this debate is whether democracy as a political system is viable in a context of great social inequality. It is no accident that this question has come into focus and acquired urgency at a time when populist candidates have proliferated: Estrada, FPJ, and all the other "stars" in the political firmament occupying and running for lower offices. It would be a mistake to dismiss the one side, the restrictions camp, as simply elitist. Theirs are concerns that have long attended the institution of popular democracy. Even John Stuart Mill (1861), an advocate of universal enfranchisement, thought that certain restrictions to the franchise were necessary to mitigate the danger of "too low a standard of political intelligence." He cited a minimum of education (being able to read, write, and do basic math), paying taxes, and being off the dole.

To some extent, informants' frustration with democracy is bound to a particular political moment. When I interviewed them in early 2010, their sense of political efficacy was at its nadir, having been worn down by all the scandals of the Arroyo administration. It would rebound with Aquino's election in May of that year, then attain a new height with Duterte's election in 2016. I would argue, however—vicissitudes of public opinion notwithstanding—that the middle class's frustration with democracy is durable. It is durable because it grows out of a structural situation, not a conjunctural one; that situation is democracy in a deeply, categorically unequal society. The middle class experience this situation as electoral siege. As members of the middle class see it, they possess moral authority by virtue of their education and autonomy from political inducements, yet they find themselves outvoted by the *masa*. The *masa* elect people like Estrada who hamper the progress of the nation as a whole. The middle class suffer keenly as a result of such bad political choices. They watch gains erode, opportunities vanish, and the future darken. Hence their question of why the *masa* should get the same political rights as their betters is not an idle one. They have earned the right to ask it. But theirs is a story we must counterbalance with the urban poor's account of their own political straits.

# SEVEN

# The Politics of Recognition

In this chapter, I address the puzzle of Estrada's support among the poor in Metro Manila. I argue that the poor support Estrada because they perceive him to be sincere, someone who truly cares about them in a field of politicians who merely use them for electoral gain. They see him as sincere not because of his patronage, his celebrity, his political machinery, or any specific populist tactic, but because of the quality of his political performance. What the poor recognize, specifically, is a pattern of conduct distinguished by the negation of stigma. This conduct resonates with them because it forms part of a coherent performance. The poor perceive Estrada as treating them with consideration and respect not just during election season but consistently and "naturally," as an expression of a deeply held disposition toward the poor.[1]

Most explanations of populist appeal emphasize the political skill of leaders. My bottom-up approach highlights the political savvy of supporters—specifically, their ability to distinguish between similar, even standardized, political performances. In general, my data contradict a view of the poor as politically shallow and susceptible to demagoguery. Rather, they feature the poor acting out of a different not deficient knowledge. Once we take into account what the poor actually see in Estrada, a picture emerges of them not as political dupes but as conscien-

---

1. In Garrido (2017), I elaborate the same argument but with reference to the broader literature on populism and with the aim of developing a more sophisticated account of populist style.

tious political actors operating within the bounds of distinct but well-grounded criteria.

## The Puzzle

Why did the urban poor respond so strongly and so enduringly to the populist appeals of Joseph Estrada? His support among this group remained relatively stable even throughout his impeachment trial and ouster. During his trial, the urban poor exhibited "a pattern of disbelief" regarding the various corruption charges against him (Bautista 2001). According to the results of one survey conducted in Metro Manila, the difference between the percentage of the highest class and the percentage of the lowest class finding the charges against Estrada credible was an average of nearly forty points during his trial and thirty points after his ouster (SWS 2001a). Following Estrada's ouster, his ratings on trust plummeted across the nation, declining sharply in Metro Manila, except among the poor. Their trust in Estrada remained virtually unaffected. Even the more highly educated poor in Metro Manila (those with some college education) were more likely to disbelieve the charges against him than were their less educated counterparts nationwide. Overall, Metro Manila's urban poor demonstrated higher levels of trust in Estrada than did the poor nationwide and the urban poor outside the metropolis. This same finding from surveys by two different research organizations led one scholar to conclude that the urban poor in Metro Manila constituted Estrada's "staunchest constituency" (Bautista 2001, 25).

The urban poor's support for Estrada is puzzling for three reasons. First, Estrada was bad for them, at least in terms of their material interests. His poverty reduction program was severely limited in scope, targeting a mere 0.0008 percent of the nation's poor (Choguill 2001, 9). When it came to housing, he prioritized the interests of real estate developers over those of the urban poor (Constantino-David 2001). Overall, the poor's access to health, education, and other social services deteriorated during his presidency (Balisacan 2001). In contrast, his successor, Gloria Arroyo, issued ninety-four proclamations between 2001 and 2006 awarding land to nearly two hundred thousand urban poor families (Wehrmann and Antonio 2011), more than any other president before her and certainly more than what Estrada had done. And yet in the slums where I did research, Estrada is the one whom people cited for helping them.

Second, Estrada was strongly opposed by traditional leaders of public opinion: political leaders (former presidents Fidel Ramos and Cory Aquino), leaders of the Catholic Church, business leaders, and a broad and powerful swath of civil society. In the face of such opposition, the urban poor's support for Estrada remained strong.

Third, Estrada had been ousted, imprisoned, and convicted of plunder. These demerits did not disqualify him in the eyes of the poor, however. He came in second in the 2010 presidential race largely because of their support. The puzzling nature of this support is thrown into relief by the failed populist campaign of another candidate in 2010, Manuel Villar. Villar, a real estate developer and senator, overcame humble origins to become one of the wealthiest people in the Philippines. His campaign touted his poor background and portrayed him as someone who represented the poor. A prominent Villar ad featured child slum residents singing against squalid backdrops. They asked, "Have you ever swum in a sea of garbage? / Spent Christmas on the street? / That's our question, / Are you really one of us?" The lyrics described Villar as the one candidate who understood their plight and truly cared for them. Villar appeared on a popular midday game show and gave away free houses to contestants, made extensive use of celebrity endorsers, and even put his frail, eighty-six-year old mother on TV to plead his case. In short, he drew copiously from the populist playbook. His support dropped soon after Estrada entered the race, late and underfunded. Despite leading early on, Villar ended up finishing third behind Estrada, winning only half as many poor votes despite having outspent him nearly two to one (SWS 2010b). Estrada's lead was even larger in Metro Manila, where he won three times as many votes as Villar (Comelec 2010) and lost to Benigno Aquino III by a much smaller margin: seven hundred thousand votes versus 4.5 million nationwide.[2] Why did the poor support Estrada and not Villar? Why Estrada and not Arroyo? These comparisons suggest that simply deploying populist tactics is not enough to win the support of the poor. The poor have to recognize a leader's appeals as credible. But why do they?

## Prevailing Explanations

Prevailing explanations of the urban poor's support for Estrada emphasize both structural push factors and the pull of charismatic leaders. On

2. Amando Doronila, "Poor's Clamor Shows in Binay, Estrada Votes," *Philippine Daily Inquirer*, June 21, 2010.

the one hand, scholars underscore the urban poor's availability: their precipitous growth since World War II and their lack of institutional representation as a result of the erosion of traditional patron-client ties (Nowak and Snyder 1974), the decline of the Left as a political force (Magno 1993), weak labor unions (Hutchinson 2012), and political parties being in service of personalities rather than aggregate interests (Hutchcroft and Rocamora 2003). On the other hand, scholars point to various sources of Estrada's appeal as a political leader. Four distinct explanations of this appeal are usually given, often in combination.

One, the urban poor support Estrada because of his patronage. He used his power as patron in chief to respond directly to the particular demands of urban poor groups (Bautista 2001). This is true in specific cases, but overall, Estrada did little for the poor in Manila during his term as president (Choguill 2001). This fact is reflected in my data, as we will see. Other politicians, meanwhile, did more for the poor but never truly won them over. Take Arroyo, for example. The early years of her administration were hailed as "a golden age for the urban poor" particularly in Metro Manila, and yet despite her patronage, she remained deeply unpopular among them. This is not to say, of course, that patronage does not matter, or that Estrada's lack of accomplishment would not have come to matter had he remained president instead of being ousted after two and a half years in office. Panfichi (1997) has argued that while people may initially support a populist leader for expressive reasons, their continued support depends on the leader's delivery of concrete improvements in their lives. (In other words, it is possible that Estrada's ouster prolonged his high level of support among the urban poor because it meant that he never had to account for the policy shortcomings of his administration.)

Two, the urban poor support Estrada because of organizational ties. Karaos (2006) cites the role of political organizations in the mobilization of the urban poor in Edsa 3. Political brokers linked the community organizations of the poor with pro-Estrada politicians and organizations operating at the metropolitan and national levels. While Karaos focuses on mobilization, we might extend her argument to explain the poor's support for Estrada generally as a result of being embedded in pro-Estrada political networks. This argument crumbles, however, once we adopt a comparative lens. "Explanations that focus on clientelism," Thompson (2010, 162) writes, "cannot tell us why . . . presidential candidates considered to have the best 'political machinery'"—such as Villar and the Arroyo-backed candidate Gilberto Teodoro—failed. Teehankee (2010) points out that Villar had built up an extensive political network during his time as House Speaker and president of the Senate. Teodoro, meanwhile, had access to the combined machinery of the two administration parties (Lakas-CMD and Kampi) representing 70 percent of all the governors, congressmen, and mayors across the country (150). And yet both lost soundly to candidates (Aquino and Estrada) who relied primarily on their popularity. In Estrada's case, we see organizations following popular support rather than forming it. For example, according to Karaos (2006), the poor in the National Government Center East area of Quezon City supported Estrada in 1998 despite their federation endorsing his opponent. Eventually, the federation itself came to support Estrada against the objection of the NGO that had helped organize it. While organizational ties may have played a role in mobilizing the poor, my data show that informants conceived their support for Estrada largely independently of and, in some cases despite, such ties.

Three, the urban poor support Estrada because of his screen persona as "defender of the oppressed." We have already encountered this explanation. It is not just popular among the middle class, however. A number of Philippine scholars have advanced it as well (Bautista 2001; Flores 1998; Hedman 2001; Tolentino 2010). The contention, once again, is that the urban poor recognize themselves in Estrada's screen persona.

To be sure, Estrada's screen persona increased the poor's familiarity with him and may have predisposed them to sympathize with him. It helped make him someone they felt they knew. But this is not to say that the poor support Estrada primarily because of his screen persona. His screen persona has long been superseded by his political one. At the time of fieldwork, Estrada had been a politician for forty years. He held office from 1969 until his ouster in 2001, remained in the political spotlight over the following decade, and assumed office once again in 2013. Most of his movies, meanwhile, had debuted before the average slum resident had even been born (93 percent of them came out before 1980, and the average resident is probably around thirty years old). In short, while Estrada's screen persona may be a factor in his political performance, there is good reason to doubt that it constituted the basis of his support among the poor. As my data show, informants knew Estrada and evaluated him on the basis of his political persona.

Four, the urban poor support Estrada because of his "populist style"—a manner of acting and speaking that served to invite popular identification. This style was the effect of certain tactics, notably, an antielite line and behavior that both alienated the middle class and endeared him to the poor, who saw him as unaffected and approachable (Karaos 2006). This explanation provides the most purchase on the question of Estrada's support, but it, too, falls short. It cannot tell us why the poor support Estrada and not other politicians employing similar tactics. In general, an explanation that hinges on populist tactics cannot distinguish between successful and unsuccessful cases of populism. After all, even unsuccessful populists employ the same tactics. To account for the distinctiveness of Estrada's style, we need to look beyond his tactics at their reception. We need to take into account the views of the poor rather than simply assume, as top-down approaches tend to do, that the poor automatically respond to populist appeals. A bottom-up approach enables us to identify the logic of the poor's support for Estrada.

## Estrada's Sincerity

To explain the urban poor's support for Estrada, I focus on three elements: collective expectations, expressive coherence, and social milieu.

### Collective Expectations

Estrada's conduct is received within a particular context. It derives its revelatory quality by breaching two expectations held by the urban poor. One, the poor expect to be discriminated against because of their stigma as squatters, and, two, they expect to be used by politicians for electoral gain, courted for votes and quickly forgotten. By negating one expectation, Estrada overcomes the other.

As my data show, the poor respond to a pattern of conduct distinguished by the negation of their stigma. They see Estrada as treating them with consideration and respect. This conduct would be unremarkable toward most other groups, but given the stigmatization of the urban poor, it becomes imbued with symbolic power. Acts of consideration—frequenting slums, touching and hugging the poor, eating with them—become especially significant. They convey recognition. Recognition is experienced as revelation. Regular experiences of discrimination instill feelings of shame, timidity, anxiety, and unworthiness in situations of class interaction. Acts negating that sense of stigma, therefore, extract a sense of debt and inspire feelings of affection, including love and devotion. Thus, Estrada breaches a second expectation: electoral exploitation. He is seen as caring about the poor regardless, not because, of elections. He is seen as sincere. Sincerity, in this sense, is a social product and not, as conventionally understood, an individual property. It involves the correspondence, not between an internal state and an external aspect—"between avowal and actual feeling," in the words of the literary critic Lionel Trilling (1972, 2)—but between the collective expectations of a particular audience and the leader's performance.

### Expressive Coherence

Estrada's sincerity is irreducible to certain tactics—and this is why it's so hard to simulate. His tactics are effective because they are part of a coherent performance. A performance in Goffman's sense (1959) comprises all the activity that serves to influence a given audience, including expressions given (verbally) and given off (bodily), as well as expressions directed toward the audience and those that occur unintentionally. The success of a performance, which is to say, its credibility, depends on its expressive coherence. Expressive coherence has to do with how well all the activity constituting a performance comes together to produce a distinct impression. It requires that a performance be seen as consistent and natural. Consistency implies a commitment to a particular "line" or view of things across various settings and situations and over time. Naturalness implies both ease in the part one is playing and a performance seemingly free of artifice, contrivance, or obvious exertion.

Goffman points out that performances are vulnerable to all sorts of disruptions, discrepancies, and misrepresentations that threaten to undermine their coherence. Given the difficulty of expressive control, the most credible performances are those that, having been inculcated through constant practice, come off automatically and unconsciously. Such performances reflect, Goffman (1959, 74) writes, not adherence to a script, but "command of an idiom, a command that is exercised from moment to moment with little calculation or forethought." The expressive coherence of Estrada's populist performance underwrites the effectiveness of his tactics. Arroyo employed populist tactics, too, but the effectiveness of those tactics was fatally undercut by the incoherence of her populist performance.

A focus on expressive coherence explains the distinctiveness of Estrada's appeal but not its durability. If performances are constantly subject to being undermined, then how has Estrada's populist persona withstood such grave threats to its coherence?

### Social Milieu

In *A General Theory of Magic* ([1902] 1972), Marcel Mauss makes the argument that magic "works" because everyone in a particular social milieu believes that it does. They adhere as a group to the ideas and feelings associated with magic. There is a general consensus about the reality of magic. Its efficacy is taken for granted. "The collecting together of this kind of committed group," he writes, "provides a mental atmosphere where erroneous perceptions may flourish and illusions spread like wildfire; miracles occur within this milieu as a matter of course" (132). To say that Estrada's sincerity is collectively recognized is not simply to acknowledge its recognition by a collection of individuals. It is to say, rather, that recognition is a collective phenomenon with effects that follow from its social nature. Specifically, belief in Estrada's sincerity is articulated, strengthened, and spread through social interaction within particular milieus, in this case slum areas in Manila.

Social interaction makes belief in Estrada's sincerity more definite. As Gamson (1992) found, people construct collective orientations in conversation. Estrada, being a public figure, is someone that most people feel able to talk about. The segregation of the urban poor in slum areas facilitates conversations among people occupying a similar social position. When the urban poor talk about Estrada, being similarly predisposed, they tend to corroborate one another's accounts. Social corroboration invests belief with authority. Belief grows beyond individual and household opinion and takes on the proportion of a collective representation; that is, it becomes a social fact.

Social corroboration over time makes belief in Estrada's sincerity more durable. Sincerity in politics, like artistic value, is a quality revealed in the long run. A judgment of sincerity takes time to form because expressive coherence takes time to judge, especially in contexts where people are predisposed to doubt. A performance may come undone over time as inconsistencies accumulate and undermine its coherence. Reputations, though, are made through talk over time. After a while, the persona conveyed by a coherent performance acquires durability, or a capacity to withstand expressive threats. A durable or schematic understanding of a person or object has the effect of anchoring perceptions of it. New information about that person or object is interpreted according to established understandings, and contradictory information may be discarded or discounted.[3] My informants largely accept Estrada's sincerity as a matter of fact, and this "fact" guides their interpretation of the events surrounding his ouster.

Social interaction has the effect of both diffusing and disciplining views on Estrada. Social ties convey degrees of social pressure, from pressure to conform to public opinion to the outright censure of dissent. They also convey news and stories across broader networks. The concentration of the urban poor in slum areas and the spread of these areas across the metropolis create a distinct network of slums. Mobility across this network means more extensive interaction among the urban poor and the wider spread of information about Estrada. Moreover, the clear delineation of this network presents a political opportunity, one that Estrada in particular has exploited to the fullest. He has plied the network of slums for decades and, in the course of circulating, cultivated staunch loyalty in a number of areas. In these places, his groundwork has resulted in informally organized support. What matters here is not the poor's interaction with Estrada, which, perforce, will be limited, but their interaction with one another in spatially bounded social contexts.

## The Logic of Support

On the way to one of my field sites in Quezon City, I would often pass a group of squatters camped on the strip dividing the highway. Some six or seven shelters thrown together out of plywood and canvas clustered tightly, as if marooned on the narrow island. A banner draped over one shelter pleaded: "We're victims of Ondoy. Don't let us become victims of demolition as well" (fig. 7.1). One day I decided to investigate. The squatters used to live along a nearby creek but had been flushed out by Typhoon Ondoy some months earlier. With nowhere else to live, fifty-four families relocated to the median strip, the only available land in the area. They wrote a letter to President Arroyo. She responded, instructing the Presidential Commission on the Urban Poor (PCUP) to handle their case. A number of them had already been moved to a provincial site where land had been demarcated into lots. The rest would follow after the upcoming elections, I was told, because the head

---

3. On anchoring, see Schneider (1991); Sherman, Judd, and Park (1989); and Tversky and Kahneman (1974).

**FIGURE 7.1** Victims of Tropical Storm Ondoy.
*Source*: Author, 2010.

of PCUP was running for Congress and wanted to ensure their support. (The head of PCUP, meanwhile, told me that he was waiting for the school term to end.)[4] I asked them whom they liked for president. Erap, of course. But why, I pressed; it was Arroyo who had helped them. Why not vote for the candidate she backed? To them the answer was obvious, but to me not at all.

Support for Estrada was high across all four sites, including those without pro-Estrada political organizations (table 7.1). Indeed, even some members of avowedly anti-Estrada organizations supported him. Several members of N3T, a federation of community organizations operating in San Roque, supported Estrada despite their organization's official opposition. N3T is allied with the communist movement, and its members were mobilized to attend Edsa 2. I was surprised, therefore, when N3T's treasurer defended Estrada in front of its president, who, minutes earlier, had just denounced him. In De la Rama as well, two informants felt they had to attend Edsa 2 as members of organizations that opposed Estrada, but privately they supported him. In short, orga-

4. Interview with Percival Chavez, former head of the Presidential Commission on the Urban Poor, December 7, 2009.

Table 7.1 Organizational ties and support for Estrada by field site

| Site | Ties to pro-Estrada organization? | Informants supporting Estrada |
|------|-----------------------------------|-------------------------------|
| San Roque | Yes, San Roque Community Council | 21/28 (75%) |
| Old Makati | Yes, Makati City Hall | 28/29 (97%) |
| Holy Spirit | No | 15/19 (79%) |
| De la Rama | No | 22/28 (79%) |

nizational ties appear to matter more for mobilization than for actual support.

My informants largely supported Estrada for the same reason: he was good for the poor. They cited programs bearing his name and, in San Roque, a promise he made long ago to grant them the land they were occupying. It turned out, however, that only six people had benefited personally from Estrada's programs or patronage. With so little to show for their support, why did they persist in believing that Estrada was good for them?

As I pursued the question further, my informants shifted their emphasis from Estrada being good for the poor to Estrada being a good person, someone who really cared about the poor. He was characterized as kind, compassionate, humble, approachable, and unaffected. "He doesn't act superior," Anita said. "He treats everyone equally." Informants described him as actively recognizing them. "He sees us" (*marunong tumingin*, literally, "he knows how to look [at us]"), in contrast to the "rich," who look down on the poor or pretend not to see them. This conception of Estrada, as a good person and therefore sincere, only defers the question further. Why did informants see him in this light?

In place of an explanation, informants offered accounts of Estrada's interaction with them personally or with the poor generally as evidence of his character. These stories commonly depict Estrada as someone who treats them with consideration and respect. For example, Linda, a resident of La Peral Compound, a slum colony in Makati, recounted approaching Estrada for help. What stood out for her was not just the fact that he gave it but that he did so in a way that "didn't embarrass us."

"I saw that he helped the poor a lot, and that he would help you if you really needed it. When my husband was sick, we went to Estrada's house in Greenhills. Thank God he didn't embarrass us!"

"You went to see him?" I asked.

"We went to his house."

"And he helped you?"

"Yes sir, and he didn't embarrass us. I tell you the truth. The guard let us in."

"Even if you weren't from San Juan?"

"Yes, sir. Four of us older folks. I brought with me a handful of bills. My husband was at Makati Med. He had had a stroke but we couldn't afford his medicine. Someone invited me to go with them to Estrada's house and ask for help. That's why we went. Thank God he received us. He gave us medicine and even money to commute home."

A little later in the interview she returned to the topic: "I'm not the only person Estrada helped. He helped a lot of us. That's the thing with him. You can't just approach other presidents like that because you feel uneasy. But with him you can talk about personal things. He'll even ask you, 'What's the problem, *nay* [mother]?' I mean to say that he doesn't see you as being rich or poor. He just sees you as equal. That's why I admire him. And that's why if he'll run [for president] again, he'll have my complete support. I speak the truth."

I interviewed Doreen and Beng along the built-up bank of the Pasig River. We sat on plastic chairs under a dirty tarp. The smell of sewage was overpowering. You could almost see the vapors rising from the dead river. The two older women were some of the remaining residents of Tripa de Gallena II in San Isidro, Makati. The settlement was in the process of being demolished. (It was for their own good, residents were told. The location had been classified a hazard.) As we talked, people walked by carrying their belongings in rice sacks and *bayongs* (bags woven out of palm fronds). They were piling them in an open area outside the settlement for transport to who knows where.

The women explained Estrada's appeal with respect to their everyday discrimination and political exploitation. It was in this context that his conduct stood out as exceptional. Doreen said: "You approach a rich person for help. They won't turn around. They won't acknowledge you."

"Like you're not there," I said.

"Like you're nothing."

They took turns telling me stories of being mistreated at the hands of "rich people." "Well, politicians are the same way," Doreen attested. "When they're campaigning they're always around. They come back and come back. But once they're elected *ni-hay, ni-ho!*"

"So you feel used?"

"Yeah."

"But you're saying Erap's different?"

"Erap really wants to help the poor," Beng asserted.

Doreen began, "When he speaks it's—"

"From the heart," Beng finished.

"For the *masa*," Doreen continued. "He opens himself up to us."

"But not other politicians?" I asked.

"They just pretend. Once they're in office, they don't care anymore."

"They just use you."

"Of course, because they need us. That's why they pretend."

I heard the same thing from Lilian and Tina, two women from San Roque. "The rich saw Estrada as stupid and uneducated," Lilian said. "I say that it's not education that makes you sincere [*totoong tao*, literally, a real person]. It's that a person has heart and loves his fellow man. You see, the way it is, sir—take the president now—politicians focus only on the rich. When it comes to the poor—"

"Nothing," Tina laughed bitterly.

"It's like they're ashamed of you," said Lilian.

"But Erap's different?" I ventured.

"That's the way we feel," Lilian said. "When Estrada was president, he came to visit us a lot. He gave us hope. [He said] 'While I'm president, maybe I can help make North Triangle yours.' Of course, we know that he's just one person, but he wanted to help. It's not that we idolize him."

"You mean because he used to be a movie star?"

"Oh, no, we don't see him that way. It's more important to us that his service [*paglilingkod*] is sincere."

I looked to Tina for confirmation.

"I didn't vote for Estrada," she said. "But I saw for myself. I saw that even if he were high up he would lower himself. He would bring himself down to the lowest person."

"When he visited?"

"Yes. He would reach down to the lowest person. That's why we love him and why he has so many supporters. We aren't fans. When he was a star, he had a lot of fans. But now, because of the way he serves, he has a lot of supporters."

These sentiments reveal a distinct logic of support. The significance of Estrada's conduct, which amounts to little more than treating the poor decently, lies in contravening two expectations. One, the urban poor expect to be discriminated against because of their poverty and particularly because of their status as squatters. Two, the urban poor expect to be exploited politically. They view politicians as attending to them mainly to procure electoral support and not out of any abiding commitment to their welfare. When asked about Estrada, nearly half my informants made this point, unsolicited, to distinguish him as truly exceptional. The key to Estrada's appeal lies in his strategic breaching of these two expectations. By overturning the first, he overcomes the second. By negating the poor's stigma, he is seen as less interested in politics than in helping the poor, and so his populist line is taken to be sincere.

This logic is corroborated by existing research on the political views of the Philippine poor. Surveys show that the poor regularly cite helpfulness or being pro-poor as an important quality of a good leader (Pulse Asia 2009; SWS 2001b). According to a qualitative study conducted by the Institute of Philippine Culture (2005, 81–85), the poor identify a politician as being pro-poor by attending to "his or her deeds before, during, and after elections" (in other words, not just during campaign periods). These deeds encompass more than just projects and patronage to include visibility and attentiveness, "personally and immediately responding to people's needs . . . , and patiently listening to and consulting with [them]." Politicians who treat the poor with dignity and respect are taken as truly having their interests at heart. In Schaffer's (2008, 137–38) study of election reform, he observed that many of his urban poor informants "judged candidates on their concrete acts of caring." For them, "bad politics is a politics of callousness and insult, while good politics is the politics of consideration and kindness."

Estrada's appeal, however, cannot be reduced to "acts of caring." He is not recognized as sincere just because he visits slums and attends personally to the poor. It matters whether these tactics articulate with the rest of the activity comprising his performance. Ultimately, it is the coherence of his populist performance that gives the impression of sincerity.

## Expressive Coherence

I argue for the importance of expressive coherence by way of showing what expressive incoherence looks like. The case of Arroyo illustrates that successful populist performances defy simulation. It serves to highlight the distinctiveness of Estrada's performance by contrast.

## Arroyo

In the months following Edsa 3, Gloria Arroyo vigorously courted the poor in Metro Manila. She adopted a populist persona—posing as Ate Glo (Big Sis Glo) or Gloria Labandera (Gloria the Laundress)—and employed the personalistic tactics that had distinguished Estrada. "Ate Glo now offers to fix roofs and repair street alleys, sells rice cheap, drags doctors to free clinics, and where she could, pledges to bless the poor with land and a home of their own—in time" (Mangahas 2001). Noting Arroyo's strenuous wooing of the poor, one journalist quipped: "Gloria's put on a denim jacket. She's wearing a T-shirt and eating with her hands in front of the media. If she doesn't stop trying to be like Joseph Estrada, the day after tomorrow she'll grow a mustache!" (Reyes 2001). Despite her exertions, however, Arroyo remained unpopular among the poor in Metro Manila and, over the long run, grew increasingly so (SWS 2015). Her unpopularity was certainly evident on the ground. Arroyo lavished attention and money on San Roque. She built a health center and two schoolhouses there. She also promised to grant residents the land, as Estrada had. For all her beneficence, residents described her as "plastic," or insincere. "When it burned here," Jaylyn recounted, "Gloria came to visit but no one paid her any mind."

"We knew we had to move on," Pilar said, "but our hearts remained with Erap."

Denis Murphy, director of the development nongovernmental association Urban Poor Associates, reported a similar reaction in the slum community where his organization worked.[5] "GMA [Gloria Macapagal Arroyo] has done more for the squatters in Baseco than any other president, but they haven't warmed to her. . . . In our survey, Erap won three to one. He's never even visited!" Why did the poor resist Arroyo's populist overtures?

In her early years, Arroyo's unpopularity was attributed to a "charisma deficit" (Coronel 2003). Observers pointed to a number of contingent factors, including her lack of empathy, a dour demeanor, and her thinly veiled political maneuvering. (The malfeasance that would sully her reputation irremediably had not yet become a factor.) Understanding sincerity as attributed on the basis of a performance enables us to conceive the problem more systematically, that is, in terms of expressive incoherence. Allow me to sketch an explanation along this line.

5. Interviewed December 3, 2009.

One, Arroyo's performance appeared contrived and unnatural. There was a discrepancy between the populist persona she assumed and her "personality" as perceived by the urban poor. The persona came to be seen as merely a mask worn to suit ulterior (electoral) purposes. In Baseco, Denis Murphy observed her manner undermine her patronage: "She proclaimed land and housing for eight hundred people, but she wouldn't stop to talk and say hi. She had on a sour face." Given her unnaturalness in the role of woman of the people, her efforts to push a populist line seemed disingenuous. In San Roque, Renato and his two companions remembered Arroyo being ill at ease during her visit. They noticed how little she interacted with residents and how well guarded she was the whole time. They took issue with the fact that she didn't actually enter the slum. She didn't make her way into the interior but merely skirted its periphery.

"Gloria came by here but didn't enter," said one of Renato's companions.

"Gloria was too scared to enter," agreed the other.

"She was scared to enter even with a whole battalion of soldiers and police deployed all around her," Renato said.

"Not like Erap."

"He came without a bodyguard."

"Without even a bodyguard?" I asked, surprised.

"Well, there was an escort vehicle," Renato clarified, "but not so many police like with Gloria."

"She didn't even enter," his companion said.

"She didn't *enter* enter," Renato said, "but she did get on a stage [set up at the edge of San Roque]."

"So many soldiers. Even up in the trees."

"She didn't even want to take the stage," said the other companion. "She was so scared."

"Of what? A sniper?" I joked.

"Yeah, something like that," Renato said. "That's why there was a whole battalion."

"This was the time it burned here," his companion recalled.

"It burned here and she came to visit but stayed right over there by Philippine Science [the high school]. She didn't really enter."

"Well, what did she say?" I asked.

"I don't know. She just looked around at the burned structures."

The men discussed the uptick in the number of fires in San Roque recently. They speculated that the fires were being started deliberately.

"Did Gloria start them?" my research assistant joked.

"No," said one companion, smiling.

"Nah," said the other, smiling.

"I don't know," Renato said. "We're all Erap supporters here, after all."

We burst out laughing.

Arroyo's performance also suffered from inconsistency, across various settings and situations and over time. Her populist persona was not sustained. Over the course of little more than a year, it was succeeded by other personas: reformer, modernizer, and herald of a "strong republic," taking a hard line against crime and corruption and serving as America's zealous ally in the war on terror. These personas catered to other audiences. Moreover, the timing of her attentions was suspect. She issued land proclamations primarily in the run-up to elections. Around 75 percent of all the proclamations made in 2004, for example, were issued in time for elections in May (Wehrmann and Antonio 2011). Such maneuvering was not lost on the urban poor—indeed, they had come to expect it—and it contributed to their impression of Arroyo's populist performance as politically motivated at bottom.

The coherence of her populist performance was undermined for good by the events surrounding her election in 2004. In late 2002, amid dismal poll numbers, she vowed not to run for president after finishing Estrada's term. The declaration, as loud and clear a disavowal of politics as any, redounded to her credit. The tactical nature of this move was revealed, to her lasting discredit, when she entered the race nine months later. She won the election but was discovered to have meddled with the results. She apologized on TV for her indiscretion, and it is this apology that informants kept bringing up when we talked about Arroyo. They would mimic her nasal delivery of the words "I'm sorry" with palpable disdain. What upset them was the emptiness of the words, their sheer inadequacy compared to her violation. For them, her puny apology had become emblematic of a populist performance rendered incoherent to the point of irony. Because they were convinced that she cared nothing for them, they failed to recognize everything she had done. Evelyn, for example, wrote off Arroyo's visit to San Roque as compelled and her construction of a schoolhouse as having come to naught.

"It's like she doesn't care about us," Evelyn said.

"Doesn't care?"

"Not one bit from what we've seen."

"But she did visit," I pointed out.

"She did but only because of our bishop. The bishop kept asking her to visit, but she was scared to because of what people here might do to her. This is Erap City, after all."

"Erap City?"

"Yeah. Gloria knew that people here are pro-Erap. It wasn't until the bishop assured her that she would be taken good care of that she agreed to come. He talked with all the leaders here, and they promised to give her a chance. It was also our chance to show her what conditions here were like and what *we* were like—I'm sure not at all the way she imagined."

"Did her visit lead to anything?"

"Well, yes. She had a schoolhouse built over there." She pointed in its direction. "Isn't that right, Manang Laring?" The old woman nodded. "But with our barangay being so corrupt, the money for it ran out after three years."[6]

### Estrada

A few months before the presidential elections in 2010, I accompanied Estrada along with a number of other politicians running under his party on a campaign sortie through four towns in the Laguna and Batangas provinces south of Metro Manila.[7] We traveled by tour bus and van along the highway. Upon arriving at one of our stops, Estrada and the other politicians would transfer to the back of a pickup truck outfitted with speakers that would then process through the town's main road. From the back, the politicians would wave and distribute campaign paraphernalia while the speakers blasted pop tunes rewritten as campaign jingles. Occasionally the truck would stop and the politicians would take turns addressing the crowd. They also made formal presentations at a resort, town hall, and public square. In these presentations, the comedian Marissa Sanchez would warm up the audience by telling jokes and leading chants: *Erap pa rin! Erap pa rin!* (Still Erap! Still Erap!). She would sing and get the politicians to dance with her on the stage. This was followed by a number of speeches delivered according

---

6. We might surmise that gender played a role in Arroyo's inability to carry off a populist performance. I cannot discount it, but in specifying its role we should recall that another woman, Corazon Aquino, was able to play the populist successfully. She was another president beloved by the poor for her sincerity. Furthermore, among my informants, both women and men overwhelmingly supported Estrada. In fact, a greater proportion of women supported him than men: 88 percent compared to 74 percent. Of course, it may be claimed that a gendered conception of leadership operating on a cultural level (a valorization of the macho leader, say) influences both men and women equally. This may be true, but given its operation at such a high level of determination, it is hard to show with my data—it did not appear to figure in informants' accounts of Arroyo's illegitimacy—and thus may require a different approach to uncover.

7. A slideshow consisting of pictures and video clips of the events discussed in this section can be viewed at http://www.patchworkcityarchive.com.

**FIGURE 7.2** A woman laying hands on Estrada, much as one would on a religious icon. *Source*: Author, 2010.

to political pecking order: town mayor, provincial governor, one or two congressional candidates, the vice presidential candidate, and, finally, after about three interminable hours, Estrada himself. His script was more or less the same each time. He would thank the *masa* profusely for their continued support, he would take shots at Arroyo and Villar, and he would plead for the *masa*'s help in the upcoming elections. He never spoke for very long or grew particularly animated. He told a few jokes and twice joined in a duet with the emcee. His performance was self-assured, certainly, but not especially exciting. It seemed incommensurate to the adulation he received from the crowd; the enthusiastic cheering and loud applause, the grasping to lay hands on him or on one of the slight things—calendars, caps, posters, bracelets—he threw at them, the look of enchantment on their faces (fig. 7.2).

I also observed the campaign rallies of two of other presidential candidates, Noynoy Aquino and Gilberto Teodoro. As productions, these were far more spectacular. They were much larger in scale—one took place in an open field and the other in a stadium—and enhanced by effects: fireworks, showers of confetti and balloons at key moments, and towering, deafening sound systems. The entertainment routines were more elaborate and polished and starred celebrities at the height of their popularity. The candidates spoke with greater energy and urgency. Of course, the difference may come down to these being different types of events, a sortie versus a rally, or it may speak to the Estrada campaign's relative lack of funding. My point is simply that, for a politician ascribed a kind of magical power over the poor, Estrada in the flesh and in action came off as disappointingly ordinary. I was looking for the dramatic gestures said to distinguish charismatic leadership: Gaitan's frenzied oratory, Evita's high-flown declarations of love, Bucaram's taboo-smashing stunts. I had waited the whole day, watching intently for something to seize upon, some clue to Estrada's hold over the poor.

Something did happen, which, while hardly spectacular, yielded the glimmer of an insight. It happened at the end of the day, after all the formal events had been concluded, and we were on our way back to Manila. The entourage stopped for dinner at a fancy Chinese restaurant. After dinner, Estrada walked out of the restaurant to find that a small crowd had gathered to greet him. There were about ten to fifteen people; from the look of it, sidewalk vendors and street children. They had probably seen the vehicles plastered with Estrada's face parked outside the restaurant and had come out of curiosity. They would never enter the restaurant, of course—they would never be allowed inside—and so they simply waited outside to see. Out he came. They started chanting *Erap pa rin, Erap pa rin,* but shyly, circumspectly, perhaps out of fear that their sudden presence would be seen as intrusive. One or two of the braver ones called out more loudly "Idol!"[8] Without the slightest hesitation or change of aspect, Estrada walked into the crowd, took their hands, and thanked them for their support. He gestured to an aide who knew enough to board the tour bus and retrieve campaign paraphernalia, which Estrada then distributed before disappearing into the bus. The scene lasted no more than two or three minutes, and, on the face of it, nothing happened. Estrada had certainly not done anything out of the ordinary. He probably did nothing that his presidential rivals, finding themselves in similar circumstances, would not also have done. And yet it was clear from the beaming faces of the crowd that, from their perspective, something extraordinary had happened.

What struck me was how naturally he carried himself. He did not pretend that he was not tired, a seventy-three-year old man who had spent the previous fourteen hours campaigning, or act any differently than a moment before when dining among his friends. I came to understand much later that the poor took his familiarity for acceptance.

8. *Idol* is Filipino slang for "person I look up to."

"Erap will accept you no matter how filthy you are," Sandra told me. "Other politicians will take your hand but afterwards they will wash theirs with alcohol." Having come to expect discrimination, they regarded Estrada's acceptance of them as nothing short of extraordinary. His appeal did not derive, as I had thought, from a set of tactics that he alone deployed. This was a power that the poor attributed to him. Their recognition constituted his authority over them.

Acts of consideration like the one I had observed were evaluated not in isolation but in the context of a coherent performance. Such acts had been rendered consistently over the course of a long political career. This consistency conveyed Estrada's commitment to the poor more effectively than any declaration or gift. In the eyes of the poor, Estrada was never not Erap. His consistency stemmed from the simplicity of his political persona. His performance had a one-note quality encapsulated by his campaign slogan—"Erap is for the poor"—but it was a note he sounded repeatedly. His undistinguished speeches were not self-contained but echoed a line that had come to distinguish him over the course of his forty years in politics, and thus they resonated with his audience. He had sounded this line even before becoming mayor of San Juan in 1969. The movie star Joseph Estrada justified his entry into politics as a way of paying back a debt of gratitude to the *masa*, the main audience of Tagalog movies. "I know who put me where I am now," he told the writer Nick Joaquin (1977). "The *bakya* crowd. . . . It's time for me to repay them for what they have done for me and I can only repay them by serving them" (18).[9] In the years following, Estrada not only articulated this line repeatedly; he enacted it with an apparent indifference to municipal boundaries and election periods. My informants in San Roque claimed that Estrada had groceries delivered to their community every year on his birthday, and that he had been doing this since his time as mayor of San Juan in the 1970s and 1980s and had continued doing so even after his ouster in 2001. I don't know if this is true, but what matters is the perception that his help, because of its consistency, simply reflected his goodness and had nothing to do with politics.

## A Mental Atmosphere

While I was in the field, I showed informants Estrada's mug shot to elicit aspects of their support that my questions had failed to bring

---

9. The *masa*. *Bakya* is a wooden clog associated with the lower class.

out. Seeing the photograph triggered an outpouring of emotion among many informants. Some reached out to caress the photograph; some asked if they could keep it; some, suddenly angry, decried the treatment of Estrada; a handful wept; one woman remembered, with evident solicitude, that at the time of the photograph, Estrada had been down with a cold. I showed the picture to Nerissa, a resident of the De la Rama settlement in Parañaque. "Goose bumps," she said.

"Ma'am?"

"Goose bumps. Look, look!"

She raised her arms, and indeed, they were impossible to miss: dozens of tiny, well-defined bumps on both arms. She insisted that I feel them, and so I ran my fingers along the ridges.

When I showed the picture to Sandra, who ran a rice stall along Samonte Street in Holy Spirit, she began to cry. "I remember this," she said, sobbing. We sat behind several trays containing different grains of rice. When a customer approached the stall, I thought that I had better explain to her that it wasn't me who had made the rice vendor cry. I showed her the picture. She simply nodded, as if the image explained the matter, and proceeded to fill a bag with rice from one of the trays. She put money on the table and left. By this time, Sandra had recovered somewhat. "It's because he's made out to be a criminal," she said.

Upon seeing the picture, Laverne clapped her hands and exclaimed, "Oh, I'm so happy!" She told me that she had once seen Estrada give a speech in Tondo. She had been feeling ill at the time and hadn't planned to go, but her friend dragged her to the event. When Estrada took the stage, she began to shriek with excitement. Her friend looked at her and said, dryly, I imagine: "You must be feeling better."

"And it's true," Laverne admitted. "Estrada makes me happy."

As these reactions suggest, support for Estrada involves more than simply an assent to his leadership; his supporters feel bound to him personally. Many of them expressed feelings akin to religious devotion. Although I featured individual reactions, I don't think that people feel this way independently of one another. I make the case here that this devotion is a product of the particular mental atmosphere of many slum areas in Manila.

When I spoke with informants in groups, they tended to echo one another's feelings about Estrada. They responded to their neighbors' accounts of Estrada's sincerity by affirming them and reciting their own accounts. The effect of such corroboration was to make belief in Estrada's sincerity a social fact. By invoking it, informants affirmed their solidarity as Estrada supporters.

I was visiting Wilma in a slum area along Zuzuarregui Street. She had prepared a meal for me (noodles and Coca-Cola). When she brought out the food, I joked that we should invite Estrada to join us. Wilma's friend Annie, struck by the idea, interjected:

*"Hoy, hoy, hoy,* Erap used his hands. He just washed them, not with soap, just with water. Then he ate with his hands. I saw him do it in Lucban."

"I saw him do the same thing in Romblon," Wilma said excitedly. "He just washed with water."

"It was seafood, and there was fresh fish. That's why he used his hands."

"He crushed the tomato like this"—Wilma pretended to squeeze a tomato with her fingers—"and put it all over the fish."

"Like this?" I asked, squeezing my own imaginary tomato.

"Yes!"

"He really ate with his hands," Annie continued. "It's true. That's why I love him! My neighbors laughed at me. 'What happened to your eyes?' [they asked]. It's because I felt sorry for Erap. They kicked him out of Malacañang. When I watched it on TV, I had to have a towel with me. I cried and cried."

"Me, too," Wilma said dolefully. "All of us in Romblon."

Annie and Wilma observed Estrada eat separately. They watched his ouster separately. By sharing accounts, however, something happens. Their feelings build up: something as mundane as Estrada eating with his hands had made an impression on someone else; Estrada's ouster made another person feel just as despondent. The discovery that their feelings extend beyond themselves and are widely shared solidifies their adherence to a particular perception of Estrada. This perception, being corroborated, becomes more real for them; that is, it appears objective. This type of interaction multiplied many times over forges a common sense about Estrada. His love for the poor comes to be taken for granted. While visiting Annie and Wilma, for instance, I met a man with a goiter, his neck swollen to the size of a melon. The man insisted that I take a picture of his face and deliver it to Estrada. He was absolutely certain that Estrada, once made aware of his condition, would help him—that, in the thick of a presidential campaign, with only a picture and the name of a slum, Estrada would find the man and help him.

Some people dissented from the "public opinion," of course. Of the 104 people I interviewed, nine did not support Estrada, and another nine claimed not to bother with politics or felt unqualified to give an opinion. Of those who did not support him, some never liked Estrada, seeing him as having been unfit to become president in the first place. Others had grown disenchanted with him. They were persuaded by the verdict against him—that, indeed, he had received illegal kickbacks. In either case, the conclusion was the same: Estrada was using the poor just like other politicians. "Look, I'm poor," Jonathan said. "But I saw that what he did was wrong. The money he took from *jueteng*, it didn't come from the government. It came from the poor."

"They proved in court that he was corrupt," Manuel reasoned, "and so the people who ousted him were right." Whether because of ouster, arrest, or conviction, whatever authority Estrada once commanded had evaporated. He was no longer exceptional, the real thing among fakes, but just another politician. Jonathan, Manuel, and other dissenters saw Estrada in the same light the middle class saw him: as corrupt and rightly deposed. This was how the media largely portrayed him. What is remarkable, then, is just how few informants saw him in this way.

We can explain this disproportion with respect to the collective nature of belief. Slum residents faced social pressure to recognize the "fact" of Estrada's sincerity. They could dissent but not always without repercussions. For example, I was interviewing Noel and his boyfriend Gem in San Roque. We were seated on stools along one side of a common area. A man passing by overheard Noel describe Estrada as corrupt. The man, visibly upset, interrupted our conversation.

"Prove it! Prove it!" he demanded.

"Stop," Noel said.

"Prove it! Prove it!"

We tried to ignore him and continue with the interview, but he remained standing over us.

"Prove it! Can you prove that Estrada stole? You're an idiot!"

"Erap stole!" Noel exploded. "There's a case against him!"

"Not anymore," Gem said quietly. It had come out in the interview that the couple disagreed on Estrada. Noel looked crestfallen.

"It's because you're crazy," the passerby said. "Crazy!" He turned to me. "Don't listen to him. He's crazy. Ask anyone around here." He turned around abruptly and walked away.

I tried to pick up where he left off, but before I could, the stranger, unable to help himself, came back.

"Don't listen to that guy! You won't get anything from him. Don't hang around this mental case." To Noel he yelled, as if shooing away a dog, "Hoy!"

Another passerby, attracted by the fuss, intervened. "You're not the one being interviewed," she reprimanded the man. "It's those two."

The man walked away. The woman muttered something under her breath and also left.

The man came back yet again. "Erap was the best president we've ever had," he said. "That's who I'm voting for."

"If he's so great, why was he put in jail?" Noel retorted.

The man snorted and walked away, for good this time.

"If he was so great," Noel repeated meekly, "he shouldn't have been put in jail, right?"

In the slum areas where I did research, believing in Estrada's sincerity and not believing in it were not equally likely to be adopted as beliefs for the simple reason that the two beliefs were unequally appraised; one carried authority or collective weight, while the other, as a result, invited incomprehension, disapproval, and, as we just saw, censure.

The "fact" of Estrada's sincerity anchored informants' perceptions of the events surrounding his ouster. They interpreted the allegations of corruption against Estrada not as undermining his populist persona but as malicious attacks directed against him because of his populism— and hence all the more reason to close ranks. The charges were fabricated or flimsy, they claimed. So he took money from *jueteng* operators. What's the big deal? There are lots of corrupt politicians. Why single out Estrada? He was targeted, they maintained, because he focused on the poor or because he lacked education, English fluency, and social polish. He was betrayed by his friends and political allies. In Marietta's reckoning: "They said he was a drunk. We don't see it. They said he was incompetent and that he lacked education. That's why they took over. They said a lot of things but we don't believe them. Whatever they say he is, it doesn't matter." Belief in Estrada's sincerity, having become durable, dictated how his supporters handled threats to the coherence of his populist persona. They actively parried them.

Consequently, informants interpreted Estrada's ouster in a way that contrasted sharply with the dominant account. Some informants saw his ouster as voluntary, even heroic. "That's why I got goose bumps," Nerissa explained. "I saw it on TV. [Estrada said,] 'I'll step down; just don't hurt these people.' He sacrificed himself because he didn't want to see people get hurt." Others found Estrada's ouster utterly incomprehensible and cast around for reasons to explain it.

"I just don't understand it," Geraldo said.

"Maybe the people who ousted Estrada think differently from you," I suggested.

"Maybe. I've also heard that they were paid [to attend Edsa 2]."

"Paid?"

"Oh, yeah. They were paid to attend."

"You're talking about Edsa 2?" I clarified. I thought that perhaps he was referring to Edsa 3, the demonstration following Estrada's arrest. The media widely portrayed these demonstrators as transported and paid.

"Of course!"

## The Politics of Recognition

If Estrada's appeal were reduced to the deployment of standard populist tactics, then it would be hard to distinguish him from other politicians employing similar tactics. I have argued that the poor appraise populist tactics to see whether they are substantiated by a genuine disposition toward them. What they actually respond to is the successful performance of sincerity. To the poor, Estrada's conduct is distinguished by the negation of their stigma; hence, he is seen as someone who cares about them beyond electoral considerations. His conduct resonates because it is taken as part of a coherent performance. The poor perceive him as treating them with consideration and respect not just during election season but consistently and "naturally," as an expression of a deeply held disposition favoring them. Moreover, belief in Estrada's sincerity is collectively held. It is articulated, strengthened, and spread through social interaction such that it becomes a property of particular social milieus—in this case, slum areas in Metro Manila. The inhabitants of these milieus tend to take Estrada's sincerity for granted. This belief anchors their perception of him, and they actively parry threats to it. Nonbelievers or holdouts, meanwhile, face social pressure to conform to "public opinion."

Sincerity is a political logic that obtains within a particular relationship, that between Estrada and the poor in Metro Manila. Outside Manila, sincerity is probably less important than traditionally dominant logics such as regionalism and clientelism. Estrada's alliances with political dynasties better explain why he carried regions such as Palawan and Cagayan in 2010. His prosecution of an "all-out war" against Islamic insurgents during his presidency better accounts for his support among Christians in Mindanao. It is in Metro Manila, where class relations are most intense, that perceptions of Estrada's sincerity clearly mattered.

In this context, we might speak of a politics of recognition among the urban poor. On the one hand, the urban poor have become more demanding of equal treatment; on the other hand, they face greater discrimination than ever as squatters. The result is a contradiction keenly felt between the gospel of democracy and the reality of social inequality. For example, I interviewed three taxi drivers along an alleyway somewhere deep inside San Roque. There were no plastic stools around, so we simply squatted on the ground to talk. Ruel told us about a difficult passenger.

"I had this one passenger—I knew she was rich by the way she dressed—who wanted to be dropped off at a spot where you couldn't stop. I said, 'Ma'am, I can't do that. If they catch me, it's a 750 peso fine.' She said, 'That's why I'm taking a taxi, so that I don't have to walk.' She just kept on insisting. Anyway, I dropped her off at the spot where you're supposed to drop people off. She got mad and said, 'Do you know who you're talking to?'"

The other drivers groaned. They had all been accosted with the line before.

"I said, 'Ma'am, you haven't introduced yourself. So how would I know who you are?'"

We laughed.

"She cursed at me, 'You have no education!'"

"How rude," said Eddie, one of the other drivers.

"I said, 'Ma'am, I know that you're educated, but use it to do the right thing.' I said, 'I may not have a lot of education, but I'm following the law.' She just slammed the door."

"You turned it around," Eddie said admiringly.

"You were in the right," I added.

"Yeah, well, I'm still the one who loses out," Ruel said ruefully.

Ruel had a strong enough sense of equality to tweak his passenger's assertion of social hierarchy. This sense of equality does not simply result from democratic institutions being in place and from the poor having an equal right to vote. It is learned from the experience of being treated with relative equality in some class relationships. Ruel, for example, followed his story of discrimination with one of egalitarian treatment. "Not all rich people are like that," he said about his haughty passenger. "I used to work as a family driver and I had this one boss who didn't care about my place in society. If he saw something wrong with you, he'd tell you. But he'd also ask you to tell him if you saw something wrong with him. He was a good guy, real sincere." As I argued in chapter 5, these "exceptions" provide a model of moral behavior. They enable the poor both to indict bad behavior and to recognize good behavior. As we've seen in this chapter, the poor don't just evaluate their employers in this way but political leaders as well.

In the case of Estrada, the link between feeling recognized and being represented is clear. Upon receiving news of Estrada's impending arrest, Myrna spent a week sleeping on the sidewalk outside his house. She wanted to be there to "protect" him. I asked her why he meant so much to her. "We gained a voice when he became president," she said. "He listened to the complaints of us small people. He listened." Analytically, we might distinguish between two moments: "He listened to us" and "We gained a voice." Informants felt that Estrada recognized them in a way that alleviated their feeling of oppression and affirmed their sense of dignity. They responded by recognizing his authority over them—which is to say, of course, that they endowed him with that very authority. It is at this moment that Estrada came to be seen as representing them.

I want to be clear about what a politics of recognition is doing in this case. It is obviously not improving the urban poor's material lot. Rather, its power lies in its affirming their worth as human beings. It must be understood, therefore, against the backdrop of widespread and increasingly insufferable discrimination. Recognition succeeds in annulling the stigma if not the reality of poverty. While this cannot be enough, it is clearly something. Too many observers make nothing of it. They evaluate Estrada's populism using only a material yardstick and, on this basis, inevitably conclude that the poor had been fooled. This assessment misses what for many informants was the most important thing. Recognition is socially transformative. With Estrada's election in 1998, informants described being momentarily elevated. With his ouster, Salvador recalls, "we went back to being poor."

# EIGHT

# Dissensus

I saw Edsa 3 myself, although, at the time, I didn't realize what I was seeing. We emerged from the Shangri-La Plaza in Ortigas in the early afternoon on Tuesday, May 1, 2001. My date and I had caught a matinee of the latest Keanu Reeves movie. There, in front of us, a scattering of people looking exhausted were marching down Epifanio de los Santos Avenue. I thought at first that it was a workers' rally given the date, Labor Day in the Philippines. Checking my phone, I found a series of uninspected text messages and missed calls. My aunt wanted me home immediately. The "rally" had turned violent, she texted. The demonstrators had attacked Malacañang, the presidential palace. *Could this be them?* I wondered, incredulous. I had thought the demonstration was over. That's why I went out on a Tuesday, because I had stayed in the whole weekend on account of Edsa 3.

When people first started gathering around the shrine following Estrada's arrest on April 25 (the previous Wednesday), my uncle dismissed the demonstrators as *hakot*, that is, as "pulled" by pro-Estrada politicians—transported to the shrine, fed, and paid. "Just look at them!" he said, referring to how "ugly" they were, how poor. These people were clearly bought, or worse, they were fanatics. After the fourth or fifth day of the demonstration (we didn't know what to call it yet), insouciance turned into alarm. Net 25, the official channel of the Iglesia ni Cristo (INC), a religious group supporting Estrada, showed a massive crowd. It took the camera several seconds just to pan its breadth.

"Camera trick," my uncle groused. By Monday, alarm gave way to relief. The government announced that a deal had been brokered with the INC and El Shaddai, two religious groups supporting Estrada. They had agreed to pull out their people. The newspapers had hailed the end of Edsa 3. Then what was it I was seeing?

On the bus ride home, the scale of the emergency became clear: there was smoke on the horizon, military vehicles on the road, and more demonstrators making their way in desultory fashion toward various destinations. Years later, pursuing the topic as a graduate student, I came to realize not only what I had seen but also how much I had missed.

In this chapter, I show the two Edsa 3s, one in the minds of Manila's middle class and one in the minds of the urban poor, the former a product of political manipulation and the latter an expression of people power. The two sides mobilized different facts in support of their respective interpretations. The middle class pointed to demonstrators bused in and paid, their destructive behavior, and the coup plot hatched on their backs. The urban poor pointed to the sheer number of people gathered around the Edsa shrine, their participation despite personal cost and risk, and the sense of *communitas* among them. While the two sets of facts are not mutually exclusive, each party attends to only one set in their depiction of Edsa 3, and thus we end up with incommensurable objects.

It's clear that the two Edsa 3s follow from the middle class and urban poor's different views of Estrada. The middle class saw Estrada as corrupt and incompetent. They couldn't imagine why anyone would turn out to support him of their own accord. Clearly, the Edsa 3 demonstrators were paid or bound by clientelist obligation or else simply duped. The urban poor saw Estrada as someone who genuinely cared about the poor. His ouster may have been unjust, but his arrest was intolerable. Clearly, people took to the streets out of a real sense of grievance.

Edsa 3 describes a situation of dissensus. Remember, the parties in dissensus disagree on the nature of an object, here Edsa 3. Remember, too, that for Rancière dissensus represents politics in action. It involves dominant and excluded segments of society in contention. It interrupts consensus or a social order where the will of the one segment normally prevails while the voice of the other is muted or discounted. The interruption is politically significant because it makes the excluded group visible (and audible) as political actors. It shows them capable of "speech," that is, of making claims on society as a group. The aim of the chapter is to keep the urban poor's claims in view, to keep these claims from being swallowed up by various efforts to reinstate consensus, whether spatial, political, or historiographical.

I proceed by juxtaposing the two Edsa 3s. I narrate the dominant account based primarily on coverage of the event in the *Philippine Daily Inquirer*.[1] I narrate the subaltern account based on the testimony of organizers and urban poor participants.[2] To be clear, juxtaposition is not a means of "correction"—of balancing the perspective of Edsa 3's opponents with that of its exponents—in an effort to get at the whole truth. The point is to show that the truth is not unitary, that there are two truths at stake, and that by keeping both in view (mindful, of course, that one is at greater risk of occlusion than the other) we are better able to grasp the landscape of contention.

## The Dominant Account

With the prospect of Estrada's arrest looming, partisans began to hype the idea of an Edsa 3. By mid-April, hundreds of urban poor supporters had gathered outside the gates of his subdivision. The notion of an Edsa 3, nevertheless, struck the *Inquirer*'s editorial board as absurd: "The opposition would have us believe that the masses would rise up to protect the arrest of a deposed president against whom an overwhelming amount of evidence of graft and plunder was presented during the Senate impeachment trial. . . . Do [they] think so low of [them]?"[3] By April 25, the crowd, now inside the subdivision, had grown to ten thousand people. It had entered North Greenhills and surrounded Estrada's compound. Following Estrada's arrest, the protestors transferred to Crame, the military camp where he was being held. They found their pathway blocked by police barricades, however, and diverted to the Edsa shrine. Notably, they had not planned to stage another Edsa—that is, a demonstration in the mold of Edsa 1 (ousting Marcos) or Edsa 2 (ousting Estrada). "Why should we?" an organizer with the People's

---

1. The *Inquirer* is the country's most widely read newspaper, as well as the one preferred by the middle and upper classes in major urban areas (see "Inquirer Top Choice of ABC1 Readers," *Philippine Daily Inquirer*, May 11, 2015). I also consulted the *Philippine Star*, another popular broadsheet, and drew on existing accounts, particularly *Inquirer* journalist Amando Doronila's chronicle of Edsa 3 in the last chapter of *The Fall of Joseph Estrada* (2001). Finally, I reviewed about an hour of television footage of the march on Malacañang acquired from the ABS-CBN network.

2. Of my informants, 49 of 104 participated in Edsa 3.

3. "Erap's Arrest," *Philippine Daily Inquirer*, April 17, 2001.

Movement against Poverty asked journalist Glenda Gloria (2015) in 2001. "That's not our Edsa."

The number of demonstrators massed around the Edsa shrine grew exponentially. It reached three hundred thousand by April 29. Over the course of its seven days (April 25–May 1), the *Inquirer* estimates that Edsa 3 involved around 1.5 million people.[4] In comparison, Edsa 2 probably involved fewer than one million. On its first day alone, according to de Quiros, it was already as big as Edsa 2.[5] Although mainly comprising the urban poor, the demonstration was significantly enhanced by the addition of members from two religious organizations that supported Estrada, the Filipino Christian church Iglesia ni Cristo and the Catholic charismatic sect El Shaddai. Each group commanded several million followers across the country. The members of these two groups, in the *Inquirer*'s account, comprised the "backbone" of the demonstration.

Edsa 3 was denounced from the start as "a parody and mockery of Edsa."[6] The *Inquirer* balked at even referring to it as Edsa 3. The demonstrators were largely discounted as *hakot*. The word means to load or carry, but in this context it meant that the demonstrators were brought by politicians to swell the crowd. They were "collected, delivered, fed, and paid" (Doronila 2001a, 222). A columnist for the *Star* dismissed them as a "rent-a-crowd."[7] Reporters cited the procession of buses depositing people around the shrine, the distribution of rice meals in Styrofoam boxes, the discovery of coupons redeemable for cash along Epifanio de los Santos Avenue, and, later, reports of politicians disbursing money to urban poor organizers. The quality of the demonstrators was also disparaged. They were described in editorials and op-eds as "hooligans," "vandals," and "thugs," as "rabid," "an unthinking throng," and "blind Erap fanatics." Widely circulated text messages deriding them were published as front-page news.[8] A few samples of these:

Let's go to Edsa and protest. Please wear shorts, undershirt and slippers, bring a fan, knife, iron pipe, ice pick and rocks. Don't bring money. There will be money.

---

4. Carlito Pablo and Dave Veridiano, "AFP Ready to Crush Erap Coup," *Philippine Daily Inquirer*, May 1, 2001.

5. Conrado de Quiros, "Again, the 'Dumb' Masa," *Philippine Daily Inquirer*, April 30, 2001.

6. "Parody of People Power," *Philippine Daily Inquirer*, April 28, 2001.

7. "Is It 'Poor People Power,' EDSA Tres, or Just Plain Hakot Power?" *Philippine Star*, April 27, 2001.

8. J. F. Caneday and F. Gallardo, "Text Wars, Erap Jokes are Back," *Philippine Daily Inquirer*, April 29, 2001.

Calling all the unwashed and ignorant, the toothless and unclothed, let's prove we have no brains—go to Edsa.

You can now shop, carry lots of cash, drive alone even in dark areas, holduppers etc. are busy at Edsa.

To be sure, not everyone bought the *hakot* narrative completely. The columnists Conrado de Quiros and Dean Bocobo stand out for being reflective, rather than defensive, in the midst of the event. Bocobo went to investigate for himself:

For some reason, I could not sleep on Friday night, so I ventured out into the crowd at 2:30 a.m., by which time most *hakot* mercenaries must have left. There seemed to be at least as many sincere people there as at the height of last January's rave parties [i.e., Edsa 2], though with a decidedly different taste in politics as entertainment. It seemed to me many really wanted to be there, not because they are *tarantado* [foolish] or *mangmang* [ignorant] or *bayaran* [paid], which they are uncharitably being called in text, e-mail, and full page ads by the perfumed crowd. Maybe, the text jokes are just nervousness over the unexpected turn of events, a whistling in the digital dark, reflecting an innate fear of a mob to which one does not belong.[9]

Early into the demonstration, particularly April 26–28, reporting focused on the "desecration" of the Edsa shrine. *Desecrated, profaned*—these were the words Catholic Church officials used to describe the shrine's occupation. Demonstrators had taken down "the flag of the Holy See [replacing it with a pro-Estrada banner], clambered up the bronze statue of the Virgin Mary, spray-painted the walls, and dumped trash on a marker for People Power II."[10] The rector of the shrine pleaded with them to leave, but to no avail.[11] "This is private property," he told them, insinuating, perhaps, his view of them as squatters. "Check City Hall and you'll see this has a land title." De Quiros remarked on "the long row of women washing clothes" on one side of the highway, with the clothes then "strung up in various parts of the shrine." It was like "a bizarre parody of a bucolic scene of women by the *batis* [stream]." "If Edsa wouldn't come to Payatas [a dump site and slum area]," he mused,

9. Dean Jorge Bocobo, "Common Ground," *Philippine Daily Inquirer*, April 30, 2001.

10. Christian Esguerra, Gerald G. Lacuarta, Carlito Pablo, and Christine Avendaño, "Protestors Accused of Vandalism," *Philippine Daily Inquirer*, April 27, 2001.

11. Blanche Rivera and Christian Esguerra, "Edsa Reclaimed by Edsa II Forces," *Philippine Daily Inquirer*, May 2, 2001.

"Payatas would come to Edsa."[12] Another columnist made use of the same trope, the shrine being transformed into a slum, to underscore its abasement: "There was evidence that some families had taken to living on the roof of the shrine throughout the five days that the pro-Erap forces "occupied" it. There were makeshift tents and folding beds, as well as soggy lengths of cardboard that had apparently been used as mattresses. And what did they use as bathrooms? Noli [a member of the cleanup crew] found a shabby lean-to, fashioned from cartons set against the fiberglass roof, and beneath it human waste. The folks had literally been shitting at Our Lady's feet."[13] The amount of trash collected on Saturday, April 28, made the front page: five truckloads before noon.[14] The article depicted the scene with relish: "Humans—and human waste—are scattered on the pavement. The air is vivid with the stench and spill of urine and phlegm. Mats and folding beds abound. Litter is everywhere. . . . Passersby who checked out the protest action had to fight from throwing up at the sight of the trash and the human waste, which were already drying in the heat. Empty water bottles, banana peels, corn cobs, barbecue sticks, plastic bags and other food refuse littered the area."

The major TV stations ignored the demonstration at first. They claimed that the demonstrators were chasing their TV crews away. The reporters that were there had taken to wearing Estrada paraphernalia—armbands and caps—as *anting-anting*, or protective amulets to ward off harassment. The demonstration was broadcast around the clock, however, by the Iglesia ni Cristo channel Net 25. Until that point, the channel had mainly featured religious programming.

As the numbers of people amassing at the shrine grew, a "rally" that, by one police chief's account, "did not appear to have any organizers" acquired "representatives."[15] Politicians who had aligned with Estrada during the trial grafted themselves on to the crowd, reportedly supplying them with food and money out of a kitty that had been established by Estrada cronies (Doronila 2001a, 225). They stoked the crowd by exploiting the class divide between Edsa 2 and Edsa 3. One senatorial candidate "known for his penchant for designer suits and impeccable grooming" rallied the people by chanting, "Long live the smelly!

---

12. Conrado de Quiros, "Inherit the Wind," *Philippine Daily Inquirer*, May 10, 2001.

13. Rina Jimenez-David, "Cleaning Up," *Philippine Daily Inquirer*, May 3, 2001.

14. Blanche Rivera, "Sea of Humanity Yields 5 Trucks of Trash," *Philippine Daily Inquirer*, April 28, 2001.

15. Volt Contreras, Blanche S. Rivera, and Agnes E. Donato, "Erap Allies Mass at Edsa," *Philippine Daily Inquirer*, April 27, 2001.

Long live the stinky!" and went on to denounce those who say "that *we* smell," making himself one of the crowd.[16] One of Estrada's sons exhorted the demonstrators to "take over" the financial center of Metro Manila. J. V. Ejercito led a contingent of about two thousand demonstrators into the downtown area of Makati City, where they set up a stage in front of the Philippine Stock Exchange. "If you run into mestizos," he told them, "flick them on the nose!"—presumably to flatten them and thus efface one symbol of their class-cum-racial power, that is, their high-bridged noses.[17] Estrada, meanwhile, appeared to be in good spirits. Panfilo Lacson, the Philippine national police chief, visited him in Crame and reported that Estrada told him that he had had a wet dream the night before. "His blood pressure must be OK," Lacson surmised.[18]

By Sunday, April 29, the *Inquirer's* coverage had taken a darker turn. The outlines of a coup plot had surfaced. Millions of pesos had reportedly been earmarked to buy the support of ranking officers in the military. The armed forces commanded by Estrada's political allies were to join the demonstration and lead an attack on Malacañang, the presidential palace. The military and police were put on red alert, and an anticoup task force formed. Two thousand troops stood at the ready with helicopter gunships, tanks, and other combat vehicles at their disposal. On April 30, the *Inquirer* warned that the country was "sitting on the edge of civil war."[19] The very next day, however, nearly all the major dailies ran banner headlines declaring Edsa 3 finished (see fig. 8.1). What happened?

The coup plotters had split into two factions, one in favor of marching on Malacañang and the other opposed to it. The moderate faction had apparently prevailed. Perhaps more important, Arroyo had persuaded the head of the Iglesia ni Cristo, Eraño Manalo, to rein in his followers. She had agreed to his demand that Estrada be put under house arrest. Net 25 stopped broadcasting the demonstration. It is unclear whether a deal had also been reached with El Shaddai, the other religious group supporting Estrada, but it backed out as well. The withdrawal of these two groups, the purported backbone of Edsa 3, led

16. Dona Z. Pazzibugan, "Dong Extols the Virtue of Bad Smell," *Philippine Daily Inquirer*, May 1, 2001.

17. Alcuin Papa, "Erap Loyalists Storm Makati," *Philippine Daily Inquirer*, May 1, 2001.

18. "Erap Nag-Wet Dream sa Selda—Lacson," *Philippine Star*, April 28, 2001.

19. Amando Doronila, "Country Sitting on Edge of Civil War," *Philippine Daily Inquirer*, April 30, 2001.

STORY BELOW, COLUMN 1

## SME workers: Modern slaves

By RAMON T. JIMENEZ
*(First of two parts)*

EMIL, age 16, works as a gas station attendant. He is paid P150 for working eight hours, but sometimes when asked to work for two or more hours, he is not paid any overtime premium. If he refuses, many boys from the nearest squatter

SME/A18

e-mail: feedback@inquirer.com.ph · website: www.inq7.net

# PHILIPPINE DAILY INQUIRER

## BALANCED NEWS, FEARLESS VIEWS

TUESDAY, MAY 1, 2001 ** 54 PAGES 3 SECTIONS VOL. 16 NO. 142 P15

## Show of force set at Mendiola today

By C. AVENDAÑO, N. BORDADORA, J. CANUDAY AND A. MELLEJOR

LABOR Day today marks the coming together again of workers, big business, government and cause-oriented groups, this time to protect the gains of the People Power II uprising last January.

SHOW/A18

# WHY POWER GRAB FAILED

## Moderates Angara, Puno, Zamora, JV Ejercito prevail over hot heads

By AMANDO DORONILA, ROCKY NAZARENO AND DONA PAZZIBUGAN

A PLAN to storm Malacañang with a human wave of Edsa demonstrators in an attempt to grab power was aborted on Sunday evening following a "split" of opposition leaders over the attack, according to a confidential report to President Macapagal-Arroyo.

WHY/A6

## Erap blames Miriam for march idea

By CARLA P. GOMEZ
PDI Visayas Bureau
AND CHRISTINE HERRERA

BACOLOD CITY—Joseph Estrada yesterday said it was not he, but Sen. Miriam Defensor-Santiago who had started President Macapagal-Arroyo to step down in his loyalists would storm Malacañang.

ERAP/A19

BY NIGHTFALL Monday, the vigil in Mendiola starts with a Mass, a prelude to the Labor Day, anti-Estrada rally today to be mounted by the Edsa II forces.

AT THE END of the day, only heaps of garbage remain as INC members leave Edsa after five days of protesting the arrest of ex-President Estrada.

## INC pulls out of Edsa; Net 25 has last hurrah

By CHRISTINE HERRERA AND ANDREA L. ECHAVEZ

NET 25 returns to its well-deserved slumber.

After a closed-door meeting yesterday with the executives of President Macapagal-Arroyo, Iglesia Ni Cristo Executive Minister Eraño Manalo ordered a stop to the round-the-clock live coverage in the PMI-owned dzEC and Net 25 of what had been billed as "Edsa III".

Manalo, perceived to be a longtime ally of ex-President Joseph Estrada, also ordered the pullout of his flock from the Edsa Shrine, ending a six-day INC rebuild that requested anti-

INC/A7

## AFP, PNP keep faith with gov't

By CARLITO PABLO, CHRISTINE HERRERA AND TJ BURGONIO

UNDER intense pressure from the Estrada camp to support its cause, the military and police kept faith with the government that they helped install in January, and remained loyal to the chain of command.

The Armed Forces of the Philippines is not for sale. Armed Forces Chief of Staff Gen.

Dominador Villanueva asserted yesterday amid persistent reports that the anti-Macapagal forces were offering huge bribes to military officers and soldiers to turn against the government.

In an apparent effort to undercut fears that the military is no mercenary army, the AFP defined its operational plan to protect the government as "Oplan Righteous Cause".

AFP, PNP/A6

## NBI eyes sedition charges

### Miriam, JPE, Gringo, Ping facing probe

THE NATIONAL Bureau of Investigation is closely studying the inflammatory speeches made by four senatorial candidates of the Puwersa ng Masa preparatory to the possible filing of sedition charges against them.

NBI Director Reynaldo Wycoco said on radio yesterday that six-beleaguered Senators Miriam Defensor-Santiago, Juan Ponce Enrile and Gregorio Honasan and Panfilo Lacson—all PnM candidates—were being put under surveillance and their remarks at the loyalist rallies at Edsa studied.

The candidates, as well as other allies of Joseph Estrada, have been inciting the protesters at Edsa to storm Camp Crame, where the ex-president was briefly held, and Malacañang in order to force President Macapagal-Arroyo to step down.

SLEEPLESS at the Palace, the President's husband, Mr. Mike Arroyo, is still up at 5 a.m. Monday after a long day's night.

NBI/A6

THE MORNING after the night before, the most critical in the 100 days of President Macapagal-Arroyo's administration.

## AFP ready to crush Erap coup

By CARLITO PABLO AND DAVE VERIDIANO

"CRUSH the march."

That was the order reportedly issued by the Philippine National Police and the Armed Forces top brass to their men in the middle of the night yesterday as the number of Edsa protesters reached an estimated 1.5 million.

The military will stop supporters of ousted President Joseph Estrada from marching on Malacañang, declared Gen. Dominador Villanueva, chief of staff of the Armed Forces of the Philippines.

"Whatever it takes to protect this government, we are going to do it," Villanueva yesterday said, when asked about the AFP's response to a plan by Estrada supporters to troop to the Palace.

Villanueva made the pledge as the AFP augmented its combat troops and hardware in Metro

AFP/A7

NABABANTOT AT NABA BAHO DAW TAYO? IKAW RIN?!

## Dong extols virtue of bad smell

By DONA Z. PAZZIBUGAN

"MABUHAY ang mabahate! Mabuhay ang mabahong eLong live the smelly! Long live the stinky!"

With that memorable, Dong/A7

observers to believe the demonstration to be all but over. An *Inquirer* columnist who had infiltrated the crowd close to midnight on April 30 reported texting his friends: "Sleep well, I was at Edsa III. Their physical numbers are less and their spirit is much less." He continued: "I took my advice and went to sleep. At about 2:30 a.m., Linggoy woke me up with a text message. 'Erap forces moving west on Ortigas and Santolan.' I was wrong!"[20]

On May 1, at around two in the morning, a contingent of fifty thousand demonstrators marched to the presidential palace. They used dump trucks to breach the five cement barricades along the ten-kilometer stretch from the Edsa shrine to Malacañang. They torched news trucks, police cars, and ambulances. They "divested [construction sites] of lead pipes, hollowblocks [cement blocks], wooden planks, stones—anything that could be used as a weapon."[21] Riot police, caught off guard and greatly outnumbered, could do little to halt their progress. Some were disarmed. The marchers proceeded down Mendiola, the avenue leading to Malacañang, splitting into three groups and approaching the palace from different directions. In the face of their advance, the Edsa 2 forces that had gathered along Mendiola to defend the palace retreated behind the walls of a nearby college. The marchers reached the gates of the palace just before dawn. The crowd spanned an area nearly a kilometer in length, the stretch from the Mendiola Bridge to Malacañang's Gate 7.

Television footage shows demonstrators chanting "Gloria step down," "Erap return," and "Edsa Tres." Men clustered around a dead comrade and painted their hands with his blood. People were singing the national anthem and mugging for the TV cameras circulating among them. A thin line of police had interposed themselves between the demonstrators and the gate. A man with a megaphone was desperately pleading with them. To do what? They remained unmoved. Over time, the line thickened with military troops. At around 10:30 a.m., combined police and military forces moved to drive away the demonstrators, pushing them back with shields and truncheons. The demonstrators scampered away. Some turned around to hurl stones. The cameras, now behind the troops, show them firing overhead and shooting

20. Manuel A. Alcuaz Jr., "Leaderless and Manipulated," *Philippine Daily Inquirer*, May 14, 2001.

21. Jerome Aning, Armand N. Nocum, and Dave Veridiano, "6 Dead, 113 Hurt in 12-Hour Battle of Mendiola," *Philippine Daily Inquirer*, May 2, 2001.

tear gas canisters into the crowd. The stalemate had devolved into a street battle. Back in the shrine, around two hundred demonstrators remained. An eyewitness described them as "huddled around radios, listening to the coverage of the march on Malacañang. But when they heard news of how the soldiers and police were turning away the mob, one by one, they started to drift away."[22] The *Inquirer* reported six people dead and 113 injured.

The march was portrayed as orchestrated from above. According to the *Inquirer*, Estrada's political allies had provided the dump trucks used to ram the police barricades. They had released instigators into the crowd. They had supplied the marchers with drugs and alcohol. Two of Estrada's sons had joined the march early on but escaped as it neared the palace. The "attack on Malacañang" was well planned, Doronila reported (2001, 239–40). "The frontline, for instance, was composed mostly of women, who gave way to rows of tattooed thugs and shirtless men, some supplied with drugs and liquor, who battled the police and smashed barricades." The marchers were armed, addled, and bloodthirsty. Some of those arrested tested positive for *shabu* (crystal methamphetamine): "One Estrada loyalist, his eyes bloodshot, stopped at the 7-Eleven outlet on J. P. Laurel Street and Nagtahan and brandished a club. He shouted at the terrified customers inside: 'We won!'"[23] Elsewhere in Manila, a gambler was stabbed in the chest and killed for saying that the march would come to nothing.[24]

My middle-class informants largely viewed the demonstrators in accord with the dominant account: as *hakot*. Indeed, the fact appeared self-evident, something that could be seen simply by *looking* at them.

They were hooligans and people brought in and paid. You could see it!

The Edsa 3 crowd was really ugly. We saw it on TV and the newspapers. They were just being manipulated.

We saw them bused in. We saw it! We were on the flyover along Ortigas and you would see bus upon bus upon bus. Edsa along White Plains all the way to the Noynoy monument, bus upon bus upon bus. It was nothing like Edsa Dos where people really came on their own.

22. Rina Jimenez-David, "Cleaning Up," *Philippine Daily Inquirer,* May 3, 2001.
23. Aning et al., "6 Dead."
24. Alcuin Papa, "Erap Fanatic Kills Critic," *Philippine Daily Inquirer,* May 2, 2001.

## The Subaltern Account

### *Pulled yet Propelled*

My urban poor informants tell a different story. It is true that many of them were able to participate because outside organizations provided transportation and thus were literally *hakot* or brought, but it is also true that going to Edsa was something they *wanted* to do. They described their participation as *kusang loob*, or voluntary. They emphasized their own agency: their desire to go, the costs they incurred by going, and the hardship they endured as a result. They spoke of the pain of their part being reduced to nothing in the mainstream portrayal of Edsa 3 as *hakot*.

Informants were mobilized in various ways. Mobilizing organizations played a significant role, but there are also numerous examples of self-mobilization, of neighbors undertaking the trip to Edsa themselves. In Makati, someone from the city hall arranged for six jeepneys to take the residents of D. Gomez Street to Edsa. Some of La Peral's residents were ferried by "a group coming from San Juan," possibly the People's Movement against Poverty. Melanie went with her neighbors, one of whom owned a truck. They took whoever wanted to go with them.

The San Roque Community Council arranged for the transportation of its members. According to the members of a competing community organization, SRCC leader Edwin Nakpil received money from Jinggoy Estrada. He used the money, they claimed, to pay demonstrators. I asked two SRCC officers about this.

"I heard that the people who participated were—"

"Paid!" Jolene and Didi said in unison. They had heard the allegation before.

"I've never taken money to attend a demonstration," Jolene averred.

"What about being made *hakot*?"

"It's true that we organized jeepneys to take people [to Edsa]," Didi said.

"People were *hakot*," Jolene continued, "insofar as they needed a way to get there. We gave them a ride, but they wanted to come."

"So it's not true what they say?"

"It hurts to hear people say those things," Didi said. "We were fighting for something that we believed in, but then it comes out that we were merely paid. That's not true. People went because they wanted to go."

In Holy Spirit, the barangay provided a ten-wheeler truck to take the residents of Kasiyahan Street to Edsa. The Aglipayan church took the residents of Samonte Street in several jeepneys. For a group coming from Zuzuarregui Street, participation in Edsa 3 was a family affair. Annie and her brother took their families. I spoke with Annie, her sister-in-law Mariette, and Mariette's eighty-three-year-old mother, whom I'll call, as the newspapers did, Lola Rebelde (Rebel Grandma). I interviewed them separately. Their story is worth recounting because it highlights the sense of agency attending every aspect of participation.

The two families, outraged by Estrada's arrest, took to Edsa in a show of protest. It was the first time that any of them had participated in a political demonstration. They were impressed by the number of people that showed up and felt moved to help them however they could. They went back to Zuzuarregui and pooled their money, managing to raise around 2,500 pesos (US$50). They used the money to prepare *pansit* (noodles), *pandesal* (bread rolls), ice water, and candy. They took the food in Mariette's truck and returned to Edsa, where they distributed it to demonstrators. This made Annie happy. Being at Edsa made her happy. She remembers not wanting to leave but having to, finally, because her husband had a doctor's appointment he couldn't miss. The others decided to stay, her children included. They wanted to see if the march would push through. It did, and they joined it.

Waiting at a red light in Sampaloc, the police pulled them over and made them disembark the truck. The Erap streamers decorating the truck had probably given them away. While they were being questioned, Mariette claims, the police planted rocks and pipes and lewd anti-Arroyo signs in the cab. This "evidence" was used as a pretext to arrest them. They were brought to Crame, the military camp. They were distraught. Upon learning that bail had been set for 12,000 pesos (US$240) per person, they began to despair. How could they possibly afford so large a sum?

Estrada, himself detained, had groceries and new clothes sent to the eighty-nine prisoners held at Crame. Lola Rebelde happily recalled receiving a duster and panties. She carried on as if Estrada had gifted them to her personally. Eventually, Arroyo paid them a visit. The newspapers show her in a denim outfit, her arm around Lola Rebelde. She is leaning in, head bowed, listening to her. Apparently, Lola was asking Arroyo to have her daughter's truck released. It had been impounded by the police. Annie, visiting her family in Crame, asked the president to have the police return her cooking pot. She was still paying the installments on it and would be crushed if it were lost. The pot was returned, the food inside it spoiled. Following Arroyo's visit, the women were transferred from Crame to a Department of Social Welfare and Development office in Alabang. After about a week, they were visited by Lito Lapid, a politician and former movie star. Arroyo had enlisted him as her representative to the *masa*. Lapid announced that they were free to go. In all, they had been incarcerated for nine days.

Back in Zuzuarregui, Mariette clipped the picture of her mother, Lola Rebelde, talking with Arroyo and framed it. She shows it to everyone who visits. It's not the fact that her mom had an audience with the president that makes her proud. It's the fact that they took to the streets on behalf of *their* president. "I can hold my head up high," she said. "No one paid me. I went there to help people."

In De la Rama, I couldn't find anyone who participated in Edsa 3. It was easier to find people who had participated in Edsa 2. It wasn't that the residents didn't support Estrada. They did in the same numbers as elsewhere. It was the fact that they lived twenty-two kilometers away from the shrine, and no organization had stepped in to provide them with a means of getting there. The residents who had participated in Edsa 2, though, had been brought there by outside actors. Efren had to drive his boss there. Leonisa went as a member of an NGO that provided transportation and food. She claims not to have known what the demonstration was all about and regrets her participation. This makes her a textbook example of *hakot*, except in this case it was for Edsa 2.

The presence of mobilizing organizations, whether local or external, made a difference in participation. They facilitated the participation of residents in Makati, San Roque, and Holy Spirit. Their absence in De la Rama, meanwhile, prevented its residents from participating. As informants tell it, however, these organizations played an enabling role, not a compelling one. They did not pull informants to participate so much as provide them with a means of doing so. Informants were already propelled by a sense of grievance.

### The Grievance at the Core

Doreen and Beng are discussing Estrada's ouster. They remember one detail vividly: Estrada's departure through the rear of Malacañang, the entrance opening to the Pasig River. He boarded a ferry and took it to the opposite bank, where a coterie of vehicles was waiting to escort him to his residence in San Juan. It's a detail that seemed unimportant at first, an informant's stray memory of the event. I took notice when

informants kept bringing it up. It became clear that this was an incident they not only remembered but held on to.

"They didn't even let him exit through the front. He had to go
through the back and ride a boat," Doreen said.

"They made him go through the back. Of course you feel sorry for
him!" said Beng.

"We all watched him and what they did to him. Waving buh-bye to
all the fishes," she laughed. "Because there was no one there."

"You really feel bad for him because they made him go through the
back. You feel bad. You want to cry. Why did they do that to him?"

"It's as if he were a bad person."

"He was hiding because he knew that what he did was illegal," Beng
laughed.

"It's like they think he's a bad person," Doreen repeated.

"Why didn't they give him the chance to go out front?"

"Yeah, why through the *back*? Arroyo shouldn't even get to go out
through the back but through the toilet!" Everyone laughed. "Or the
roof!" We could barely contain ourselves.

"Then suddenly a helicopter will come . . . with a rope for her neck!"
Beng blurted out through laughter. "Dragging her body. We'll be the
ones happy." We settled down, caught our breath, and then, as if she
had just remembered something, said in Cebuano, *"Ay naku. . . . Pastilan!"* ("Ah, well. . . . Dammit!").

*"Pastilan gyud!"* ("Dammit, indeed!")

I argue that the grievance driving the demonstrators was fundamentally a class grievance. It implicated their identity as poor people and
squatters. It wasn't just that they saw Estrada's ouster as unjust; it was
that they saw him as mistreated and responded to this out of their own
sense of discrimination. In their eyes, he was wronged by being tried
on such trivial charges. He was wronged by being singled out in a field
of corrupt politicians. He was wronged by being deprived of due process. He was wronged by being made to exit, ignominiously, through
the back door. He was wronged most flagrantly by being arrested, his
mug shot broadcast for all the world to see. Informants found the image humiliating. Benito complained: "It was embarrassing that that
would be done to the president of the Philippines, that he would be
treated like a murderer, like a criminal. Actually, I cried when that happened. Why? Because they didn't even show him respect. Even if he
had done something wrong, show him respect. Then they broadcast it
on TV. Why not keep it private? They humiliated the president of the

country. The way he looked, broadcast not only in the Philippines but all over the world. How shameful, not just for him but for all of us."

"It wasn't right what they did to him," Elena protested. "It wasn't right. It was as if he wasn't a person."

"Wasn't a person?" I asked.

"They didn't show him any respect. If they were going to remove him, why not do it the right way? Why force him out? Why put him in jail?"

The urban poor reacted so strongly to the image, I suggest, because they identified with Estrada's humiliation. They knew what it felt like to be diminished and discredited as a bad person. They commiserated with him. "I was crying. All of us were crying." Tina said, recalling Estrada's departure through the back of Malacañang. "He looked so miserable. It was terrible his being driven away like that." There was something, moreover, about Estrada being mistreated that made them feel more intensely degraded. Estrada represented them, but he wasn't like them. He wasn't a "small person [*maliit ng tao*]," as informants liked to call themselves. He was a big one, the biggest, a sitting president, and, as we saw in the previous chapter, someone who embodied the prospect of their recognition as equal members of society.

"You asked me who organized Edsa 3," said Von Mesina, a leader of the National Urban Poor Coalition. "GMA did. Not us." He meant that Arroyo had moved to arrest Estrada with little consideration of his urban poor supporters. She had assumed, like everyone else, that they had moved on or that they lacked sufficient political conviction to protest. She had counted on them simply accepting the latest development. After all, they had always done so before. This time was different, I have argued, because Estrada's "mistreatment" resonated with an experience of discrimination that had been building up over the decades into something combustible. This mistreatment was as self-evident to my urban poor informants as the *hakot* demonstrators were to my middle class ones. "I saw with my own two eyes how he was harassed," Myrna insisted. "I saw it!" Estrada's arrest was the wrong that sparked Edsa 3. "That's the reason we rebelled."

As it unfolded, Edsa 3 became about more than just Estrada's mistreatment; it became about the poor's. The disparagement of the demonstrators in the media galvanized them. Von remembers listening to the radio around the time of Estrada's arrest. "The things they were saying about the poor," he exclaimed. "On the air! They were calling them stinky and toothless. They don't understand how the poor think. The poor may not have money, but they still have a sense of dignity.

Don't insult them! While they were saying those things, we were say-ing [to the radio]: 'The reason we don't have teeth is because you don't pay us enough to afford dentures!'" He laughed. "The reason we're dirty is because we're cleaning your cars and taking out your trash!" Such disparagement clarified the class identity of the demonstrators as poor people and squatters. It made their discrimination the subject of contention. It made Edsa 3 about their right to be heard. The following section bears this out as I document the event from the perspective of its participants.

### The "Real" Edsa 3

My urban poor informants depicted a different object from what was in the media and in the minds of the middle class. The "real" Edsa 3, to them, was an expression of people power. It was not defined by politicians and religious groups but by ordinary demonstrators who took to Edsa out of grievance and stayed, despite the cost and risk to themselves, because their cause was just. With this object in mind, the stream of buses along Edsa was evidence not of *hakot* but of the depth of people's support for Estrada; the distribution of food in Styrofoam boxes was evidence of the outpouring of support.

The true object was carefully delimited. The shrine was made filthy, but this could be explained as a consequence of the sheer number of people there. The nearby mall, moreover, had closed its doors to them—it had remained open during Edsa 2—and there were no porta-ble toilets during the first few days of the demonstration. Carmen was sorry for contributing to the filth but faulted the situation: "It wasn't out of rudeness; we had no choice. We had to shit right there because of all the people. We couldn't move. That's the truth. We had to piss on the spot because all we had room to do was crouch."

The presence of drugs and thugs was portrayed as the work of out-siders. Some informants claimed that the government had released prisoners into the march in order to discredit the marchers. They could tell, they say, by their tattoos. (The *Inquirer* reports that one politician accused another of sending criminals and drug addicts to join the march. The accused politician, however, was an Estrada ally.[25]) The real demonstration was largely peaceful. Indeed, the real violence was done to the demonstrators, not by them. They were the ones who were shot

25. Christian V. Esguerra, "Asistios Brought in Addicts—Malonzo," *Philippine Daily Inquirer*, May 2, 2001.

at, teargassed, hosed down, and beaten. The People's Movement against Poverty counted more than eighty casualties. The official figure is six.

The real Edsa 3 was marked by a spirit of *communitas*. People were dancing and singing and sharing food with one another. Informants spoke of Edsa 3 in the same way that the middle class, the media, and scholars alike spoke of Edsa 2: as a "vanguardless, decentralized, and spontaneous uprising" (Bautista 2001, 7). Following, I present different reflections on this object by informants occupying distinct vantage points: members of the PMAP, the purported organizers of Edsa 3, on their view from the frontlines; a community leader from San Roque on the march to Malacañang; and an ordinary demonstrator on the breakfast at the presidential palace held for incarcerated demonstrators and their families.

View from the Front Lines

The members of the People's Movement against Poverty were banking on Estrada's arrest leading to something. They didn't know what, but they wanted to capitalize on the outrage it was sure to cause. The group shuttled people from Tondo and the National Government Center area in Quezon City to Estrada's subdivision of North Greenhills. Estrada partisans provided them with funding and vehicles. Following Estrada's arrest, Lumbao led the demonstrators to Crame. The plan was to extract Estrada from the military camp with help from the inside. When this help failed to come through, Lumbao diverted the demonstrators to the Edsa shrine. I tell the story of what happened there through the eyes of PMAP officer Cynthia Villarin.

I spoke with Cynthia at the Tapa King restaurant along Commonwealth. I had met her along with Lumbao and the other PMAP officers at the Gerry's Grill on Tomas Morato. My understanding of the events marking Edsa 3 remained shaky, so I reached out to her. She obliged me with a blow-by-blow account. I recount it here, supplementing it in parts with testimony from my Gerry's interview with Lumbao and the others.

"I got word that Estrada would be arrested around noon or 1 p.m. [on April 25] and that we had to go to Greenhills. People were already there sleeping on the streets. They had just shown up. The police were blocking vehicles traveling along Edsa. I called Ronald and told him to find another route. I was coming from the NGC area and had eleven jeeps with me. The police stopped three of them with flags, but the rest were able to make it through. When I got there, Ronald told me to turn around and head to the Edsa shrine. I did. There were only about two hundred people there all scattered around. Our flag was up. Girlie was there and Marlon. By the time Ronald arrived, there were already a thousand people at the shrine. We set up a stage and speakers. After about thirty more minutes, the one thousand became five thousand. It happened so suddenly. The police had left us alone because they didn't think that a lot of people would show up, but by 9 p.m. there were three hundred thousand. That was the first day alone! On the second day, the Iglesia came. Net 25 showed up and covered the demonstration full-time. People kept coming and coming."

They were mostly "ordinary people and ordinary organizations," Lumbao added. They weren't activists or the kind of people who made it their job to protest. "You know how I know?" he asked me. "The 'slogan' of Edsa 3. People were chanting 'Gloria *pok-pok*, Ramos *supot*'" (Gloria's a slut, Ramos a dick—an uncircumcised one to be precise).

Cynthia shushed him immediately.

"No, that's what they really said," he replied, deadpan.

"Gloria, Gloria, *labandera* [washerwoman]," Ronald Coronado began to sing to the tune of "Glory, Hallelujah." Another "slogan."

"We couldn't come up with that chant if we tried," Lumbao said. "We *wouldn't* come up with it!"

"It's because they were angry," Coronado said.

"It came out of their anger," Lumbao agreed. "But don't you think it's catchy?"

First husband Mike Arroyo was asked about Edsa 3 on the talk-radio AM station DZBB, Cynthia recalled. "He said, 'The demonstration? It's nothing. Those people are uneducated. They stink. They don't bathe. They're drug addicts. It's the politicians telling them what to do. They're just paid.' And then, on Channel 7 and Channel 2, what do they show? People fighting for food. Sure, that happened, but it couldn't be helped. That's what they showed though, not how it normally was. . . . Like Chowking gave a truck of *siopao* [pork buns]. The truck brought it to the shrine, and it was automatic. People started distributing the *siopao* among themselves. Group leaders would say, 'Give that out, call your friends, give some to the people over there.' One person would get his share and then the next."

She marveled at the outpouring of support: "There was so much food. I know, I was the person who signed for it." She named Chowking, Jollibee, Goldilocks, Red Ribbon, and Julie's Bakeshop as donors. In fact, there was *too much* food. "We had to send it elsewhere. We sent three jeepsful to urban poor communities along Commonwealth."

"The people made the decision to march, not us," Cynthia insisted. Von Mesina said the same thing. The politicians were divided. Some exhorted the demonstrators to charge Malacañang while others counseled calm. "So who decided to march?" asked Von. "Not PMAP but the people. They just needed to see the flag of an organization ready to risk their lives along with them."

"We set out the night of April 30," Cynthia recounted. "We had garbage trucks and jeepneys leading the way. People were marching behind them. Ronald was in the front, but we moved him back because we were afraid he would get hurt. . . . There were cement barricades all along the way. Really heavy ones. We pushed them aside like they were cardboard boxes. . . . The police fired teargas at us. People picked up the canisters and threw them back. They were different colors— pink, violet, yellow—and really, really hot. People had to use towels to pick them up, and after tossing them would shake their hands from the heat. At one point, the wind changed direction and brought the gas back to the police. Can you believe it? They started running away!"

Marlon Uson of PMAP remembered the Edsa 2 forces blockading Mendiola Bridge. They had gathered to defend the palace, said a labor leader quoted in the *Philippine Star*.[26] "They stood there, arms locked," Marlon recounted. "When they saw us breaking through the barricades they fled to San Beda [a nearby college]. We had to stop our own people from chasing them inside. We formed a human chain to keep them out. If they got in, that would be the end of them. So if you ever interview Chito Gascon [an Edsa 2 leader], tell him to thank PMAP—and Marlon in particular—for saving him."

Cynthia remembered the snipers: "I counted seven. There were two on the roof of C'est la Vie. What are those? I was wondering. I saw a mint-green light coming out of their guns. That's how I knew there were two of them. Are those snipers? I can't say I was scared because I couldn't imagine that they would start shooting us.

"Police officers or soldiers joined us along the way. I think they were police officers or soldiers because they had guns with them, but they were dressed in civilian clothes. When they saw other police officers, they'd greet them: '*Hoy, pare!*' ['Hey, buddy!']. It was like *Braveheart*. By dawn, we were at Gate 7.

"Ronald had lost his glasses. He can't see without them. He dropped them and someone had stepped on them. He also lost one of his san-

26. Mayen Jaymalin and Sandy Araneta, "Workers Set Big March to Mendiola," *Philippine Star*, May 1, 2001.

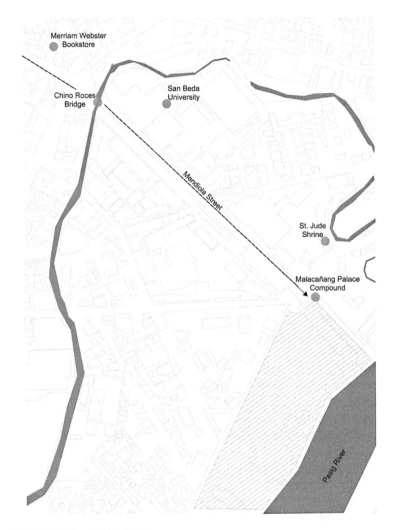

FIGURE 8.2  The marchers' route.

dals so he was walking around barefoot on one foot. We told him to go
home and fetch another pair of glasses. He was about to go when Golez
[Arroyo's national security adviser] fired tear gas into the crowd. Maybe
he had to do it himself because the PSG [Presidential Security Group]
and soldiers didn't want to do it. The canister landed under Gate 7 and
kept twirling and twirling there, spreading gas. I had to tell Ronald because he couldn't see. [She laughed.] We were running toward St. Jude
[a nearby church] when, two or three meters away, this guy falls flat on

the ground. This part of his face [she points to his left cheek] had been blown off. I couldn't believe it!"

I stopped her, incredulous. "What?!"

"The guy had been shot and the bullet came out right below his ear. His blood splattered all over us. Ronald almost fell on top of the guy. 'Oh, fuck, Tsay!' he said. 'Fuck you, Bok,' I said. 'Let's get out of here. They aim to kill us.' We ran scared. We heard shots being fired into the crowd. Everyone was running. I found two of our guys and told them to take Ronald with them. They hid out in St. Jude. Marlon and the others retreated to San Beda. I ran up Mendiola and ducked into the Merriam-Webster bookstore.

"When I came out, my companion and I saw an ABS-CBN van there.[27] 'Wait a sec,' he said. 'Let's turn over this truck before we go.' 'I don't think we can,' I said. Well, we did. Other people saw us pushing and helped us. Once it flipped over, they kicked in the windows. They found pipes and began to smash it. People were doing that to all the ABS-CBN vehicles they saw." She chuckled. "I saw four down on my way home: the one on Mendiola, one near San Sebastian, one in front of FEU [Far Eastern University], and one near PRC. I was walking so fast it felt like I was skating. I kept thinking about the guy whose head had been blown off.

"At home, I turned on the TV and watched [the marchers being dispersed] on the news. 'Maybe I can still go back,' I thought. [She laughed.] 'I can bring more people with me.' Then I saw names flash on the TV: Enrile, Miriam, Lacson, Gringo Honasan—and Ronald! They were wanted for inciting the march. Something else: Ronald had seven PMAP officers with him. I was one of them. Ka Lope called, 'Tsay, hide for a while. Leave your house. It's too dangerous.' It didn't feel like I was in danger. Well, it didn't matter. I had to attend a graduation at the PICC [Philippine International Convention Center] that evening. When I was there I got a call. 'Don't come home. There are people here asking about you.' I went home anyway because I didn't have any clothes. How could I escape without clothes? I got home and, sure enough, there were men there from the NBI [National Bureau of Investigation]. You know what happened? The people in my neighborhood drove them away. They surrounded them and started yelling at them, 'She's not a bad person. Get out of here!' They started throw-

27. ABS-CBN is a major broadcast network in the Philippines. Edsa 3 forces accused it of portraying the demonstration negatively.

ing rocks. The men got scared and left. I went into hiding for a few weeks.

"When I got back, the barangay summoned me to meet with [the NBI men]. They were all *J*s: Jimmy, Joel, Jaime, and another *J*. They offered me a position in return for testifying against Ronald. My old position at the National Anti-Poverty Commission—or I could be a consular officer at the Philippine embassy in Taiwan. They offered PMAP twenty million pesos (more than US$400,000). The condition was that we couldn't organize or join any mass actions against Gloria. We'd have to use the money to go into business or something. We had to stop causing trouble. We refused, and they stationed soldiers in [the NGC area].

"They put Ronald in prison for almost a year and a half. Crame first, maximum security, then city jail. He's out now on bail. They charged him with rebellion. [Nine others, all senators, were accused, but] he was the only one convicted."

"Well," Ronald said matter-of-factly, "I *am* the most handsome."

I asked Cynthia how many people were killed at the march.

"Over eighty according to our sources. We collected reports from different areas and added them all up. Those are just the ones we know about. There are probably more. We used to commemorate them by retracing our steps from Edsa to Mendiola every May 1. We'd lay flowers for them along the way. Now we don't even do that anymore."

The Poor People's March

Edwin Nakpil has been a community organizer in San Roque since the 1990s. He led a group from San Roque to Edsa 3. He gives an account of their march to Malacañang on May 1, 2001.

"Some groups didn't want to march to Malacañang. I said to my group, if we don't go to Malacañang, if we don't make ourselves heard, then this demonstration won't amount to anything. Maybe they didn't hear us at the shrine because we were an assorted lot: organized groups, unorganized people who only cared about Estrada, politicians who came to make speeches. We have to storm Malacañang in order to make ourselves heard! This opportunity may never come again. When people heard about the march, people who lived in the slums along our route, from San Juan all the way to Manila, they came out to see us. They wanted to see what was going on. At first, they came out of curiosity, but then they became believers. It wasn't just about Erap anymore but about something deeper. It was about exposing social problems. It was about expressing love of country. There were so many of us! We overturned this huge construction vehicle, a grader, or was it a bulldozer? We flipped it over and burned it.

"When we crossed the Chino Roces [Mendiola] Bridge, people went in different directions. Some continued along Chino Roces, some took another route to Malacañang, some took yet another. If you had an aerial view, if you were to look down on us from above, it would look like we were surrounding Malacañang on all sides. We had no leader. Well, there were a lot of leaders but no one wanted to speak up for all of us. We were all too scared! There were snipers on the buildings along either side [of Mendiola]. We knew they were snipers because we saw their guns had lasers. It was dark. All the streetlights had been turned off. They had set up barricades along the road, those iron rail fences used in construction. As we broke through them, the soldiers and police just stood aside and watched. They just watched and did nothing. There were a lot of them. Some of them, out of fear, left their guns, and, out of fear, people took them. Others were unwilling to harm their fellow poor. These were their relatives and their friends, and if they didn't know them, they could identify with them. 'Would you kill your neighbor?' 'Oh, this is too much.'

"Groups that had been a part of Edsa 2 were gathered along Chino Roces [in an attempt to defend Malacañang]. People were sent ahead of the crowd to get them to leave lest they be injured or killed. But they had nowhere to escape to and people were already coming in from all sides, so they ducked into a school [San Beda College]. People saw them go inside the building and wanted to get them. We stopped them. We said, 'Let's not bother with them. They're not our enemy. We came here to make ourselves heard.' [Those Edsa 2 groups] should thank us. The people were really angry and some of them just wanted to go crazy.

"Along the way, we saw [Senator] Angara's truck. One of his men was speaking through a loudspeaker: 'Let's leave! We might die here!' The leaders got mad at him and said: 'Get out of there! You're already dying of fear. Go home!' Then we commandeered his truck. Now we had a sound system!

"When we got to Malacañang we put away all our sticks—barbecue sticks, deadly weapons if need be. We threw them away to prove that our message was pure. We left behind a mountain of sticks for the police to see. Dawn broke and we saw that we were literally at the gate of Malacañang. One step away. Just a road between us. It's like, here we were, there's the gate, a road in between, what, six steps? There was the gate. Just go in. 'What do we do now, Mang Edwin?' My God! I couldn't be speechless at a time like this. What if they charge? There were snipers, ready to fire! Imagine all the people, not quite a million but hundreds of thousands. Chest to chest, elbow to elbow. You can't retreat. There's just no space for it. So we had no choice. Some of the old people started crying: 'We're going to die here.' 'Let's go home because I can't breathe.' 'But where will we pass? And if we retreat now we may be more likely to die.' And then I heard this woman say, 'Fine. If we die, we die.' [He laughs.] Just like that. 'If we die, we die.'

"We started to pray. After praying, we planned to sing the national anthem and then stage a program. We were bluffing for time. When we could move forward, we would. We were so scared. While we were praying, even before we had finished, it began to rain tear gas. A lot of tear gas. Then they started shooting. *Pak! Pak! Pak! Pak! Pak!* Rubber bullets, but they still hurt. It's like you've been shot with a slingshot. It's like . . . ah, it hurt! It's like you've been poked with the end of an iron rod. But the tear gas was worse. They wanted us to disperse, but how could we fall back? It's like we were ants trying to back into a whale. When the tear gas fell, you would just hear this *shhhh, crash.* It made the hair on your skin stand on end. Then a sound you won't forget your whole life, this howl. The cry of thousands of people roaring, *Huuuuu!* When I turned to look, I was teargassed myself. I saw people waving like the sea. A lot of screaming and crying. Other people got mad and wanted to fight back. A little later the helicopter came. It had a missile. A missile! It was about this long, right there on the side of the helicopter. It was just like a movie. The helicopter went like this [he makes a swooping motion with his hands followed by a shrieking noise], *Eeeeee!*

"We looked for what we could find. Water, even sewer water. A lot of people were hurt. A little boy got caught inside the barbed wire and died there. He was trampled while stuck. Finally, things quieted down. The Red Cross showed up. They didn't know what to do with all the injured. [The media said,] 'Their eyes are red, they're drug addicts!' As if your eyes wouldn't be red too if you were just teargassed! 'Why are you naked?' We took off our clothes to wet them and have something to cover our eyes with. The discos and nightclubs gave us water. Customers and even the GROs [hostesses] helped out. They brought us water and some even joined us.

"Around ten o'clock, I got word that someone from the media wanted to interview me and that I should go to him. I was holding up the flag of our party list and my companion was holding up the Philippine flag. I left my flag with him and went over to where I was supposed to go, but the guy who had asked me to come over wasn't there. I saw the guy who was supposed to interview me, but it didn't look like he wanted to interview me. I've been fooled, I thought. When I got back to my group, the guy I had left my flag with was dead. Shot in the head. Someone said it was because he turned the Philippine flag upside down and raised it. Isn't that the signal to attack? So they shot him, *pak*! Other people said that it was me they wanted to shoot. The guy who had told me about the interview had found out and led me away so I wouldn't get killed. Or maybe it was all just a coincidence.

"By noon, things looked bleak. Our chance to take Malacañang had gone. People were on their knees praying, screaming, huddled together in groups. I said to myself, this is desperation. It's suicide. I couldn't take it and went home. I watched the rest on TV. I got mad because this wasn't what we wanted. People were burning and destroying things. They had been hurt and needed to do these things. That's my version of the story. Now many years have passed. After it happened, we tried to bring together all the forces that made up Edsa 3. But they were so disparate, we couldn't do it. And now, instead of . . . now I'm portrayed as the villain. That's my version. There are other versions and you should seek them out. They differ in details and in the overall sense they make of Edsa 3. Other groups may see things differently, but we have our own name for the march: the Poor People's March. May 1 was the Poor People's March. Will it happen again? Again and again."

Breakfast at Malacañang

Annie, whom we met before, was part of the contingent from Holy Spirit that went to Edsa as a family. Recall that her family members were arrested and incarcerated. Arroyo, in an effort to woo the poor in the days following Edsa 3 (and preceding a senatorial election), invited the people who had been arrested and their families to have breakfast at the presidential palace. Annie recounts the event.

"They told us to dress up so that it wouldn't be so obvious that we were squatters. I made sure to look good that day. I took a long time in the bathroom and really washed up well. I used makeup and even bought perfume even though I couldn't afford it. When I left the house, I could have been mistaken for a schoolteacher! Our escorts came wearing uniforms. They were soldiers. We traveled by convoy with a military truck in the lead. The cars didn't even stop at the red light. They went straight through. I never imagined that the time would come when I could simply blow past a red light. Who can do that? And we went so fast.

"Shit, the palace was gorgeous! It felt like I was dreaming going up the stairs because the carpet was so soft. It was so nice to step on. I can die now that I've been to Malacañang. The tables were beautiful. They were carved and covered with nice things. And it was cold. You didn't have to fan yourself. You could eat and eat and not begin to sweat. No wonder Gloria won't resign even though everyone wants her to. Her life here is really nice. She has so many servants. They probably even bathe her.

"They invited hundreds of people. It was like everyone who attended Edsa 3 was there. At least everybody they put in jail. Although most people dressed up, some people didn't really comb their hair. There were people who looked like they hadn't bathed. Some people brought their kids even though we'd been told not to.

"They liked me because I talked a lot. They gave me a paper and asked me to read it in front of everybody. 'Oh, no,' I said, 'I'm not used to public speaking.' 'Don't worry,' they said. 'The media won't be there.' But they were. The dining hall was full of media people taking our picture. The paper said that I promise never to cause trouble like that [Edsa 3] again. That's not how I really felt! I didn't protest to cause trouble; I did it for my country. But I couldn't say that, I couldn't just come up with something on my own, and so I just read the speech. Before I knew it, it was over, and people were clapping. I read it, but I didn't mean it. I wanted to tell the truth. Later I threw the paper away—even though I usually take care to keep such things—because I didn't want to think about it. I felt terrible.

"We were seated at President Arroyo's table along with the head of the DSWD [Department of Social Welfare and Development] and [Police Chief] Aglipay. After I spoke, Aglipay was clapping loudly for me. He said, 'Missus, do you often attend these sort of gatherings?' 'No, sir,' I said, 'this is my first time.' 'Well, you were very impressive.' Then President Arroyo said—in Tagalog, not English—'Let's eat!' I didn't eat at first because I didn't know how to do it properly. Our spoon and fork were gold; how were we supposed to eat? Gold! I looked at the president to see how she ate. I see, you take the tissue [napkin] and spread it out on your lap. You take the bread with your fork and slice it with your gold knife. I had to see how they ate, of course, because they knew better than us. We used to be squatters (not anymore, though). [Arroyo] took her fork and used it to put ham on her bread, and then she put her fork down and began to eat. Well, that's what I did, too, so I wouldn't look like an idiot. Us, we just use our hands to eat bread. We even dip it in our coffee. If they saw us doing that they might say, 'What is this? Where are these people from?' So I just did what they did.

"Breakfast was one *pandesal* [bread roll], fruit salad, ham, and a cup of hot coffee. I thought, 'One *pandesal*? That's not enough.' It was a big *pandesal*, but I could have eaten four of them. They said we could have more, but I was too embarrassed to ask. They might call me greedy. Other guests arrived who were more important than we were, and so I said to the president, 'Madam, I'll just move over to the other table.' 'No,' she said. 'Stay right there.' There was a lot of small talk at our table but I stayed quiet. I was embarrassed. They might say, 'Who does she think she is?'

"They gave my mother-in-law PhilHealth [insurance]. They gave everybody who hadn't finished school a four-year scholarship. My son cried when he found out because now he could finish. I was proud, and I won't forget that of all the presidents of the Philippines President Arroyo is the only one I've shaken hands with. She hugged me and I took her hand. She said that I was her guest of honor. I was excited at the time, but I don't feel that way anymore. She was good to me, and she took care of us, but to tell you the truth, I can't bring myself to like her. It felt like she wanted something from us. What bothers me is having read that paper. I wouldn't do it again. They didn't tell me that I would have to give a speech. They only told me once I got there. If I had known, I would have made them listen to how I really felt. Then I wouldn't feel so bad about it now.

"I don't even want to vote anymore. My vote's wasted. I voted for Estrada and they brought him down. I was glued to the TV when that happened. You know, my eyes were so swollen from crying. I didn't even eat. When he waved goodbye [from the ferry on the Pasig River], I cried and cried. Even if he didn't say anything, just the picture of him looking like he didn't really want to leave. . . . I'm poor, that why I love him. When my sons were locked up in Crame, he was the one who sent them food. Briefs for the men, panties and dusters for the women, and a lot of food."

## Why Dissensus Matters

Once Edsa 3 had been crushed, political and civil society leaders moved to reestablish consensus spatially and politically. The Edsa shrine was hosed down by firefighters, scrubbed by cleaning crews, and disinfected with bleach.[28] Some days later, a group of clergy and lay citizens calling themselves the Mendiola Angels retraced the route taken by the demonstrators in their march to Malacañang to "sanctify" it.[29] These measures suggest a house blessing, or perhaps an exorcism. As if this were not enough, about a week later, the archbishop of Manila moved to "reconsecrate" the shrine with a healing mass. He staged a go-round of apologies. He asked the poor's forgiveness for the church's neglect, business-sector representatives apologized for their excessive lifestyles, politicians allied with Estrada were held responsible for working the poor into a frenzy, and an urban poor representative was on hand to apologize for the "desecration" of the shrine.

Sympathy for the poor had become popular again, as reflected in the editorials and letters to the editor in both the *Inquirer* and the *Star*. Pundits stressed the work of conscientization. Someone dropped leaflets from a private helicopter over slum communities reputed to have turned out for Edsa 3.[30] The four-page leaflet titled "What the People Should Know" argued for the necessity of Estrada's ouster and, therefore, the illegitimacy of Edsa 3. It was clearly intended to discredit Estrada, but the inclusion of his mug shot—the face that launched a thousand jeeps—only underscored the depth of dissensus between urban rich and poor.

With senatorial elections approaching on May 14, Arroyo campaigned to win over the poor in traditionally paternalistic fashion. Reports of the military raiding slum communities and rounding up truckloads of youth gave way to coverage of her distributing land titles in slums.[31] She even commissioned another popular movie star turned politician, Lito Lapid—dubbed "the *masa* tranquilizer"—for help in wooing the poor. "Makes sense," the *Inquirer*'s editorial board quipped. "It would take another actor to gain the support of the pro-Estrada masses."[32]

Perhaps the most significant effort to reestablish consensus was historiographical. It consisted of narrating Edsa 3 as supplementary to the story of Edsa 2. The event was relegated to the concluding chapter, epilogue, or postscript of books on the ouster of Estrada. It functioned as the ominous coda of an otherwise celebratory account. This lit-

28. Rivera and Esguerra, "Edsa Reclaimed by Edsa II Forces," May 2, 2001.

29. Norman Bordadora, "Church Asks Poor's Forgiveness," *Philippine Daily Inquirer*, May 12, 2001.

30. Carlito Pablo, "Anti-Erap Leaflets Rain on Erap Turf," *Philippine Daily Inquirer*, May 4, 2001.

31. Volt Contreras, Jerome Aning, and Andrea Trinidad-Echavez, "Truckloads of Tondo Youth Rounded Up," *Philippine Daily Inquirer*, May 5, 2001.

32. "Days of May," *Philippine Daily Inquirer*, May 21, 2001.

**FIGURE 8.3** Gloria Macapagal Arroyo: "Is this all I need to remove? Chicken!"
*Source*: Pol Medina (published in *Philippine Daily Inquirer*, May 20, 2001).

erature is sizable. It includes commemorative documentaries, at least two coffee-table books, a slim volume of poetry, and a music album. Writing Edsa 3 under the sign of Edsa 2 reinscribes the usual, unequal weighting of the actors involved.

Narrating Edsa 3 alongside rather than under Edsa 2—that is, in terms of dissensus—recalibrates our vision, keeping in view the things Edsa 3 made visible. The urban poor became visible to the middle class as cohabitants of the same urban space and not just encroachers and criminals, people to help, or the help. Specifically, it made confronting the social and political divide between them unavoidable. In the wake of Edsa 3, one *Inquirer* columnist remarked: "Isn't it amazing that in this day and age there still exist undiscovered islands in our archipelago? In early May we discovered one such island: a colony of smelly, boisterous and angry people. They are the poor among us."[33] Another described the "discovery" of the poor in the following way: "It felt like someone had rammed his fist through my home's painted walls, exposing decaying breams overrun by termites."[34]

33. Leandro V. Coronel, "Discovering the Poor," *Philippine Daily Inquirer*, May 19, 2001.
34. Rina Jimenez-David, "Getting at the Rot," *Philippine Daily Inquirer*, May 4, 2001.

Second, Edsa 3 made the urban poor visible to themselves. We might finally speak of class consciousness in E. P. Thompson's sense. The crucible of Edsa 3 clarified shared grievances and a common stigma. It heightened the poor's consciousness of themselves as a group. Notably, it did so primarily through spatial mechanisms: optically, by affording them the sight of so vast an assembly of people united not only in cause but, to a large extent, also in station. It did so, moreover, through the experience of transgression. If consensus manifests in the imposition of boundaries, then dissensus involves their transgression. The fact that urban poor demonstrators occupied the Edsa shrine for a week and managed to make it all the way up to the gates of Malacañang some fifty thousand strong—heretofore an unimaginable feat—represented a kind of victory in itself. Edwin Nakpil made this clear:

We broke the barbed wire on the way to Malacañang, my friend and I. We used pliers to cut it and wooden planks to ford it. I won't forget. That was our "payment." We shouted, "Long live the revolution of the small!" That's it. I'm paid up. It's over. We did it. The revolution of the small that no one had prepared for. Who knew that Erap would be the reason behind a revolution where we were able to take power? Even if all that meant was breaking the barbed wire and entering an area that we couldn't have entered before.

Despite Edsa 3's failure to reinstall Estrada, we should not overlook its significance as a demonstration of the urban poor's political agency. A display of class identity on this scale was simply unprecedented.

Finally, dissensus makes visible class division as a constitutive dynamic of Philippine politics. The official historiography tells a story about the people taking action against a corrupt president. This is a familiar story pitting civil society against retrograde rulers, whether corrupt leaders or an entrenched political class. Essentially, it's a story about political modernization, and it lines up with the standard reading of Philippine politics in terms of patrimonial or elite democracy. This rubric directs what we look for, what we see, and how we make sense of it. It can also keep us from seeing dynamics falling outside its framework. By keeping dissensus in view, however, we get a different story, one about how the "people," invoked monolithically in the standard story, are actually divided along class lines. This story shows civil society to be an exclusive project. With this story in mind, we are better able to appreciate the long shadow cast by Edsa 2 and 3 across election after election: in 2001 with the election of Estrada's wife and three of the alleged coup plotters to the Senate, in 2004 with the near election of FPJ, and in 2010 with the comeback candidacy of Estrada himself.

We are better able to recognize the importance of class division in shaping contentious politics. Edsa 3 may have been an exceptional occurrence, but it is for this reason that we are better able to discern class dynamics normally occluded by social and political entanglements. In the event of Edsa 3 we see class division crystallize. To lose sight of it would represent a loss of understanding.

# Conclusion

## When Is Inequality Felt?

When do the poor feel that they're squatters? When Erap Estrada is put in jail, not when their shanties are being demolished. They feel that they're squatters when they see that their president can be jailed just like that. They realize, "Motherfucker! That's why they treat us like nothing. It's because we're nothing to them!"

RONALD LUMBAO

Class division in Manila is more pronounced than ever. It is evident in the interaction between slum and enclave residents, in the physical and symbolic partitioning of urban space, and in the character of contention over Estrada and Edsa 3. We might expect class division to track with growing poverty and inequality, but it does not. Poverty incidence in Manila declined precipitously between 1985 and 2015, from nearly 30 percent to less than 4 percent (table 9.1).[1] Income inequality spiked around the time of the Asian financial crisis in the late 1990s but declined slightly overall within the same period. It is likely also the case that class division is more pronounced in Manila than elsewhere in the country, and yet both poverty and income inequality in the metro region are significantly lower than in the Philippines as a whole. Class division, in other words, cannot simply be a function of the extent of inequality. We need a sociological account to explain it.

1. These figures may be understated as a result of an unrealistic poverty threshold, as Ofreneo (2013) claims, but their direction is clear.

Table 9.1 Poverty incidence and income inequality in Manila and the Philippines, 1985–2015

| | Poverty incidence (%) | | Income inequality (Gini index) | |
|---|---|---|---|---|
| Year | Manila | Philippines | Manila | Philippines |
| 1985 | 27.1 | 49.2 | 0.44 | 0.45 |
| 1988 | 25.1 | 45.4 | 0.44 | 0.46 |
| 1991 | 16.6 | 45.2 | 0.45 | 0.48 |
| 1994 | 10.4 | 40.6 | 0.43 | 0.47 |
| 1997 | 8.5 | 36.9 | 0.49 | 0.51 |
| 2000 | 11.5 | 39.5 | 0.48 | 0.51 |
| 2003 | 7.8 | 33 | 0.47 | 0.50 |
| 2006 | 4.7 | 26.6 | 0.43 | 0.48 |
| 2009 | 3.6 | 26.3 | 0.41 | 0.46 |
| 2012 | 3.9 | 25.2 | 0.40 | 0.46 |
| 2015 | 3.9 | 21.6 | 0.39 | 0.44 |

Source: NSCB (various years).

Tilly (1998) points to the organization of inequality. He argues that the institutionalization of unequal relations, specifically exploitation and opportunity hoarding, promotes categorical distinctions. In the book, I have focused on the spatial organization of inequality. What distinguishes Manila is not that it is more unequal than the rest of the country but that it is richer. It contains eight of the ten richest cities in the Philippines and has an average per capita income 1.6 times higher than the rest of the country (Virola 2010). It is where most of the upper and middle class live. Their concentration alongside a larger population of relatively poor people (on whose labor they depend) brings about a peculiar ecology of inequality involving a particularly intensive form of segregation. We see rampant enclavization along with the growth and dispersal of slums. The spatialization of the urban poor and middle class in slums and enclaves makes class boundaries sharper. The interspersion of slums and enclaves drives boundary imposition. Thus, we see the housing divide become salient as a class divide. Note, though, this is different from a relative deprivation argument where concentration leads to starker contrasts and a stronger sense of social inequality (see Festinger 1954). It is not just the concentration of rich and poor that is at issue but their interspersion. It is not just social comparison at work but categorically unequal interaction. And it is not just the urban poor's sense of relative deprivation that is aggravated but their sense of discrimination.

Bourdieu (1984, 1987) emphasizes the representation of inequality as categorical. Class becomes real when it's represented, credibly, as a way of making sense of experience. He identifies two mechanisms of representation: boundary making and delegation (cathexis with a spokesperson who then comes to symbolize the group). I have taken up both of them. In part 1, I focused on boundary imposition. I showed that enclave residents feel besieged and thus compelled to impose spatial boundaries on slum residents. For slum residents, the regular imposition of boundaries makes a sense of discrimination a common sense. Thus, we see class boundaries clarify along the housing divide and the urban poor and middle class emerge as class actors—not as labor and capital but as squatters and villagers. In part 2, I focused on class formation both through and against Estrada. These two modes of class making are linked. By putting them together, we are better able to make sense of Lumbao's assertion in the epigraph that the urban poor felt acutely degraded with Estrada's arrest.

Being poor, Simmel ([1908] 1965) observed, is more than just a material situation. It is a disvalued social status. Under interspersion, the urban poor are reminded of this status regularly. Estrada's political performance was powerful because it negated their stigma as poor people and squatters. It is not just that he treated them decently but that he did so consistently and naturally, giving the impression that his attentions were sincere rather than instrumental. Estrada not only won the urban poor's support; he also became someone into whom they poured their aspirations as a class. Because of this they took his mistreatment personally. Through him they reexperienced their own mistreatment but with the greater force and clarity that comes from seeing it dramatized before them and from watching it happen to someone with whom they identified.

I said this would be a book about the relationship between the urban poor and middle class, and it has been, but it has *also* been, necessarily, a book about inequality, specifically, about when inequality is *felt*. Among the various concepts I've cobbled along the way, from interspersion to dissensus, the central one, undoubtedly, is categorical inequality. I find the concept useful because it enables us to distinguish simple inequality from social division, classes on paper from real classes. Further, it enables us to see different types of interaction—efforts to uplift as well as to exclude—as possessing the same form and thus having a similar effect. I like it, finally, because it captures the gist of my empirical concern: the nature of the relationship between the urban poor and the middle class. These groups are separated by more than just economic capabilities. The urban poor, the *masa*, are seen as deficient not just in terms of housing, tenure security, income, and education but, above all, in terms of civility. Quijano (2000) and other coloniality scholars portray the class divide as a recapitulation of the colonial divide distinguishing a modern from a benighted people. Hence the moral charge of the class boundary—the repugnance with which the middle class treat the urban poor, the fear of pollution, as well as the civilizing imperative. This social structure is as indispensable to the study of cities in the Global South as race is to the study of American cities. As we have seen in the case of Manila, its impact is profound. A categorical inequality of this sort—essentially dividing "civil" from "uncivil" society—shapes more than just class interaction but urban space and the character of democracy.

## Class Differences in the Experience of Democracy

The current president of the Philippines, Rodrigo Duterte, has been called a populist, but his populism is very different from Estrada's. Estrada drew a line between rich and poor; Duterte's line cuts between discipline and disorder. His is the politics of "I will," as Curato (2016) aptly put it. This politics separates law-abiding citizens from rule breakers and rule benders, the corrupt and criminal. Randy David, a Philippine sociologist and *Inquirer* columnist, described Duterte on the stump: "Duterte regales his listeners with stories of his frustrating encounters with a dysfunctional national government and how he deals with these to produce tangible results in Davao City. . . . What is urgent, he says, is that we restore order and respect for authority. He laments the fact that criminals, drug peddlers, and corrupt public officials have been able to act with impunity by exploiting the weaknesses of the judicial system. In this manner, he articulated the exasperation and desperation that people experience in their daily lives."[2] Duterte is certainly vulgar. He has joked about joining in the gang rape of an Australian missionary and publicly cursed Barack Obama, UN Secretary-General Ban Ki-moon, and Pope Francis. Like Estrada, his vulgarity conveys a disdain for polite society. But it is also differently articulated with the rest of his performance; it bespeaks an immovability of will rather than incompetence.

"Dutertismo" appeals to both the middle class and poor. Walden Bello (2016) characterized the groundswell of support for Duterte as "an electoral insurgency." Traveling the country on his own campaign for Senate, he recounts the excitement around Duterte's candidacy. People waited for hours in the sweltering heat, homemade posters in hand, for

2. "Dutertismo," *Philippine Daily Inquirer*, May 1, 2016.

him to arrive. Support for Duterte picked up even before he had formally announced his candidacy and despite him saying, repeatedly, that he would not run. After Mindanao, where Duterte's bailiwick, Davao City, is located, his support was highest in Metro Manila. The percentage of people in Manila preferring Duterte for president jumped from 7 percent to 40 percent in the year preceding the election (Holmes 2016, 34). Since his inauguration in June 2016, Duterte's administration has been controversial to say the least. The centerpiece has been a ruthlessly prosecuted war on drugs that has claimed more than twelve thousand lives in two years.[3] Duterte has also pursued a more independent foreign policy, pivoting away from the Philippines' historical alliance with the United States. He has authorized the burial of the late dictator Ferdinand Marcos in the Heroes Cemetery despite popular opposition. He has taken steps to remove corrupt officials, cut bureaucratic red tape, improve public infrastructure, and regulate labor contracting. At the time of writing (two years into Duterte's six-year term), his approval rating remains extraordinarily high, at close to 80 percent (Pulse Asia 2017).

Just because class has become less salient as a political identity, it does not follow that class relations have become less important in shaping politics. The class-cum-housing divide is something Estrada clarified, not created. It is a structural problem. Keeping it in view, therefore, enhances our understanding of Philippine politics. In this case, it can help us parse the social bases of Duterte's support.

"The Duterte phenomenon is not a revolt of the poor," Teehankee (2016, 72) observed; "it is elite-driven. It is the angry protest of the wealthy, newly rich, well off, and the modestly successful new middle class (including call centre workers, Uber drivers, and overseas Filipino workers abroad)." His claim is based on several polls. In the run-up to the election, the upper and middle classes (ABC in an A-through-E scheme) were opinion leaders. They showed the strongest support for Duterte's candidacy early on and throughout the race (fig. 9.1). The exit poll from the 2016 presidential election shows Duterte to have won the most votes among the upper classes and people with college degrees or higher. Compare these results with the exit poll from Estrada's election in 1998 (table 9.2). Class support for Duterte and Estrada describes intersecting trajectories. Support for Duterte is highest among the upper and middle classes, while for Estrada it is highest among the lower classes. The upper classes have continued to support Duterte

---

3. Human Rights Watch, "Philippines: Duterte's 'Drug War' Claims 12,000+ Lives," January 18, 2018.

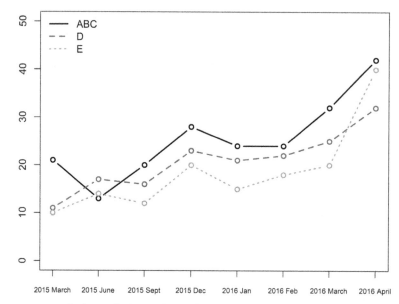

**FIGURE 9.1**   Preference for Duterte by social class in the lead-up to the 2016 presidential election (percentage).
*Source*: Pulse Asia (2016).

Table 9.2 Support for Estrada and Duterte by social class in the 1998 and 2016 presidential elections (%)

|  | Estrada (1998) | Duterte (2016) |
|---|---|---|
| Margin of victory | 40 | 39 |
| *Class support* |  |  |
| Upper and middle class (ABC) | 23 | 46 |
| Lower middle class (D) | 38 | 40 |
| Lower class (E) | 48 | 35 |

*Sources*: Mangahas (1998) and SWS (2016).

postelection. Surveys show that people with the highest levels of education generally express the most trust in and satisfaction with his administration (SWS 2017a, 2017b). Why? What accounts for his support among the middle class?

Teehankee (2016), Thompson (2016), and other scholars (Casiple 2016; Curato 2017; Timberman 2016) interpret Duterte's middle-class support as a repudiation of elite politics and, in particular, of the Aquino administration's "liberal reformism" (a "bourgeois" story line, Thompson writes, hailing democracy, the fight against corruption, and good governance as the country's top priorities). They argue that Aquino's efforts to eradicate corruption, despite some gains, did not go far enough. These efforts, moreover, were politically biased. Aquino targeted political enemies while sparing allies. The sense developed among segments of the middle class that a stronger medicine was required, hence they rejected Aquino's chosen successor, vice president Manuel "Mar" Roxas, along with other establishment candidates running in 2016. Knowing what we do about class relations, we know that this cannot be the whole story.

We saw that the middle class in Manila perceive threats coming from above and below. The middle class decry the elite capture of democratic processes but also and just as vehemently "*masa* capture." The middle class complain about being shaken down by traffic cops, having permits held up for want of grease money, being crowded out of sidewalks by street vendors, and of course having to fend off squatters from their property. Its members pay their taxes dutifully, and yet in their view, politicians down to the barangay level cater to the poor. These politicians get elected not because they are especially competent or virtuous but because they possess "*masa* appeal." This experience of being besieged both territorially and electorally is a crucial part of the story, but it is overlooked by an explanation focused on elite politics.

Philippine politics is mainly understood through an elite democracy framework dividing the polity into elite and people (Kerkvliet 1995; Quimpo 2005). The elite consist of "corrupt caciques, predatory oligarchs, and bosses" (Quimpo 2005, 241). By employing politics to further particularistic aims, elites are seen as distorting democracy. This framework emphasizes elite action. A kindred framework called contested democracy emphasizes popular counteraction and highlights the role of civil society and people power. The elite-cum-contested, democracy framework is predominant for a reason. It gets at a central dynamic of Philippine politics. It is limited, however, by its treatment of "the people" monolithically. In fact, it tends to generalize from the experience of the middle class and so-called civil society. It is limited, in other words, because it fails to take class differences into account.

These differences, as we know by now, are significant. The middle class and urban poor may agree that big-time or elite corruption is a problem, as are crime and even drugs (although drugs are nowhere near as big a problem as Duterte has made them out to be[4]). But otherwise

---

4. According to the UN Office on Drugs and Crime, the drug use rate in the Philippines is 1.7 percent. The global rate is much higher, at 5.2 percent (Quimpo 2017).

the middle class cite bureaucratic extortion, squatter encroachment, poor infrastructure, and bad traffic as evidence of political dysfunction. For the urban poor, the leading evidence is different. It is being discounted by politicians, government agencies, and courts; it is being exploited by employers; it is being denied a right to the city. Thus, while the urban middle class and poor may both identify political dysfunction as a problem, they do not necessarily understand the same things by the term. They may both extol political will but would see it used toward different ends. A class analysis keeps these differences in view and provides a necessary corrective to the elite democracy framework.

A recent survey showed satisfaction with democracy to have reached an all-time high, at 86 percent, not long after Duterte's election (SWS 2017c). This finding, taken by itself, is misleading. High levels of satisfaction with democracy now and during the Aquino administration do not erase the ten-year stretch spanning the Estrada and Arroyo administrations, when satisfaction levels were abysmal. They broke 50 percent, barely, in just two out of thirty-one surveys between 1999 and 2009 (fig. 9.2). Indeed, taking the longer view, the population's satisfaction with democracy appears remarkably fickle, varying significantly with each administration. The more telling statistic may be that only 61 percent professed to "always prefer democracy," whereas 19 percent "sometimes prefer authoritarianism." To me, this suggests an ambivalence toward democracy, and even an openness to less democratic, or at least less liberal, forms of government. Having attended to the urban poor's and middle class's different experiences of democracy throughout the book, we are in a good position to explain this ambivalence and to tell a more complex story about each group's relationship with democracy.

If democracy made Estrada's presidency possible because it empowered the urban poor electorally, then frustration with democracy led to Duterte's election. His support among the middle class is not simply a reaction to the Aquino administration's shortcomings. It grows out of a sense of electoral siege, a sense of being beset by *masa* candidates, of feeling bound to support Arroyo as the lesser evil, and of disillusion in the wake of Edsa 2. These feelings came to a head during the Estrada and Arroyo periods. By viewing support for Duterte in light of this experience, we are better able to understand why civil society has shown so little outrage and failed to mobilize broad based opposition against his drug war—twelve thousand casualties in two years! It is because his efforts represent an answer, not to the drug problem specifically or to problems of crime and corruption, but to the problem of democracy. In this sense, the drug war is emblematic of an effort to impose discipline

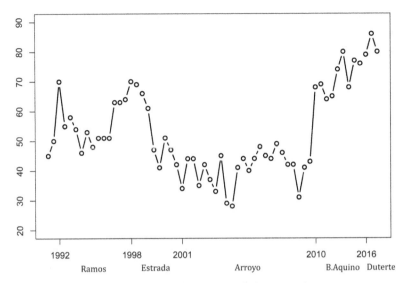

**FIGURE 9.2** Satisfaction with the way democracy works (percentage).
*Source:* SWS (2017c).

on democracy. The idea of discipline may appeal to both the urban middle class and the poor, but it resonates more strongly with the former. The urban poor construe the problem of democracy differently. They put greater stake in broadening the democratic ethos. As we have seen, however, these two political imaginaries are difficult to reconcile. I suspect that the tension between them will define the landscape of contention for some time to come.

## Dissensus: Not a Solution but a Way of Posing the Problem

To think with an enlarged mentality means that one trains one's imagination to go visiting.
ARENDT (1992, 43)

### The Activist's Dilemma

"Estrada and his backers have been able to do something that has eluded the left for decades," Walden Bello (2001) remarked, "and that is to organize the people along class lines into a powerful mass movement."

Indeed, some in the Left, recognizing Estrada's power over the poor, have sought to use him as an organizing tool. "We don't have anybody

**235**

like Hugo Chávez," said Von Mesina of the National Urban Poor Co-alition. "If people on the left are using Mao Zedong and Lenin, why not Erap?" "And just who is Erap?" he asked rhetorically. "Take Noynoy [Aquino]. They say he embodies the struggle between good and evil [the evil being corruption]. That's a bourgeois line. What did Erap say? Our society is divided between rich and poor. That's a proletariat line. There it is. Even if we say Erap isn't sincere, you can use that line against the elite and even to unmask him."

"You're saying that Erap's just a symbol."

"He's just a symbol! Use him as such. Personally," he chuckled. "I don't believe Erap is pro-poor at all."

Even the PMAP approached Estrada as a means to a greater end. The group seeks deliverance from poverty through a nationalist revolution. Estrada was to be its trigger.

"Did Erap believe in your cause?" I asked Lumbao.

"We didn't dare ask him that. We argued among ourselves about how we could use him for the purpose of organizing, and, eventually, how we could turn him against himself if he wasn't really sincere [in his commitment to the poor]."

"You didn't think Estrada was sincere?"

"At the time we didn't care. What was important was what he stood for. We believed it and the masses believed it, so we organized around it. . . . When we campaigned for him to be vice president, we just asked for Lucky Me [noodles] and 555 [sardines]. Nothing more. If he wins, then we won't bother him. We just asked that we be allowed to orga-nize in his name. We organized people that believed in *Erap para sa Mahirap*. That's what they gave us but didn't know they gave us. I didn't ask for a position. None of us did. But they let us organize and we used his name for our cause. We believed that he could live up to his image and that we could push him if he didn't. Who he was in real life was beside the point."

Another longtime activist, Edicio de la Torre (2001), pointed out the problem with this approach: "It's easy to tell the poor, 'It's not Erap you're fighting for. He's just a symbol of your aspirations. A metaphor.' But I'm sure that they will tell you, 'Metaphor? What metaphor? No, I really want him back as president.' That's the dilemma." In other words, to use Estrada instrumentally meant to miss what the poor ac-tually saw in him. It meant approaching them paternalistically, as a group whose sense of reality was not to be taken at face value and had to be guided to see things in their proper light. The problem was that it meant looking down on the poor.

De la Torre cited the media coverage of Edsa 3, "which looked down on them, indeed, if it even looked at them at all." He broadened his indictment to include the university audience. De la Torre was speaking at the University of the Philippines. A few weeks after Edsa 3, a group of activists and scholars had been convened to discuss the event. The auditorium was packed. "If we look at what happened [purely in terms of the poor chasing after a metaphor]," he said, "we look down on them, too."

"I remember a nice poster by Sister Purita from the 1970s," he continued. "It said, 'To understand is to stand under, is to look up, this is the good way to understand.'" We need to look up at the poor, he asserted. This means trying to understand what Estrada meant to them. It means trying to grasp the same objects they held on to in Estrada and in Edsa 3.

### Internal Transformation

When the leader of the Indian religious sect Santan Dal passed, Chatterjee (2004, 41–51) recounts, his followers, consisting mainly of lower-caste peasants, held on to the body in the belief that he would one day awaken. They kept it on a slab of ice in an air-conditioned room. It began to putrefy anyway, its stench pervading the neighborhood. Holding on to the body violated laws regulating the disposal of corpses, but the authorities allowed it. They did so because of politics, charged critics writing in the major dailies. A local election was upcoming, and political leaders were taking care not to antagonize Dal supporters. After about two months, the outcry scaling with the stench, the government finally moved. Five thousand police stormed the Santan Dal headquarters and seized the body. Members of the sect, incensed, alleged a miscarriage of democracy.

Chatterjee relates the incident as an example of the kind of activity constituting "political society." The Indian middle class, scandalized by such activities, react predictably: "The complaint is widespread in middle-class circles today that politics has been taken over by mobs and criminals. The result is the abandonment—or so the complaint goes—of the mission of the modernizing state to change a backward society. Instead, what we see is the imposition of the disorderly, corrupt, and irrational practices of unreformed popular culture into the very hallways and chambers of civic life, all because of the calculations of electoral expediency." They have responded to the expansion of political society in two ways, he writes. The first is by segregating themselves behind walls or within delimited spheres of activity. This strategy "seeks to preserve the civic virtues of bourgeois life from the potential excesses of electoral democracy." The second response, which he endorses, is engagement. It "does not abandon the project of enlightenment, but attempts to steer it through the thicket of contestation in what I have called political society. It takes seriously the functions of direction and leadership of a vanguard, but accepts [the necessity of political society]." To be clear, accommodation remains a kind of progressive strategy. The hope is that the process of political negotiation will prove transformative. "Even in resisting the modernizing project that is imposed on them," he argues, "the subaltern classes also embark on a path of internal transformation."

### Dissensus as Frame

The two cases presented here articulate two different visions of leadership. The Philippine activists (Ed de la Torre excepted) claim to represent the poor better than they can represent themselves. Chatterjee describes leadership as a matter of steering discussion. He would have the poor work through the democratic process but with civil society's guidance. Both views presume that the poor have to be led and take their backwardness as an impediment to development. Leadership is necessary in order to advance the development project. Democracy may be welcome, but it coexists problematically with the exigencies of progress, specifically because it empowers the backward sectors of society, whether the adherents of Santan Dal or Joseph Estrada. Lumbao and Mesina, therefore, seek to bypass the will of poor. Chatterjee would have this will be exercised but partly in order to see it transformed through politics into something more acceptable.

I wonder whether we should not dispense with the conceit of leadership altogether, bracket the development project, and prioritize a better practice of democracy. This would mean facing the reality of dissensus instead of seeking to transcend it—and not just because it makes class division visible, as I have argued. Dissensus is a way of reframing the "problem" of democracy in terms of difference rather than backwardness.

A difference framework represents a shift in focus from trying to change the poor to trying to understand them. What can understanding possibly accomplish? Understanding another person or group does not mean coming to see things their way; it does not entail agreement but serves, rather, to clarify the basis of disagreement. Understanding means attempting to put ourselves in the place of others to "get behind"—to stand under, to look up at—their perspective. Doing so requires "getting out of ourselves," as Iris Marion Young (1997) has noted, and thinking beyond our personal situation. Here the role of imagination is crucial, as Arendt (1992) indicated in the epigraph opening the section; it enables us to "go visiting." Kant claimed that taking the perspective of others into account enlarges our thought. By incorporating multiple perspectives and being able to move freely among them, our thinking acquires impartiality. Maybe so. But I would cite a different warrant for understanding. To understand is to recognize. It is fundamentally an act of respect. This by itself may not advance the development project, but it is good democratic practice. It prepares the ground for a different kind of interaction than the one I've spent the book underlining: categorically *equal* interaction. This kind of interaction does not require that actors be equal in every respect—indeed, it becomes all the more important when they are not—only that they be equal in standing, secure in their right to speak and be heard in the presence of others, even, especially, more powerful others. Isn't that what democracy means? But that would be the subject of a very different book, one, lamentably, having written this one, I have trouble imagining.

# Appendix: Selecting Cases and Getting Access

## Selecting Cases

My cases comprise four pairs of slums and enclaves in proximity. I selected them on the basis of four criteria:

*Geographical spread.* I selected cases from across Metro Manila (see figure 1.1).

*Proximity between slum and enclave.* The first three cases represent situations of immediate proximity. Phil-Am and San Roque are separated by a highway. The slum areas along Samonte and Zuzuarregui Streets lie just outside the walls of Don Antonio village. De la Rama is nestled beside BF Homes. The fourth case represents a situation of relative distance. In Makati City, the slum areas where I interviewed are in a different part of the city from the cluster of enclaves that make up New Makati. This variation enabled me to consider the role of relative proximity in boundary imposition. Specifically, I explored whether boundaries are imposed only in situations where slums and enclaves are immediately proximate. The answer, of course, is no. The general proximity of slum residents to exclusive public spaces also makes a difference.

*Fragmentation.* Two cases are located in Quezon City, which is extremely fragmented, having many more slums and enclaves than other cities in Metro Manila (see table 3.3). The other two cases are located in cities with fragmentation levels that were more typical of Metro Manila. Were slum residents in Quezon City more boundary conscious than elsewhere? Not discernably so.

Slum residents conceived a sharp boundary consciousness in every case. This finding suggests that Metro Manila, on the whole, is sufficiently fragmented to make boundary imposition a common experience.

*Political affiliation.* Of the four slum areas, I selected two known to have some affiliation with Estrada and two not known to have any affiliation with him. One of the affiliated sites was in Makati, whose mayor was running as Estrada's vice president. The other, San Roque, was a place Estrada had visited several times during his presidency. Both sites are relatively close to Estrada's bailiwick in San Juan. Meanwhile, the two unaffiliated sites are farther out: the cluster of Kasiyahan, Samonte, and Zuzuarregui Streets in Holy Spirit and the De la Rama colony in Parañaque City. As far as my informants from these sites recalled, Estrada had not visited either. This distinction between affiliated and unaffiliated sites made little difference in the end, however. Support for Estrada was comparably high across all four sites (see table 7.1).

## Getting Access

To obtain interviews with slum residents, I went through the barangays in charge of them. In two sites, the barangay captain referred me to his deputies in the area. I followed up with them and began soliciting interviews myself. In the other two sites, the captain simply gave me his blessing, and so I immediately began soliciting interviews myself.

I took care to avoid interviewing too many informants from the same area within the slum to acquire as broad a range of views as possible. I employed two strategies. In three sites, I targeted informants from different parts of the slum. Every week I would visit a different section of the slum areas to interact with new groups of residents. In the fourth site (Makati), I targeted five different slum areas around the city. In all sites, I spoke with four to five people from each new section or area until I had obtained around twenty-five interviews per site. I spent about a month in each site. Targeting different entrances and areas exposed me to different communities and organizations in each slum. In San Roque, for instance, one entrance led to a community organized by a pro-Estrada group and another to a community organized by an anti-Estrada group.

Given the public character of social life in slum areas, it was not hard to solicit for interviews. People were generally available, sitting around, vending goods, washing clothes, and tending to various duties. The slum population in the daytime, however, is heavily female and older. Thus, I made an effort to include younger men. The point, of course, is to minimize selection bias and to obtain, within the scope of a qualitative approach, a fairly representative sample of opinion.

To obtain interviews with enclave residents, I approached the home-owners' association and/or the barangay if it overlapped with the village's boundaries. I was mainly referred to residents who served in the village association or barangay council. I began with them and, from them, obtained referrals to other residents (proceeding, in other words, by snowball). I continued until I had around fifteen interviews per site (interviews were harder to get in enclaves than in slums, hence the lower target). I also found middle-class informants through personal contacts. These were professionals working in private companies and civic organizations.

My informants are fairly representative of slum and enclave residents in Metro Manila (see table A.1). The enclave residents in my sample typically possess college and postgraduate degrees and work as professionals and small business owners. The slum residents typically possess no more than a high school diploma. They work as laborers: domestics, drivers, security guards, carpenters, seamstresses, laundresses, and flexible staff in local government offices; as construction and factory

Table A.1 Informant profile

|  | Enclave residents | Slum residents |
| --- | --- | --- |
| N | 81 | 104 |
| Average age | 57 | 47 |
| *Gender (%)* | | |
| Male | 58 | 38 |
| Female | 42 | 63 |
| *Occupation (%)* | | |
| Executive/manager | 14 | 0 |
| Small-business owner | 33 | 2 |
| Professional | 36 | 2 |
| Government official (national level) | 13 | 0 |
| Manual worker | 0 | 23 |
| Vendor | 0 | 18 |
| Barangay/community organization staff | 0 | 16 |
| Unemployed/retired | 5 | 39 |
| *Final level of education completed (%)* | | |
| Postgraduate | 36 | 1 |
| College | 63 | 8 |
| Vocational | 2 | 4 |
| High school | 0 | 52 |
| Elementary | 0 | 28 |
| Less than elementary | 0 | 8 |

Table A.2 Current and previous jobs of slum residents

| Job type | Percentage |
| --- | --- |
| Low-skill service work: domestics, drivers, security guards, barangay personnel, seamstresses, laundresses, carpenters, street sweepers, etc. | 43 |
| Construction and factory work | 15 |
| Self-employed: microbusiness owners and vendors | 36 |
| Professional: call-center agents, soldiers, sailors, welders, secretaries | 5 |

workers; and as various kinds of vendors. A large proportion of them are unemployed. Table A.2 details the kind of work occupying slum residents. (I include previous as well as current jobs because so many were unemployed at the time of interview.)

Mainly, I asked informants about three topics: their interaction with the slum or enclave residents "next door," which led to discussions about social class differences; Joseph Estrada, which led to discussions about the upcoming presidential election and politics in general; and Edsa 2 and Edsa 3, that is, how they saw the demonstrations, why they participated if they did, how they mobilized, and so on.

In addition to my interviews with slum and enclave residents, I interviewed the representatives of various governmental and nongovernmental organizations, including the following:

**Government organizations**
- National Housing Authority
- Housing and Land Use Regulatory Board
- Housing and Urban Development Coordinating Council
- Statistical Research and Training Center
- Metropolitan Manila Development Authority
- Presidential Commission for the Urban Poor

**Urban poor NGOs**
- Urban Poor Associates
- Institute on Church and Social Issues
- National Urban Poor Coalition
- Community Organizers Multiversity
- Kadamay

**Political organizations**
- People's Movement against Poverty
- Pwersa ng Masang Pilipino
- Akbayan

**Business and civic organizations**

· Chamber of Real Estate and Builders' Associations
· Makati Business Club
· Rotary (two different clubs in Makati)

# References

Abaza, Mona. 2001. "Shopping Malls, Consumer Culture, and the Reshaping of Public Space in Egypt." *Theory, Culture, and Society* 18 (5): 97–122.

Abinales, Patricio N., and Donna J. Amoroso. 2005. *State and Society in the Philippines*. Lanham, MD: Rowan and Littlefield.

Abrams, Charles. 1964. *Man's Struggle for Shelter in an Urbanizing World*. Cambridge, MA: MIT Press.

Abueva, Jose V. 2001. "A Crisis of Political Leadership: From 'Electoral Democracy' to 'Substantive Democracy.'" In *Between Fires: Fifteen Perspectives on the Estrada Crisis*, edited by Amando Doronila, 78–97. Pasig City, Philippines: Anvil Publishers.

Abueva, Jose V., Sylvia H. Guerrero, and Elsa P. Jurado. 1972. *Metro Manila Today and Tomorrow*. Institute of Philippine Culture.

Abu-Lughod, Janet L. 1999. *New York, Chicago, Los Angeles: America's Global Cities*. Minneapolis: University of Minnesota Press.

Alcazaren, Paulo, Luis Ferrer, and Benvenuto Icamina. 2011. *Lungsod Iskwater: The Evolution of Informality as a Dominant Pattern in Philippine Cities*. Mandaluyong City, Philippines: Anvil Publishing.

Amoranto, Glenita, Douglas H. Brooks, and Natalie Chun. 2010. "Services Liberalization and Wage Inequality in the Philippines." ADB Economics Working Paper Series No. 239, Asian Development Bank, Manila.

Anjaria, Jonathan Shapiro. 2016. *Slow Boil: Street Food, Rights, and Public Space in Mumbai*. Stanford, CA: Stanford University Press.

Arcinas, Fe Rodriguez. 1955. "A Socio-Economic Study of Manila Squatters." *Philippine Sociological Review* 3 (1): 35–41.

Arendt, Hannah. 1992. *Lectures on Kant's Political Philosophy*. Chicago: University of Chicago Press.

Abbott, Andrew. 1995. "Things of Boundaries." *Social Research* 62 (4): 857–82.

Arugay, Aries A. 2004. "Mobilizing for Accountability: Contentious Politics in the Anti-Estrada Campaign." *Philippine Sociological Review* 52 (January–December): 75–96.

Auyero, Javier. 2001. *Poor People's Politics: Peronist Survival Networks and the Legacy of Evita*. Durham, NC: Duke University Press.

Balisacan, Arsenio M. 2001. "Did the Estrada Administration Benefit the Poor?" In *Between Fires: Fifteen Perspectives on the Estrada Crisis*, edited by Amando Doronila, 98–112. Pasig City, Philippines: Anvil Publishers.

Ballesteros, Marife M. 2011. "Why Slum Poverty Matters." *Policy Notes* (Philippine Institute for Development Studies), no. 2011-02 (January), 1–6.

Banaji, Mahzarin R., and Larisa Heiphetz. 2010. "Attitudes." In *The Handbook of Social Psychology*, edited by Susan T. Fiske, Daniel T. Gilbert, and Gardner Lindzey, 353–93. Hoboken, NJ: Wiley.

Bangko Sentral ng Pilipinas. 2017. "Key Statistical Indicators: Overseas Filipinos' Remittances." http://www.bsp.gov.ph/statistics/statistics_key.asp.

Barlow, Fiona Kate, Stefania Paolini, Anne Pedersen, Matthew J. Hornsey, Helena R. M. Radke, Jake Harwood, Mark Rubin, and Chris G. Sibley. 2012. "The Contact Caveat: Negative Contact Predicts Increased Prejudice More Than Positive Contact Predicts Reduced Prejudice." *Personality and Social Psychology Bulletin* 38 (12): 1629–43.

Basta, Samir S. 1977. "Nutrition and Health in Low Income Urban Areas of the Third World." *Ecology of Food and Nutrition* 6: 113–24.

Bautista, Maria Cynthia Rose Banzon. 1999. "Images of the Middle Class in Metro Manila." *Public Policy* 3 (4): 1–37.

———. 2001. "People Power 2: 'The Revenge of the Elite on the Masses'?" In *Between Fires: Fifteen Perspectives on the Estrada Crisis*, edited by Amando Doronila, 1–42. Pasig City, Philippines: Anvil Publishers.

———. 2006. "Beyond the EDSA Revolts: The Middle Classes in Contemporary Philippines: Development and Politics." In *The Changing Faces of the Middle Classes in Asia-Pacific*, edited by Hsin Huang Michael Hsiao, 167–86. Taipei: Academia Sinica.

Baviskar, Amita, and Raka Ray. 2011. *Elite and Everyman: The Cultural Politics of the Indian Middle Classes*. New Delhi: Routledge.

Baviskar, Amita, and Nandini Sundar. 2008. "Democracy versus Economic Transformation?" *Economic and Political Weekly* 43 (46): 87–9.

Bello, Walden. 2001. "The May 1st Riot: Birth of Peronism Philippine-Style?" *Focus on the Philippines*, May 7.

———. 2016. "Chronicling an Electoral Insurgency: 'Dutertismo' Captures the Philippines." Transnational Institute, May 19. https://www.tni.org/en/article/chronicling-an-electoral-insurgency-dutertismo-captures-the-philippines.

Benzecry, Claudio E., and Gianpaolo Baiocchi. 2017. "What Is Political about Political Ethnography? On the Context of Discovery and the Normalization of an Emergent Subfield." *Theory and Society* 46 (3): 229–47.

Berner, Erhard. 1997. *Defending a Place in the City: Localities and the Struggle for Urban Land in Metro Manila*. Quezon City, Philippines: Ateneo de Manila University Press.

———. 1998. "Globalization, Fragmentation, and Local Struggles." *Philippine Sociological Review* 46 (3–4): 121–42.

———. 2000. "Poverty Alleviation and the Eviction of the Poorest: Towards Urban Land Reform in the Philippines." *International Journal of Urban and Regional Research* 24 (3): 554–66.

Bosdorf, Axel, Rodrigo Hidalgo, and Rafael Sánchez. 2007. "A New Model of Urban Development in Latin America: The Gated Communities and Fenced Cities in the Metropolitan Areas of Santiago de Chile and Valparaíso." *Cities* 24 (5): 365–78.

Bourdieu, Pierre. 1979. *Algeria 1960: The Disenchantment of the World, the Sense of Honor, the Kabyle House or the World Reversed: Essays*. Cambridge, UK: Cambridge University Press.

———. 1984. *Distinction: A Social Critique of the Judgment of Taste*. Cambridge, MA: Harvard University Press.

———. 1987. "What Makes a Social Class? On the Theoretical and Practical Existence of Groups." *Berkeley Journal of Sociology* 32: 1–17.

———. 1991. *Language and Symbolic Power*. Cambridge, UK: Polity Press.

Brenner, Neil. 2001. "World-City Theory, Globalization and the Comparative Historical Method: Reflections on Janet Abu-Lughod's Interpretation of Contemporary Urban Restructuring." *Urban Affairs Review* 37 (1): 124–47.

Brillantes, Alex Bello Jr. 1991. "National Politics Viewed from Smokey Mountain." In *From Marcos to Aquino: Local Perspectives on Political Transition in the Philippines*, edited by Benedict J. Kerkvliet and Resil B. Mojares, 187–205. Honolulu: University of Hawai'i Press.

Bromley, Ray, and Chris Gerry, eds. 1979. *Casual Work and Poverty in Third World Cities*. Hoboken, NJ: Wiley.

Bureau of Labor and Employment Statistics. 2011. "Profile of Workers in Vulnerable Employment." *Labstat Updates* 15 (19): 1–4.

Cadiz, Gibbs. 2010. "The Rise and Fall of Manny Villar." *Gibbs Cadiz* (blog), May 2010. http://gibbscadiz.blogspot.com/2010/05/rise-and-fall-of-manny-villar-cont.html.

Caldeira, Teresa P. R. 2000. *City of Walls: Crime, Segregation, and Citizenship in São Paulo*. Berkeley: University of California Press.

Caoili, Manuel A. (1988) 1999. *The Origins of Metropolitan Manila: A Political and Social Analysis*. Quezon City: University of the Philippines Press.

Carroll, John J. 1966. "Philippine Social Organization and National Development." *Philippine Studies* 14 (4): 575–90.

———. 1968. *Changing Patterns of Social Structure in the Philippines, 1896–1963*. Quezon City, Philippines: Ateneo de Manila University Press.

Casiple, Ramon C. 2016. "The Duterte Presidency as a Phenomenon." *Contemporary Southeast Asia* 38 (2): 179–84.

Castells, Manuel. 1983. *The City and the Grassroots: A Cross-Cultural Theory of Urban Social Movements*. Berkeley: University of California Press.

Chamber of Real Estate and Builders' Associations. 2003. "Framework for Social and Economic Advancement: Recommendations." http://creba.ph/files/SocioEcoFramework-Position.pdf.

Chatterjee, Partha. 2004. *The Politics of the Governed: Reflections on Popular Politics in Most of the World*. New York: Columbia University Press.

Choguill, Charles L. 2001. "Urban Policy as Poverty Alleviation: The Experience of the Philippines." *Habitat International* 25: 1–13.

Clarke, Gerald. 1998. *The Politics of NGOs in Southeast Asia: Participation and Protest in the Philippines*. New York: Routledge.

———. 2013. *Civil Society in the Philippines: Theoretical, Methodological, and Policy Debates*. New York: Routledge.

Clarke, Gerald, and Marites Sison. 2003. "Voices from the Top of the Pile: Elite Perceptions of Poverty and the Poor in the Philippines." *Development and Change* 34 (2): 215–42.

Commission on Elections (Comelec). 2010. "Philippines 2010 Election Results." http://curry.ateneo.net/~ambo/ph2010/electionresults/index2.html.

Connell, John. 1999. "Beyond Manila: Walls, Malls, and Private Spaces." *Environment and Planning A* 31: 417–39.

Constantino-David, Karina. 2001. "Surviving Erap." In *Between Fires: Fifteen Perspectives on the Estrada Crisis*, edited by Amando Doronila, 212–26. Pasig City, Philippines: Anvil Publishers.

Coronel, Sheila S. 2003. "The Problem with Gloria." *I: The Investigative Reporting Magazine*, April–June, http://pcij.org/imag/PublicEye/gloria.html.

———. 2005. "The Unmaking of the President." Philippine Center for Investigative Journalism, July 1. http://pcij.org/stories/the-unmaking-of-the-president/.

———. 2006. "The Philippines in 2006: Democracy and Its Discontents." *Asian Survey* 47 (1): 175–82.

Corpuz, Arturo G. 2000. "Integrating Transportation and Land Use Planning: The Metro Manila Experience." In *Southeast Asian Urban Environments: Structured and Spontaneous*, edited by Carla Chifos and Ruth Yabes, 133–51. Tempe: Program for Southeast Asian Studies, Arizona State University.

Coy, Martin, and Martin Pöhler. 2002. "Gated Communities in Latin American Megacities: Case Studies in Brazil and Argentina." *Environment and Planning B* 29 (3): 355–70.

Curato, Nicole. 2016. "Politics of Anxiety, Politics of Hope: Penal Populism and Duterte's Rise to Power." *Journal of Current Southeast Asian Affairs* 35 (3): 91–109.

———. 2017. "Flirting with Authoritarian Fantasies? Rodrigo Duterte and the New Terms of Philippine Populism." *Journal of Contemporary Asia* 47 (1): 142–53.

Daenekindt, Roger, and Mary Alice Gonzales-Rosero. 2003. "How Cheap Can We Get? A Survey of the Situation of Contractual Workers in Selected

Industries in and Nearby Metro Manila." Pasig City, Philippines: Labor Rights and Democracy.

DaMatta Roberto. 1991. *Carnivals, Rogues, and Heroes: An Interpretation of the Brazilian Dilemma*. Notre Dame, IN: University of Notre Dame Press.

David, Randy. 2001. "Erap: A Diary of Disenchantment." In *Between Fires: Fifteen Perspectives on the Estrada Crisis*, edited by Amando Doronila, 148–79. Pasig City: Anvil Publishers.

Davis, Kingsley, and Hilda Hertz Golden. 1954. "Urbanization and the Development of Pre-Industrial Areas." *Economic Development and Cultural Change* 3 (1): 6–26.

Davis, Mike. 1990. *City of Quartz: Excavating the Future in Los Angeles*. London: Verso.

De Duren, Nora Libertun. 2006. "Planning à la Carte: The Location Patterns of Gated Communities around Buenos Aires in a Decentralized Planning Context." *International Journal of Urban and Regional Research* 30 (2): 308–27.

De la Torre, Carlos. 2010. *Populist Seduction in Latin America*. Athens: Ohio University Press.

De la Torre, Edicio. 2001. "'To Understand Is to Stand Under, to Look Up': Panimulang Pag-Unawa sa EDSA Tres." Forum on Understanding Edsa Tres and the State of Rebellion, University of the Philippines. http://www.up .edu.ph/oldforum/2001/5/ed.html.

Doeppers, Daniel F. 1984. *Manila, 1900–1941: Social Change in a Late Colonial Metropolis*. Monograph Series No. 27. New Haven, CT: Yale University Southeast Asia Studies.

Doronila, Amando. 1992. *The State, Economic Transformation, and Political Change in the Philippines, 1946–1972*. Oxford: Oxford University Press.

———. 2001. *The Fall of Joseph Estrada: The Inside Story*. Pasig City, Philippines: Anvil Publishers.

Dwyer, D. J. 1975. *People and Housing in Third World Cities*. London: Longman.

Elias, Norbert. (1939) 2000. *The Civilizing Process*. Oxford, UK: Blackwell.

Encarnacion-Tadem, Teresa S. 2008. "Situating NGO Advocacy Work in Middle Class Politics in the Philippines." In *The Rise of Middle Classes in Southeast Asia*, edited by Shiraishi Takashi and Pasuk Phongpaichit, 194–216. Kyoto: Kyoto University Press.

Felipe, Jesus, and Leonardo Lanzona Jr. 2006. "Unemployment, Labor Laws, and Economic Policies in the Philippines." In *Labor Markets in Asia: Issues and Perspectives*, edited by Jesus Felipe and Rana Hasan, 367–502. New York: Palgrave Macmillan.

Fernandes, Leela. 2006. *India's New Middle Class: Democratic Politics in an Era of Economic Reform*. Minneapolis: University of Minnesota Press.

Ferreira, Francisco H. G., Julian Messina, Jamele Rigolini, Luis-Felipe López-Calva, Maria Ana Lugo, and Renos Vakis. 2013. *Economic Mobility and the Rise of the Latin American Middle Class*. Washington, DC: World Bank.

https://openknowledge.worldbank.org/bitstream/handle/10986/11858/
9780821396346.pdf.

Festinger, Leon. 1954. "A Theory of Social Comparison Processes." *Human Relations* 7 (2): 117–40.

Filipinas Foundation. 1983. *Impacts of the Land Development in Makati.* Makati City: Filipinas Foundation.

Firman, Tommy. 2004. "New Town Development in Jakarta Metropolitan Region: A Perspective of Spatial Segregation." *Habitat International* 2: 349–68.

Fiske, Susan T., and Shelley E. Taylor. 1984. *Social Cognition.* Reading, MA: Addison-Wesley.

Flores, Patrick. 1998. "The Illusions of a Cinematic President." *Public Policy* 2 (4): 101–19.

Fox, Robert B., and Frank Lynch. 1956. *Area Handbook on the Philippines, Volume I.* Chicago: Philippine Studies Program, University of Chicago.

Fraser, Nancy. 1997. *Justice Interruptus: Critical Reflections on the "Postsocialist" Condition.* New York: Routledge.

Friedmann, John, and Goetz Wolff. 1982. "World City Formation: An Agenda for Research and Action." *International Journal of Urban and Regional Research* 6 (3): 309–44.

Gamson, William A. 1992. *Talking Politics.* Cambridge, UK: Cambridge University Press.

Gans, Herbert J. 2002. "The Sociology of Space: A Use-Centered View." *City and Community* 1 (4): 329–39.

Garrido, Marco. 2013a. "The Ideology of the Dual City: The Modernist Ethic in the Corporate Development of Makati City." *International Journal of Urban and Regional Research* 37 (1): 165–85.

———. 2013b. "The Sense of Place behind Segregating Practices: An Ethnographic Approach to the Symbolic Partitioning of Metro Manila." *Social Forces* 91 (4): 1343–62.

———. 2017. "Why the Poor Support Populism: The Politics of Sincerity in Metro Manila." *American Journal of Sociology* 123 (3): 1–39.

Genis, Serife. 2007. "Producing Elite Localities: The Rise of Gated Communities in Istanbul." *Urban Studies* 44 (4): 771–98.

Ghertner, D. Asher. 2015. *Rule by Aesthetics: World-Class City Making in Delhi.* New York: Oxford University Press.

Gieryn, Thomas F. 2002. "Give Place a Chance: Reply to Gans." *City and Community* 1 (4): 341–43.

Gilbert, Alan. 2007. "The Return of the Slum: Does Language Matter?" *International Journal of Urban and Regional Research* 31 (4): 697–713.

———. 2012. "On the Absence of Ghettoes in Latin American Cities." In *The Ghetto: Contemporary Global Issues and Controversies*, edited by Ray Hutchinson and Bruce D. Haynes, 191–224. Boulder, CO: Westview Press.

Gilbert, Alan, and Josef Gugler. 1992. *Cities, Poverty, and Development: Urbanization in the Third World.* Oxford: Oxford University Press.

Gloria, Glenda M. 2015. "Remembering the Iglesia-Led EDSA 3." *Rappler*, August 29. http://www.rappler.com/newsbreak/in-depth/104045-edsa-3-iglesia -ni-cristo.

Goffman, Erving. 1959. *The Presentation of Self in Everyday Life*. New York: Anchor Books.

———. 1974. *Frame Analysis: An Essay on the Organization of Experience*. Cambridge, MA: Harvard University Press.

Gonzáles de la Rocha, Mercedes, Janice Perlman, Helen Safa, Elizabeth Jelin, Bryan R. Roberts, and Peter M. Ward. 2004. "From the Marginality of the 1960s to the 'New Poverty' of Today." *Latin American Research Review* 39 (1): 183–203.

Goss, Jonathan D. 1990. "Production and Reproduction among the Urban Poor of Metro Manila: Relations of Exploitation and Conditions of Existence." PhD diss., University of Kentucky, Lexington.

Gould, Roger V. 1991. *Insurgent Identities: Class, Community, and Protest in Paris from 1848 to the Commune*. Chicago: University of Chicago Press.

Guerrero, Sylvia H. 1973. "The 'Culture of Poverty' in Metro Manila: Some Preliminary Notes." *Philippine Sociological Review* 21 (3–4): 215–21.

———. 1977. "Staying Where the Action Is: Relocation within the City." *Philippine Studies* 25: 51–56.

Gugler, Josef, and William G. Flanagan. 1976. "On the Political Economy of Urbanization in the Third World." *International Journal of Urban and Regional Research* 1 (1–3): 272–92.

Hansen, Thomas Blom. 1999. *The Saffron Wave: Democracy and Hindu Nationalism in Modern India*. Princeton, NJ: Princeton University Press.

Harms, Erik. 2013. *Luxury and Rubble: Civility and Dispossession in the New Saigon*. Oakland: University of California Press.

Harriss, John. 2006. "Middle Class Activism and the Politics of the Informal Working Class: A Perspective on Class Relations and Civil Society in Indian Cities." *Critical Asian Studies* 38 (4): 445–65.

Harvey, David. 2003. "The Right to the City." *International Journal of Urban and Regional Research* 27 (4): 939–41.

Hawley, Amos H. 1944. "Dispersion v. Segregation: Apropos of a Solution of Race Problems." In *Papers of the Michigan Academy of Science, Arts, and Letters*, edited by E. McCartney and H. van der Schalie, 30:667–74. Ann Arbor: University of Michigan Press.

Hedman, Eva-Lotta E. 2001. "The Spectre of Populism in Philippine Politics and Society." *South East Asia Research* 9 (1): 5–44.

———. 2005. *In the Name of Civil Society: From Free Election Movements to People Power in the Philippines*. Honolulu: University of Hawai'i Press.

Hobsbawm, Eric J. 1962. *The Age of Revolution, 1789–1848*. Cleveland: World Publishing Co.

Hollnsteiner, Mary R. 1969. "The Urbanization of Metro Manila." In *Modernization: Its Impact in the Philippines IV*, edited by Walden Bello and Alfonso de

Guzman, 147–74. Quezon City, Philippines: Ateneo de Manila University Press.

———. 1972. "Becoming an Urbanite: The Neighborhood as a Learning Environment." In *The City as a Centre of Change in Asia*, edited by D. J. Dwyer, 29–40. Hong Kong: Hong Kong University Press.

———. 1977. "The Case of 'The People versus Mr. Urbano Planner y Administrador.'" In *Third World Urbanization*, edited by Janet Abu-Lughod and Richard Hay Jr., 307–20. Chicago: Maaroufa Press.

Holmes, Ronald. 2016. "The Dark Side of Electoralism: Opinion Polls and Voting in the 2016 Philippine Presidential Election." *Journal of Current Southeast Asian Affairs* 35 (3): 15–38.

Holston, James. 2008. *Insurgent Citizenship: Disjunctions of Democracy and Modernity in Brazil*. Princeton, NJ: Princeton University Press.

Holston, James, and Teresa P. R. Caldeira. 1998. "Democracy, Law, and Violence: Disjunctions of Brazilian Citizenship." In *Fault Lines of Democracy in Post-Transition Latin America*, edited by Felipe Agüero and Jeffrey Stark, 263–96. Miami: North-South Center Press.

Hong, Sung Woong. 2001. "FDI in Asia in Boom and Bust." In *Globalization and the Sustainability of Cities in the Asia Pacific Region*, edited by Fu-chen Lo and Peter Marcotullio, 68–91. Tokyo: United Nations University Press.

Hoselitz, Bert F. 1957. "Urbanization and Economic Growth in Asia." *Economic Development and Cultural Change* 6 (1): 42–54.

Housing and Land Use Regulatory Board. 2014. "Residential Licenses to Sell, National Capital Region, 1981–2013." Unpublished data. Quezon City, Philippines: Housing and Land Use Regulatory Board.

Hutchcroft, Paul D., and Joel Rocamora. 2003. "Strong Demands and Weak Institutions: The Origins and Evolution of the Democratic Deficit in the Philippines." *Journal of East Asian Studies* 3 (2): 259–92.

Hutchinson, Jane. 2012. "Labour Politics in Southeast Asia: The Philippines in Comparative Perspective." In *Routledge Handbook of Southeast Asian Politics*, edited by Richard Robison, 30–52. New York: Routledge.

Institute of Philippine Culture. 2005. *The Vote of the Poor: Modernity and Tradition in People's Views of Leadership and Elections*. Quezon City, Philippines: Ateneo de Manila University.

James, Daniel. 1988. *Resistance and Integration: Peronism and the Argentine Working Class, 1946–76*. Cambridge, UK: Cambridge University Press.

Joaquin, Nick. 1977. *Joseph Estrada and Other Sketches*. Manila: National Book Store.

Jocano, F. Landa. 1975. *Slum as a Way of Life*. Diliman: University of the Philippines.

Joshi, Gopal. 1997. "Urban Informal Sector in Metro Manila: A Problem or Solution?" Geneva: International Labor Organization.

Juppenplatz, Morris. 1970. *Cities in Transformation: The Urban Squatter Problem in the Developing World*. Santa Lucia, Australia: University of Queensland Press.

Kalleberg, Arne, and Kevin Hewison. 2013. "Precarious Work and the Challenge for Asia." *American Behavioral Scientist* 57 (3): 271–88.

Karaos, Anna Marie A. 1987. "A Preface to Urban Land Reform." *Intersect* 1 (2): 1–3, 14. Quezon City, Philippines: Institute on Church and Social Issues.

———. 1995. "Manila's Urban Poor Movement: The Social Construction of Collective Identities." PhD diss., New School for Social Research.

———. 1996. "An Assessment of the Government's Social Housing Program." Occasional Paper, Institute on Church and Social Relations, Quezon City, Philippines.

———. 1998. "Fragmentation in the Urban Poor Movement." *Philippine Sociological Review* 46 (3–4): 143–57.

———. 2006. "Populist Mobilization and Manila's Urban Poor: The Case of SANAPA in the NGC East Side." In *Social Movements: Experiences from the Philippines*, edited by Aya Fabros, Joel Rocamora, and Djorina Velasco, 46–103. Quezon City, Philippines: Institute for Popular Democracy.

Kerkvliet, Benedict J. Tria. 1995. "Toward a More Comparative Analysis of Philippine Politics: Beyond the Patron-Client Factional Framework." *Journal of Southeast Asian Studies* 26 (2): 401–19.

Keyes, William J. 1976. "Land Use—and Abuse." *Philippine Studies* 24: 381–98.

———. 1979. "Economic Development and the Housing Problem." *Philippine Studies* 27: 210–30.

Knox, Paul L., and Peter J. Taylor, eds. 1995. *World Cities in a World-System*. Cambridge, UK: Cambridge University Press.

Koonings, Kees, and Dirk Krujit. 2009. *Megacities: The Politics of Urban Exclusion and Violence in the Global South*. London: Zed Books.

Lacaba, Jose F. (1970) 1983. "Notes on 'Bakya': Being an Apologia of Sorts for Filipino Masscult." In *Readings in Philippine Cinema*, edited by Rafael M. Guerrero, 117–23. Manila: Experimental Cinema of the Philippines Publications.

Lamont, Michèle. 1992. *Money, Morals, and Manners: The Culture of the French and American Upper-Middle Class*. Chicago: University of Chicago Press.

Lamont, Michèle, and Virág Molnár. 2002. "The Study of Boundaries in the Social Sciences." *Annual Review of Sociology* 28: 167–95.

Laquian, Aprodicio A. 1966. *The City in Nation-Building: Politics and Administration in Metropolitan Manila*. Manila: University of the Philippines.

———. 1969. *Slums Are for People*. Diliman: University of the Philippines.

Laquian, Aprodicio A., and Eleanor R. Laquian. 2002. *The Erap Tragedy: Tales from the Snake Pit*. Pasig City, Philippines: Anvil Publishers.

Leeds, Anthony. 1974. "Housing Settlement Types, Arrangements for Living, Proletarianization and the Social Structure of the City." *Latin American Urban Research* 4: 67–99.

Lefebvre, Henri. 1996. *Writings on Cities*. Oxford, UK: Blackwell.

Leichty, Mark. 2003. *Suitably Modern: Making Middle-Class Culture in a New Consumer Society*. Princeton, NJ: Princeton University Press.

Lico, Gerard. 2003. *Edifice Complex: Power, Myth, and Marcos State Architecture.* Quezon City, Philippines: Ateneo de Manila University Press.

Lipset, Seymour Martin. 1960. *Political Man: The Social Bases of Politics.* New York: Doubleday and Co.

Lo, Fu-chen, and Peter J. Marcotullio. 2001. "Globalization and Urban Transformation in the Asia-Pacific Region." In *Globalization and the Sustainability of Cities in the Asia-Pacific Region,* edited by Fu-chen Lo and Peter Marcotullio, 21–67. Tokyo: United Nations University Press.

López-Maya, Margarita, and Luis E. Lander. 2000. "Refounding the Republic: The Political Project of Chavismo." *NACLA Report on the Americas* 33 (6): 22–28.

Lynch, Frank. 1959. *Social Class in a Bikol Town.* Chicago: Philippine Studies Program, University of Chicago.

———. 1965. "Trends Report of Studies in Social Stratification and Social Mobility in the Philippines." *East Asian Cultural Studies* 4 (1–4): 163–91.

Magno, Alexander R. 1993. "A Changed Terrain for Popular Struggles." *Kasarinlan* 8 (3): 7–21.

Magno-Ballesteros, Marife. 2000. "Land Use Planning in Metro Manila and the Urban Fringe: Implications on the Land and Real Estate Market." Discussion Paper No. 20, Philippine Institute for Development Studies, Makati City.

Mangahas, Mahar. 1998. *SWS Surveys on the 1998 National Elections.* Quezon City, Philippines: Social Weather Stations.

Mangahas, Malou C. 2001. "The Transactional President." *I: The Investigative Reporting Magazine,* January–March, 6–11.

Marcuse, Peter, and Ronald van Kempen, ed. 2000. *Globalizing Cities: A New Spatial Order?* Malden, MA: Blackwell.

Mauss, Marcel. (1902) 1972. *A General Theory of Magic.* London: Routledge and K. Paul.

Mill, John Stuart. (1861) 2004. *Considerations on Representative Government.* Project Gutenberg EBook. https://www.gutenberg.org/files/5669/5669-h/5669-h.htm.

Mollenkopf, John, and Manuel Castells. 1991. *The Dual City: Restructuring New York.* New York: Russell Sage Foundation.

Muijzenberg, Otto van den, and Ton van Naerssen. 2005. "Metro Manila: Designers or Directors of Urban Development?" In *Directors of Urban Change in Asia,* edited by Peter J. M. Nas, 126–47. New York: Routledge.

Murphy, Denis. 1993. *The Urban Poor: Land and Housing.* Bangkok: Asian Coalition for Housing Rights.

Naerssen, Ton van. 1989. "Continuity and Change in the Urban Poor Movement of Manila, the Philippines." In *Urban Social Movements in the Third World,* edited by Frans Schuurman and Ton van Naerssen, 199–219. London: Routledge.

———. 1993. "Squatter Access to Land in Metro Manila." *Philippine Studies* 41 (1): 3–20.

National Home Mortgage Finance Corporation. 2003. "CMP Accomplishment and Program Updates." Presentation at the Symposium on the Community Mortgage Program on August 20, University of the Philippines, Diliman.

National Housing Authority. 2000. "Magnitude of Informal Settlers in Metro Manila as of October 2000—National Capital Region." Unpublished data. Quezon City, Philippines.

———. 2011. "Magnitude of Informal Settlers in Metro Manila as of July 13, 2011—National Capital Region." Unpublished data. Quezon City.

National Statistical Coordination Board. Various years. *Philippine Statistical Yearbook*. Makati City, Philippines: National Statistical Coordination Board.

Nowak, Thomas C., and Kay A. Snyder. 1974. "Clientelist Politics in the Philippines: Integration or Instability?" *American Political Science Review* 68 (3): 1147–70.

Ocampo, Romeo B. 1978. "Development of Philippine Housing Policy and Administration (1945–59)." *Philippine Journal of Public Administration* 22 (1): 1–18.

O'Donnell, Guillermo. 1999. *Counterpoints: Selected Essays on Authoritarianism and Democratization*. Notre Dame, IN: University of Notre Dame Press.

Office of the President (Philippines). 1968. "Squatting and Slum Dwelling in Metropolitan Manila." *Philippine Sociological Review* 16 (1–2): 92–105.

Ofreneo, Rene E. 2013. "Precarious Philippines: Expanding Informal Sector, 'Flexibilizing' Labor Market." *American Behavioral Scientist* 57 (4): 420–43.

———. 2015. "Growth and Employment in De-Industrializing Philippines." *Journal of the Asia Pacific Economy* 20 (1): 111–29.

Ortega, Arnisson Andre. 2016. *Neoliberalizing Spaces in the Philippines: Suburbanization, Transnational Migration, and Dispossession*. Lanham, MD: Lexington Books.

Oxhorn, Philip. 2003. "Social Inequality, Civil Society, and the Limits of Citizenship in Latin America." In *What Justice? Whose Justice? Fighting for Fairness in Latin America*, edited by Susan Eva Eckstein and Timothy P. Wickham-Crowley, 35–63. Berkeley: University of California Press.

Panfichi, Aldo. 1997. "The Authoritarian Alternative: 'Anti-Politics' in the Popular Sectors of Lima." In *The New Politics of Inequality in Latin America*, edited by Douglas Chalmers, Carlos Vilas, Katherine Hite, Scott Martin, Kerianne Piester, and Monique Segarra, 217–36. Oxford, UK: Oxford University Press.

Paolini, Stefania, Jake Harwood, and Mark Rubin. 2010. "Negative Intergroup Contact Makes Group Memberships Salient: Explaining Why Intergroup Conflict Endures." *Personality and Social Psychology Bulletin* 36 (12): 1723–38.

Patel, Sujata. 2007. "Mumbai: The Mega-City of a Poor Country." In *The Making of Global City Regions*, edited by Klaus Segbers, 64–84. Baltimore, MD: Johns Hopkins University Press.

Perlman, Janice. 1976. *The Myth of Marginality: Urban Poverty and Politics in Rio de Janeiro*. Berkeley: University of California Press.

———. 2010. *Favela: Four Decades of Living on the Edge in Rio de Janeiro*. Oxford, UK: Oxford University Press.

Philippine Statistics Authority. Various years. *Philippine Statistical Yearbook*. Quezon City: Philippine Statistics Authority.

———. 2015. "Distribution of Overseas Filipino Workers by Sex and Region." *2015 Survey on Overseas Filipinos*. Quezon City: Philippine Statistics Authority.

———. 2016. "Employment Situation in National Capital Region: October 2015." *Labor Force Survey*. Quezon City: Philippine Statistics Authority.

———. 2017a. "Employed Persons by Major Industry Group, Philippines: January 2017." *Labor Force Survey*. Quezon City: Philippine Statistics Authority.

———. 2017b. "Percent Distribution of Employed Persons by Sex, Region, and Major Industry Group: April 2016." *Labor Force Survey*. Quezon City: Philippine Statistics Authority.

Pinches, Michael D. 1985. "The 'Urban Poor.'" In *The Philippines After Marcos*, edited by R. J. May and Francisco Nemenzo, 152–63. London: Croom Helm.

———. 1987. "'All That We Have Is Our Muscle and Sweat': The Rise of Wage Labor in a Manila Squatter Community." In *Wage Labor and Social Change: The Proletariat in Asia and the Pacific*, edited by Michael Pinches and Salim Lakha, 103–40. Victoria, Australia: Monash University.

———. 1991. "The Working Class Experience of Shame, Inequality, and People Power in Tatalon, Manila." In *From Marcos to Aquino: Local Perspectives on Political Transition in the Philippines*, edited by Benedict J. Kerkvliet and Resil B. Mojares, 166–86. Quezon City, Philippines: Ateneo de Manila University Press.

———. 1992. "Proletarian Ritual Class Degradation and the Dialectics of Resistance in Manila." *Pilipinas* 19: 55–68.

———. 1994. "Modernisation and the Quest for Modernity: Architectural Form, Squatter Settlements and the New Society in Manila." In *Cultural Identity and Urban Change in Southeast Asia: Interpretive Essays*, edited by Marc Askew and William S. Logan, 13–42. Victoria, Australia: Deakin University Press.

———. 1996. "The Philippines' New Rich: Capitalist Transformation amidst Economic Gloom." In *The New Rich in Asia: Mobile Phones, McDonalds, and Middle-Class Revolution*, edited by Richard Robison and David S. G. Goodman, 105–36. London: Routledge.

———. 1999. "Entrepreneurship, Consumption, Ethnicity, and National Identity in the Making of the Philippines' New Rich." In *Culture and Privilege in Capitalist Asia*, edited by Michael Pinches, 275–301. London: Routledge.

———. 2003. "Restructuring Capitalist Power in the Philippines: Elite Consolidation and Upward Mobility in Producer Services." In *Capital and Knowledge in Asia: Changing Power Relations*, edited by H. Dahles and O. van den Muijzenberg, 64–89. London: Routledge.

———. 2010. "The Making of Middle Class Civil Society in the Philippines." In *The Politics of Change in the Philippines*, edited by Yuko Kasuya and Nathan Quimpo, 284–312. Pasig City, Philippines: Anvil Publishing.

Poethig, Richard P. 1971. "Two Views: Roofing the Urban Squatters." *Solidarity* 6 (6): 15–21.

Porio, Emma, and Christine Crisol. 2004. "Property Rights, Security of Tenure, and the Urban Poor in Metro Manila." *Habitat International* 28: 203–19.

Portes, Alejandro. 1989. "Latin American Urbanization during the Years of Crisis." *Latin American Research Review* 24 (3): 7–44.

Portes, Alejandro, Jose Itzigsohn, and Carlos Dore-Cabral. 1994. "Urbanization in the Caribbean Basin: Social Change during the Years of the Crisis." *Latin American Research Review* 29 (2): 3–37.

Portes, Alejandro, and Bryan R. Roberts. 2005. "The Free-Market City: Latin American Urbanization in the Years of the Neoliberal Experiment." *Studies in Comparative International Development* 40 (1): 43–82.

Portes, Alejandro, and John Walton. 1976. *Urban Latin America: The Political Conditions from Above and Below.* Austin: University of Texas Press.

Pulse Asia. 2001. "Class Distribution in People Power 2 Rallies in Metro Manila." Thames Nationwide Survey, February 3–5.

———. 2009. "October 2009 Nationwide Survey on Filipinos' Presidential, Vice-Presidential, and Senatorial Preferences for the May 2010 Elections." Media release, November 16.

———. 2016. "2016 Elections: First Choice Presidential Preference." Quezon City, Philippines: Pulse Asia Research.

———. 2017. "Comparative Performance and Trust Ratings of Presidents (May 1999 to September 2017)." Quezon City, Philippines: Pulse Asia Research.

Qayum, Seemin, and Raka Ray. 2011. "The Middle Classes at Home." In *Elite and Everyman: The Cultural Politics of the Indian Middle Classes*, edited by A. Baviskar and R. Ray, 247–70. New Delhi: Routledge.

Quezon City. 2008. "Updated List of Depressed Areas (in Quezon City)." Quezon City, Philippines: Barangay Operations Center, Quezon City Government.

———. 2012. "Residential Licenses to Sell, Quezon City, 1992–2011." Subdivision Administration Unit. Quezon City, Philippines: Quezon City Government.

Quijano, Aníbal. 2000. "Coloniality of Power and Eurocentrism in Latin America." *International Sociology* 15 (2): 215–32.

Quimpo, Nathan Gilbert. 2005. "Oligarchic Patrimonialism, Bossism, Electoral Clientelism, and Contested Democracy in the Philippines." *Comparative Politics* 37 (2): 229–50.

———. 2017. "Duterte's 'War on Drugs': The Securitization of Illegal Drugs and the Return of National Boss Rule." In *A Duterte Reader: Critical Essays on Duterte's Early Presidency*, edited by Nicole Curato, 145–66. Ithaca, NY: Cornell University Press.

Ragragio, Junio M. 2003. "The Case of Metro Manila, Philippines." *Understanding Slums: Case Studies for the Global Report on Human Settlements 2003.* http://www.ucl.ac.uk/dpu-projects/Global_Report/home.htm.

Rancière, Jacques. 1999. *Disagreement.* Minneapolis: University of Minnesota Press.

———. 2004. "Introducing Disagreement." *Angelaki* 9 (3): 3–9.

———. 2010. *Dissensus: On Politics and Aesthetics*. London: Bloomsbury.

———. 2011. "The Thinking of Dissensus: Politics and Aesthetics." In *Reading Rancière: Critical Dissensus*, edited by Paul Bowman and Richard Stamp, 1–17. London: Continuum.

Reyes, Jun Cruz. 2001. "Etsa-Pwera: Pagkatapos ng Mabahong Eksena." Forum on Understanding Edsa Tres and the State of Rebellion, University of the Philippines. http://www.up.edu.ph/oldforum/2001/5/Etsapwera .html.

Reyes, Marqueza C. L. 1998. "Spatial Structure of Metro Manila: Genesis, Growth, and Development." *Philippine Planning Journal* 29 (2) and 30 (1): 1–34.

Ribiero, Luis César de Queiroz, and Luciana Correa Do Lago. 1995. "Restructuring in Large Brazilian Cities: The Centre/Periphery Model." *International Journal of Urban and Regional Research* 19 (3): 369–82.

Rimmer, Peter J., and Howard Dick. 2009. *The City in Southeast Asia: Patterns, Process, and Policy*. Honolulu: University of Hawai'i Press.

Rivera, Temario C. 2001. "The Middle Classes and Democratisation in the Philippines: From the Asian Crisis to the Ouster of Estrada." In *Southeast Asian Middle Classes: Prospects for Social Change and Democratisation*, edited by Abdul Rahman Embong, 230–61. Bangi: Penerbit Universiti Kebangsaan Malaysia.

Roberto, Ned. 2002. *The Marketer's Guide to Socioeconomic Classification of Consumers*. Makati City, Philippines: Asian Institute of Management.

Roberts, Kenneth M. 2003. "Social Polarization and the Populist Resurgence in Venezuela." In *Venezuelan Politics in the Chávez Era*, edited by S. Ellner and D. Hellinger, 55–72. Boulder, CO: Lynne Rienner.

Robison, Richard, and David S. G. Goodman. 1996. *The New Rich in Asia: Mobile Phones, McDonald's and Middle Class Revolution*. London: Routledge.

Roitman, Sonia. 2005. "Who Segregates Whom? The Analysis of a Gated Community in Mendoza, Argentina." *Housing Studies* 20 (2): 303–21.

Rüland, Jürgen. 1984. "Political Change, Urban Services, and Social Movements: Political Participation and Grassroots Politics in Metro Manila." *Public Administration and Development* 4 (4): 325–33.

Sabatini, Francisco and Rodrigo Salcedo. 2007. "Gated Communities and the Poor in Santiago, Chile: Functional and Symbolic Integration in a Context of Aggressive Capitalist Colonization of Lower-Class Areas." *Housing Policy Debate* 18 (3): 577–606.

Salcedo, Rodrigo, and Alejandra Rasse. 2012. "The Heterogeneous Nature of Urban Poor Families." *City and Community* 11 (1): 94–118.

Salcedo, Rodrigo, and Alvaro Torres. 2004. "Gated Communities in Santiago: Wall or Frontier?" *International Journal of Urban and Regional Research* 28 (1): 27–44.

Sampson, Robert J., and Jeffrey G. Morenoff. 2006. "Durable Inequality: Spatial Dynamics, Social Processes, and the Persistence of Poverty in Chicago

Neighborhoods." In *Poverty Traps*, edited by Samuel Bowles, Steven N. Durlauf, and Karla Hoff, 176–203. Princeton, NJ: Princeton University Press.

Sandhu, Ravinder S., and Jasmeet Sandhu, eds. 2007. *Globalizing Cities: Inequality and Segregation in Developing Countries*. Jaipur, India: Rawat Publications.

Santiago, Asteya M. 1992. "Slums and Squatter Problems in Metropolitan Manila: An Update." *Philippine Planning Journal* 24 (1): 36–48.

Santiago, Sebastian B. 1977. "Staying Where the Action Is: Relocation within the City." *Philippine Sociological Review* 25: 45–49.

Sassen, Saskia. 1991. *The Global City: New York, London, Tokyo*. Princeton, NJ: Princeton University Press.

———. 1994. *Cities in a World Economy*. Thousand Oaks, CA: Pine Forge Press.

———. 1999. "Whose City Is It? Globalization and the Formation of New Claims." In *Cities and Citizenship*, edited by J. Holston, 177–94. Durham, NC: Duke University Press.

Schaffer, Frederic Charles. 2008. *The Hidden Costs of Clean Election Reform*. Ithaca, NY: Cornell University Press.

Schneider, David J. 1991. "Social Cognition." *Annual Review of Psychology* 42: 527–61.

Shatkin, Gavin. 2004. "Planning to Forget: Informal Settlements as 'Forgotten Places' in a Globalizing Metro Manila." *Urban Studies* 41 (12): 2469–84.

———. 2007. *Collective Action and Urban Poverty Alleviation: Community Organizations and the Struggle for Shelter in Manila*. Hampshire, UK: Ashgate.

———. 2008. "The City and the Bottom Line: Urban Megaprojects and the Privatization of Planning in Southeast Asia." *Environment and Planning A* 40 (2): 383–401.

———. 2009. "The Geography of Insecurity: Spatial Change and the Flexibilization of Labor in Metro Manila." *Journal of Urban Affairs* 31 (4): 381–408.

Sherman, Steven J., Charles M. Judd, and Bernadette Park. 1989. "Social Cognition." *Annual Review of Psychology* 40: 281–326.

Sibal, J. V., M. S. V. Amante, and C. Tolentino. 2008. "The Philippines: Changes at the Workplace." In *Globalization, Flexibilization, and Working Conditions in Asia and the Pacific*, edited by Sangheon Lee and François Eyraud, 279–312. Oxford, UK: Chandos Publishing.

Simmel, Georg. 1909. "The Problem of Sociology." *American Journal of Sociology* 15 (3): 289–320.

———. (1908) 1965. "The Poor." *Social Problems* 13 (2): 118–40.

———. (1908) 1997. "The Sociology of Space." In *Simmel on Culture*, edited by David Frisby and Mike Featherstone, 137–69. London: Sage.

Simone, Abdoumaliq. 2014. *Jakarta: Drawing the City Near*. Minneapolis: University of Minnesota Press.

Snow, David A. 2007. "Frame." In *The Blackwell Encyclopedia of Sociology*, edited by George Ritzer, 1778–80. Malden, MA: Wiley-Blackwell.

Snyder, Mark. 1984. "When Beliefs Create Reality." *Advances in Experimental Social Psychology* 18: 247–305.

Social Weather Stations. 2001a. "Survey on People Power 2 and the Change in the Presidency." February 2–7. Quezon City, Philippines: Social Weather Stations.

———. 2001b. *Filipino Voting Attitudes and Opinions: Selected Findings from SWS 1984–2001 National Surveys.* Quezon City, Philippines: Social Weather Stations.

———. 2010a. National Survey, April 16–19. Quezon City, Philippines: Social Weather Stations.

———. 2010b. "The TV5-SWS 2010 Exit Poll." https://www.sws.org.ph/swsmain/artcldisppage/?artcsyscode=ART-20160107171009.

———. 2015. "Net Satisfaction with General Performance of the National Administration." April 23. Quezon City, Philippines: Social Weather Stations.

———. 2016. "2016 Exit Poll." Quezon City, Philippines: Social Weather Stations.

———. 2017a. "Net Satisfaction in Rodrigo Duterte." Various quarters. Quezon City, Philippines: Social Weather Stations.

———. 2017b. "Net Trust in Rodrigo Duterte." Various quarters. Quezon City, Philippines: Social Weather Stations.

———. 2017c. "Satisfaction with How Democracy Works." Quezon City, Philippines: Social Weather Stations.

Soja, Edward W. 1989. *Postmodern Geographies: The Reassertion of Space in Critical Social Theory.* London: Verso.

Sovani, N. V. 1964. "The Analysis of 'Over-Urbanization.'" *Economic Development and Cultural Change* 12 (2): 113–22.

Stets, Jan E., and Peter J. Burke. 2000. "Identity Theory and Social Identity Theory." *Social Psychology Quarterly* 63 (3): 224–37.

Stone, Richard L. 1973. *The Politics of Public and Private Property in Greater Manila.* De Kalb: Center for Southeast Asian Studies, Northern Illinois University.

Stone, Richard, and Joy Marsella. 1968. "Mahirap: A Squatter Community in a Manila Suburb." In *Modernization: Its Impact in the Philippines III*, edited by Walden Bello and Alfonso de Guzman II, 64–91. Quezon City, Philippines: Institute of Philippine Culture, Ateneo de Manila University.

Stryker, Sheldon. 1980. *Symbolic Interactionism: A Social Structural Version.* Menlo Park, CA: Benjamin/Cummings Publishing Co.

Stryker, Sheldon, and Peter J. Burke. 2000. "The Past, Present, and Future of Identity Theory." *Social Psychology Quarterly* 63 (4): 284–97.

Sylvia, Ronald D., and Constantine P. Danopolous. 2003. "The Chávez Phenomenon: Political Change in Venezuela." *Third World Quarterly* 24 (1): 63–76.

Takashi, Shiraishi, and Pasuk Phongpaichit. 2008. *The Rise of Middle Classes in Southeast Asia.* Kyoto: Kyoto University Press.

Taylor, Charles. 1994. "The Politics of Recognition." In *Multiculturalism: Examining the Politics of Recognition*, edited by Amy Gutman, 25–74. Princeton, NJ: Princeton University Press.

Teehankee, Julio C. 2010. "Image, Issues, and Machinery: Presidential Campaigns in Post-1986 Philippines." In *The Politics of Change in the Philippines*, edited by Yuko Kasuya and Nathan Quimpo, 117–59. Mandaluyong City, Philippines: Anvil Publishing.

———. 2016. "Duterte's Resurgent Nationalism in the Philippines: A Discursive Institutionalist Analysis." *Journal of Current Southeast Asian Affairs* 35 (3): 69–89.

Thibert, Joel, and Giselle Andrea Osorio. 2013. "Urban Segregation and Metropolitics in Latin America: The Case of Bogotá, Colombia." *International Journal of Urban and Regional Research* 38 (4): 1319–43.

Thompson, E. P. 1978. "Class Struggle without Class." *Social History* 3 (2): 133–65.

Thompson, Mark R. 2010. "Reformism vs. Populism in the Philippines." *Journal of Democracy* 21 (4): 154–68.

———. 2016. "Bloodied Democracy: Duterte and the Death of Liberal Reformism in the Philippines." *Journal of Current Southeast Asian Affairs* 35 (3): 39–68.

Tilly, Charles. 1998. *Durable Inequality*. Berkeley: University of California Press.

———. 2004. "Social Boundary Mechanisms." *Philosophy of the Social Sciences* 34 (2): 211–36.

Timberman, David G. 2016. "Elite Democracy Disrupted?" *Journal of Democracy* 27 (4): 134–44.

Tocqueville, Alexis de. (1835) 2003. *Democracy in America*. London: Penguin Books.

Tolentino, Rolando B. 2010. "Masses, Power, and Gangsterism in the Films of Joseph 'Erap' Estrada." *Kasarinlan* 25 (1–2): 67–94.

Turner, John C. 1968. "Housing Priorities, Settlement Patterns, and Urban Development in Modernizing Countries." *Journal of the American Institute of Planners* 34 (6): 354–63.

Trilling, Lionel. 1972. *Sincerity and Authenticity*. Cambridge, MA: Harvard University Press.

Tversky, Amos, and Daniel Kahneman. 1974. "Judgment under Uncertainty: Heuristics and Biases." *Science* 185 (4157): 1124–31.

UN Habitat. 2001. *Cities in a Globalizing World: Global Report on Human Settlements 2001*. London: Earthscan.

———. 2003. *The Challenge of Slums: Global Report on Human Settlements 2003*. London: Earthscan.

———. 2011. *Innovative Urban Tenure in the Philippines*. Nairobi: UN Habitat.

———. 2016. *Urbanization and Development: Emerging Futures*. Nairobi: UN Habitat.

Usui, Norio. 2011. "Transforming the Philippine Economy: 'Walking on Two Legs.'" ADB Economics Working Paper Series No. 252, Asian Development Bank, Manila.

Veloso, Leticia. 2010. "Governing Heterogeneity in the Context of 'Compulsory Closeness': The 'Pacification' of Favelas in Rio de Janeiro." In *Suburbanization in Global Society*, edited by Mark Clapson and Ray Hutchinson, 253–72. Bradford, UK: Emerald Group.

Villegas, Celso M., and Myung-Ji Yang. 2013. "Making Narratives of Revolution: Democratic Transition and the Language of Middle-Class Identity in the Philippines and South Korea, 1970s–1987." *Critical Asian Studies* 45 (3): 335–64.

Virola, Romulo A. 2010. "The Top Cities: A Bias towards Metro Manila?" *Statistically Speaking*, September 13. Quezon City: Philippine Statistics Authority.

Virola, Romulo A., Jessamyn O. Encarnacion, Bernadette B. Balamban, Mildred B. Addawe, and Mechelle M. Viernes. 2013. "Will the Recent Robust Economic Growth Create a Burgeoning Middle Class in the Philippines?" Paper delivered at the National Convention on Statistics, Mandaluyong City, Metro Manila, October 1–2.

Wacquant, Loïc. 2008. *Urban Outcasts: A Comparative Sociology of Advanced Marginality*. Cambridge, UK: Polity Press.

Weber, Max. (1922) 1978. *Economy and Society: An Outline of Interpretive Sociology*. Edited by G. Roth and C. Wittich. Berkeley: University of California Press.

Weffort, Francisco C. 1992. "New Democracies, Which Democracies?" Working Papers of the Latin American Program of the Woodrow Wilson International Center for Scholars No. 198, Woodrow Wilson Center, Washington, DC.

Wehrmann, Babette, and Danilo R. Antonio. 2011. "Intermediate Land Tenure: Inferior Instruments for Second Class Citizens?" *Land Tenure Journal* 1: 5–25.

Weinstein, Liza. 2014. *The Durable Slum: Dharavi and the Right to Stay Put in Globalizing Mumbai*. Minneapolis: University of Minnesota Press.

Weyland, Kurt. 2003. "Economic Voting Reconsidered: Crisis and Charisma in the Election of Hugo Chávez." *Comparative Political Studies* 36 (7): 822–48.

Whiteford, Andrew H. 1964. *Two Cities of Latin America: A Comparative Description of Social Classes*. Garden City, NY: Anchor Books.

Wilson, William Julius. 1987. *The Truly Disadvantaged: The Inner City, the Underclass, and Public Policy*. Chicago: University of Chicago Press.

World Bank. 2013. "Philippine Economic Update: Accelerating Reforms to Meet the Jobs Challenge." http://documents.worldbank.org/curated/en/153551468094769606/Philippine-economic-update-accelerating-reforms-to-meet-the-jobs-challenge.

———. 2017. "Agriculture/Industry/Services, Value Added (% of GDP); Philippines." World Bank Open Data. Data available at http://data.worldbank.org.

Young, Iris Marion. 1997. "Asymmetrical Reciprocity: On Moral Respect, Wonder, and Enlarged Thought." *Constellations* 3 (3): 340–63.

Zerubavel, Eviatar. 1991. *The Fine Line: Making Distinctions in Everyday Life.* Chicago: University of Chicago Press.

Zhang, Li. 2010. *In Search of Paradise: Middle-Class Living in a Chinese Metropolis.* Ithaca, NY: Cornell University Press.

Zhao, Dingxin. 1998. "Ecologies of Social Movements: Student Mobilization during the 1989 Prodemocracy Movement in Beijing." *American Journal of Sociology* 103 (6): 1493–1529.

# Index

Page numbers in italics indicate figures and tables.

Lightning Source UK Ltd.
Milton Keynes UK
UKHW012146041119
352885UK00006B/22/P